Class Practices

This important new book is a comparative study of social mobility based on qualitative interviews with middle-class parents in America and Britain. It addresses the key issue in stratification research, namely, the stability of class relations and middle-class reproduction. Drawing on interviewee accounts of how parents mobilised economic, cultural and social resources to help them into professional careers, it then considers how the interviewees, as parents, seek to increase their children's chances of educational success and occupational advancement. Middle-class parents may try to secure their children's social position but it is not an easy or straightforward affair. With the decline in the quality of state education and increased job insecurity in the labour market since the 1970s and 1980s, the reproduction of advantage is more difficult than in the affluent decades of the 1950s and 1960s. The implications for public policy, especially public investment in higher education, are considered.

FIONA DEVINE is Professor of Sociology at Manchester University and has been a Visiting Fellow at the Kennedy School of Government, Harvard University. She is the author of *Affluent Workers Revisited* (1992) and *Social Class in America and Britain* (1997).

Class Practices

How Parents Help Their Children Get Good Jobs

Fiona Devine

University of Manchester

CAMBRIDGE
UNIVERSITY PRESS

PUBLISHED BY THE PRESS SYNDICATE OF THE UNIVERSITY OF CAMBRIDGE
The Pitt Building, Trumpington Street, Cambridge, United Kingdom

CAMBRIDGE UNIVERSITY PRESS
The Edinburgh Building, Cambridge, CB2 2RU, UK
40 West 20th Street, New York, NY 10011–4211, USA
477 Williamstown Road, Port Melbourne, VIC 3207, Australia
Ruiz de Alarcón 13, 28014 Madrid, Spain
Dock House, The Waterfront, Cape Town 8001, South Africa

http://www.cambridge.org

First published 2004

Printed in the United Kingdom at the University Press, Cambridge

Typeface Plantin 10/12 pt.   *System* LATEX 2ε   [TB]

A catalogue record for this book is available from the British Library

Library of Congress cataloguing in publication data
Devine, Fiona.
Class practices: how parents help their children get good jobs / Fiona Devine.
      p.   cm.
Includes bibliographical references and index.
ISBN 0 521 80941 X (cloth)   ISBN 0 521 00653 8 (pbk.)
1. Employees – Recruiting – Social aspects – Great Britain.   2. Employees – Recruiting –
Social aspects – United States.   3. Social mobility – Great Britain.   4. Social mobility –
United States.   5. Parents – Social networks – Great Britain.   6. Parents – Social
networks – United States.   7. Education – Parent participation – Great Britain.
8. Education – Parent participation – United States.   9. Social surveys – Great Britain.
10. Social surveys – United States.   I. Title.
HN400.S65D48   2004
305.5′13′09 – dc21   2003055142

ISBN 0 521 80941 X hardback
ISBN 0 521 00653 8 paperback

Contents

Tables

Acknowledgements

I have had huge amounts of encouragement and support from many people in the writing of this book and, quite frankly, I could not have done it without them. I could not have done the research without the crucial financial backing of the University of Manchester and the Leverhulme Trust. The University of Manchester funded the British arm of the project that allowed me to undertake interviews with British doctors and teachers in and around the city in 1996–97. Funding from the Leverhulme Trust facilitated my research with American physicians and educators in Boston and surrounds in 1998–99. I would like to convey my special thanks to Mrs Jean Cater, Secretary to the Research Awards Advisory Committee of the Leverhulme Trust, for her unfailing kindness in the administration of my research funds.

When I was in Boston, I was a Visiting Fellow at the Kennedy School of Government at the University of Harvard. I am very grateful to Professor William Julius Wilson who sponsored my affiliation and to Julie Wilson, Director of the Malcolm Wiener Center for Social Policy, who made it happen. Although I spent much of my time out and about conducting interviews while I was in Boston, I enjoyed the company of colleagues working on the Joblessness and Urban Poverty Research Program including Jim Quane, the Associate Director of the Program, Bruce Rankin, Edward Walker and Stephanie de Gonzalez. They were so welcoming and always made me feel at home. I also enjoyed the company of Pippa Norris at the Kennedy School and Mary Waters of the Sociology Department at Harvard.

I owe an enormous debt to the interviewees of this project. I love doing empirical research and I was very lucky to have the opportunity to do interviews in Britain and America. My time in America was one of the happiest in my life. All of the interviewees welcomed me into their homes and told me about their lives. They spoke to me about many of life's ups and downs with incredible candour and generosity. I could not have asked for more. They have probably long forgotten the conversations that we had. I have often wondered what they would think if they knew how much their lives have been central to mine as I have read and reread the transcripts of the interviews over the past four years. I sincerely hope that I have portrayed them honestly and fairly in the pages of this book. I hope that I have not betrayed the trust they placed in me.

I have discussed many of the ideas in this book with colleagues as I have given papers at conferences and in departments in both countries. I fear that I cannot remember all the people who have influenced my thinking. I do remember receiving comments, intriguing ideas, critical thoughts and much more from David Grusky, Barbara Reskin, Mary Waters and Nancy DiTomaso in the USA. I have been greatly influenced by the work of Rosemary Crompton, John Scott and Mike Savage in Britain. I would like to acknowledge my debt to Rosemary Crompton in particular. I have benefited from her generosity of spirit towards young colleagues in the discipline of sociology as I am sure others have too. Thanks should also go to Talja Blokland, Judy Wajcman, Geoff Payne and Mark Western for good discussions on social inequalities.

Long-standing academic friends, Graham Crow and Sue Heath, also read parts of this book for me. Graham challenged me to think straight. I tried to take on board what he said and I hope he will forgive me for not rising to a typology. Sue helped me with her expertise in the sociology of education and I hope she will forgive me for using the word 'kids'. My former Ph.D. student, Tracey Warren, provided me with lots of good comments and made me laugh as well. Judith Glover gave me some very sensible advice about the introduction too. As my research associate on another research project on voluntary activism in Britain, John Roberts has been remarkably patient about me working on this book, for which I am grateful. Sarah Caro, my editor at Cambridge University Press, has been very helpful too.

For the ten years I have been in the Sociology Department at the University of Manchester, I have worked alongside inspiring colleagues and friends. In particular, I have drawn on the intellectual stimulation and generous friendship of Peter Halfpenny, Rosemary Mellor, Colette Fagan, Mike Savage and, more recently, Alan Warde. Rosemary helped me with the titles for the chapters. We discussed many of the ideas presented here and I am sad that she died before it was finished. I miss her very much. I also want to say a big thank you to Ann Cronley, the department's postgraduate secretary, for helping me to juggle research commitments, teaching responsibilities and administrative duties in demanding times. I could not have done it without her especially during the final stages of writing this book.

I mentioned that living in America was a very happy time for me. The company of new friends was especially important and the best reason in the world for why I just have to take regular trips back. Here, I am thinking of Jim Quane (again), Galina Kirpichov, Bruce Rankin and Ishok Isik. I want to thank Pam Emerson for her companionship too. I would like to thank Sarah Smith and Frances Srulowitz for making me a part of their community in Cambridge, MA. I cannot thank Sarah enough for the warmth and love that I have always felt whenever I have stayed with her. Back in Britain, I am blessed with long-standing friends who are always good to me. Special thanks should go to Anna Grimshaw, Joanna Clarke, Rohhss Chapman and Karen Wallace-Smith. For lots and lots of fun, I have my neighbours, George, Chris, Josh, Beth and Layla Brown to thank. Josh, Beth and Layla kindly kept still for the cover photograph of this book that was taken by Mary Scanlon and Bill Green who have just joined us on Well Row in Broadbottom.

As always, I would like to thank my family – Mum, Barbs, John and Shauna, Deirds, Matt, Frankie and Ethan – for everything. A special thank you to my sister Barbs who is just great about work and life. My partner, Jim Husband, and his children, Edward and Elizabeth, have been an important source of support and encouragement too. It seems to be customary to mention the distractions of family life. I checked this out with Ed and he wants it to be known that he introduced me to 'music with attitude' (otherwise known as goth metal). This is true. I would add, however, that the pleasure of his company has rarely been a distraction. It is difficult to put into words how much I have relied on Jim's love in getting this book done. He has been very kind about it all. He is a very kind man. I dedicate this book to him.

1   Introduction

My parents were born in Ireland in 1931. My mother was the eleventh of thirteen children bought up on a small farm in Southern Ireland that passed down through her mother's side when her brothers went to America. Her father had been a valet for Lord Kenmare in Killarney and then London before returning home. When my mother finished her education at the age of sixteen in the late 1940s, she took the boat train to England where she joined some of her siblings. She spent most of her working life in London as the banqueting secretary at the Charing Cross Hotel. My father was the fourth of six children brought up in Northern Ireland. While his mother raised the children in Derry, she also made a living sewing. His father was in the British Army and, after the Second World War, he stayed in London where he was an electrician's mate until he retired. My father, I think, finished school at fifteen and then did shop work before joining the Merchant Navy at eighteen.[1] He left at twenty-one and moved to London in the early 1950s where he joined the Post Office and lived with his father. My parents married in 1959 and my three siblings and I were born soon after. Rather than bring children up in London, they moved to Bournemouth in 1968. My Dad spent a year doing odd jobs – a bread round, working in a factory – before he got back into the Post Office. My Mum did lots of jobs like child minding, working as a home help and so on. For most of our childhood, we had foreign students from various English language schools dotted around the seaside resort living with us – a vital source of additional income.

I started school in 1967. It was a tiny school in Putney, London that had about five classes of children between the ages of five and fifteen. I continued my education in Bournemouth at St Walburga's Catholic Primary School along with my sisters and brother. In the early 1970s, the tripartite system was still in operation in parts of Britain and I sat the 'eleven plus' examination to determine whether I would go to a grammar school or a secondary modern.[2] There was no expectation that I would pass and I did not. What was very upsetting at the time, however, was the fact that I got a letter on different coloured paper to my friends about going to St Thomas Moore Secondary Modern School.[3] Unbeknown to my parents, this indicated that I would not be joining my friends in the top stream doing 'O' Levels.[4] It was my best friend, with sisters already at the school, who put me right on this. At eleven, I felt ashamed and a few tears were spilt in the garden shed. All my friends went into the 'G' class while I was assigned to the 'M' class where I was expected to get a few CSEs. A desire to be with them and to be able to do O Levels fuelled a strong motivation to get into the top stream. While I was not always the best-behaved child, I mostly kept on track and was 'moved up' in the third year when I was 13. My sister, Barbara, followed me to St Thomas Moore the year after. So did my brother, much to the disappointment of my parents, since John and my younger sister, Deirdre, were always the clever ones. At least, he got into the 'G' class straight away. Finally, Deirdre passed the eleven plus and went to Bournemouth Grammar School for Girls.

Although I came seventeenth out of thirty-three for three years running, I managed to obtain five O levels – six if you include my CSE Grade 1 in Art. In 1978, I went on to do A Levels in History, Politics and Sociology at Bournemouth and Poole College of Further Education. I had a student grant from the local education authority, worked at a supermarket, the Co-op, at weekends and was a chambermaid in the local hotels during the holidays. This was a happy time and I did really well in my A Levels. Making a hash of my university applications, however, I got rejected from a number of universities. Late in the day, I wrote to the admissions officer at Essex University and I was accepted on my good results. I followed my then boyfriend to do a degree course there in 1980. I had a full maintenance grant from the local education authority again. The rest is, sort of, history. My sisters and brother did different things, of course. Barbara did a one-year typing course at the same college of further education, worked as a typist for an insurance company for a number of years and then retrained as a nurse. John also went to college although he flunked his A Levels and started work in a factory at 18. He enjoyed promotion into warehouse distribution but also experienced redundancy. Somewhere along the line, he became an operations manager for a recruitment agency in London. Like me, Deirdre went to university where she studied French and subsequently trained to be a secondary school teacher. She eventually found her niche in primary school teaching. She is a great teacher.

In many respects, this story is a classic tale of upward social mobility. The children of a postman and a housewife, we went on to become, respectively, a university professor, a nurse, an operations manager and a schoolteacher. Despite our working-class origins, we experienced mobility, to a greater or lesser degree, into middle-class jobs. This story has not been written to celebrate my personal success or that of my siblings. Nothing could be further from the truth. On the contrary, I have lots of friends and colleagues who could tell very similar family histories. I also know from my academic studies that our story is far from unique. The last major study of social mobility in Britain, conducted by John Goldthorpe and his colleagues at Oxford in the early 1970s, found that there has been considerable upward social mobility in Britain since the 1940s.[5] Prior to that, earlier research by David Glass and his associates at the London School of Economics found that while there was movement, short-range mobility was the norm, as it was difficult to move from manual to non-manual employment.[6] The later research highlighted considerable upward social mobility and, most importantly, a significant amount of long-range movement of people from working-class origins to middle-class destinations. Britain, therefore, had undergone major social change from the mid-twentieth century. Changes in the occupational structure – the growth of routine white-collar work followed by an increase in high-level professional and managerial jobs – had had a profound effect on the shape of the class structure and movement between classes.[7]

While highlighting these momentous changes, however, Goldthorpe also noted considerable stability in class relations. Children of middle-class origins were still much more likely to arrive at middle-class destinations than those kids who started from the working class. Relative rates of mobility – where the relative chances of people coming from different classes ending up in the middle classes are compared – had not changed from the 1940s. How were these somewhat curious findings about change and continuity explained? He argued that the evolution of the occupational structure and specifically the growth of the middle class meant there was more 'room at the top'.[8] There was space, in other words, for those of middle-class *and* working-class origins. That *more* people of working-class backgrounds could be found in middle-class jobs did not mean that *fewer* people of middle-class origins occupied middle-class occupations. Consequently, changes in the shape of the class structure and patterns of mobility between different classes had not made Britain a more open or meritocratic society. Where people started out very much influenced where they arrived. Class inequalities, therefore, still marred the landscape of Britain. This was true despite the development of the welfare state, and specifically the introduction of a universal education system free for all, after 1944. Attempts at equalitarian reform, such as government legislation to establish formal equality of educational opportunity in the post-war period, have failed to establish a more open society.[9]

Similar conclusions were reached from comparative research on patterns and trends in social mobility across European nations and the USA,

Australia and Japan undertaken by Erikson and Goldthorpe. They considered, for example, whether America, as a 'new nation', is exceptional in terms of unusually high levels of mobility or openness given, among other things, the substantial growth of educational provision over the twentieth century. They found high levels of absolute (upward and downward) mobility resulting from an occupational structure that had a high proportion of non-manual jobs to manual jobs. America is at the 'post-industrial' end of the European range. Even so, they emphasised that America does not have exceptionally high levels of absolute mobility in comparison to other European countries such as Britain. In relation to relative mobility rates, a greater level of openness was found in 'elite' professional, technical and kindred occupations. Again, however, they stressed that such fluidity arises from the fact that there are more such occupations in America than in European nations.[10] America, they concluded, is characterised by more mobility and is more fluid than European countries. That said, it is not an exceptionally open society when compared to other European nations like Britain. Erikson and Goldthorpe concluded that patterns and trends in social mobility in the United States are not exceptional and that America, as a 'new nation', is not that distinctive from the old European world in these respects. As in Britain, the expansion of educational opportunities has not led to a more open society.

Theoretical underpinnings to my research

When I think of my own personal experiences, and how my life is so different to that of my Mum and my Dad, what is most striking is how things have changed for the better. While my parents faced considerable constraints when they were growing up in the 1930s and 1940s, myself and my siblings enjoyed many opportunities in the 1960s and 1970s. The sociological findings on continuity, therefore, have not been easy to grasp or, at least, not initially. I have taught successive generations of students, with similar family histories, who have encountered the same problem. Yet, the idea that there is 'more room at the top' and that change and continuity coexist seems highly plausible. Both myself, and my students, therefore, have come to understand these continuities. Maybe because it does not chime with my own experience, however, my intellectual curiosity has focused on the stability of class relations in the context of change.[11] What has intrigued me is 'how is this so?' What are the processes by which class inequalities are reproduced across generations? How do members of the middle class retain their privileges and power across different nations like Britain and America? Are they, in other words, successful in reproducing advantage across time and space?

Importantly, how has the middle class proved so effective in resisting legislative attempts, especially through educational provision, at creating a more open society? Does their effectiveness make such efforts worthless? Should more or less be done? With these questions in mind, I now want to discuss the theoretical underpinnings that shaped the research described in this book.

So far, discussion has focused on an *empirical description* of the major patterns and trends in social mobility in Britain and America derived from a sophisticated statistical analysis of data from large surveys. Buried in Goldthorpe's early work on social mobility in Britain, in my view, is a very important *theoretical explanation* for the stability of class relations across time and space.[12] He argues that continuities in relative rates of mobility should be understood with reference to the desirability, advantages and barriers associated with different class positions. The relative desirability of different class positions refers to people's preferences and aspirations for certain positions. In relation to the relative advantages of different class positions, he distinguishes between three types. First, there are economic resources including wealth, income and other forms of capital such as business enterprises and professional practices. Second, there are cultural resources in the sense that Bourdieu uses the concept of 'cultural capital' to refer to the importance attached to life-long education (either of an academic or vocational kind) within the family. The issues of occupational inheritance and traditions of self-employment within families are also important here. Third, there are social resources in the sense of involvement in social networks that can serve as channels of information and influence in, for example, finding a job, as Granovetter described. Finally, the relative barriers of different classes derive from the lack of resources outlined above.

Against this background, those at the higher echelons of the class structure (the middle class) enjoy these advantages – and the power than comes with them – while those in the lower echelons (the working class) do not. Most importantly, members of the middle class are keen to hold on to their advantages and they have the power – via the resources they command – to do so. Economic resources are the most important resource because they are exclusive goods (not owned by others) that can be easily transmitted from one generation to another in comparison to cultural and social resources that are inclusive goods (which can be owned by others) that are less easily transmitted. Thus, those in positions of privilege and power 'will typically seek to exploit the resources that they can command in order to preserve their superiority'. It is no surprise, therefore, that the class structure has proved so resistant to change, for it has strong 'self-maintaining properties'.[13] Further, it is no wonder that government attempts to create an open society have proved less successful than hoped for. This theory was not developed explicitly or extensively worked out in Goldthorpe's early work. Be that as it may, I thought the explanation of how children of middle-class origins are more likely to arrive at middle-class destinations than children of working-class background was very persuasive. I became excited by the idea of doing empirical research on how middle-class parents mobilise their economic, cultural and social resources to ensure their children attain middle-class positions. It would help me grasp the stability of class relations.

These theoretical ideas were elaborated a little further in the concluding discussion to Erikson and Goldthorpe's comparative research. Again, it was argued that class stability is the outcome of advantaged individuals and groups protecting their privilege and power. They also stressed that children's mobility chances are strongly conditioned by inequalities in the economic, cultural and social resources of families that exist *before* they enter the labour market. That is to say, the mobilisation of the different resources, including the conversion of economic resources into cultural capital in the acquisition of educational credentials, is key. Further still, it was argued that resistance to a reduction in inequalities operates 'chiefly at the micro level of adaptive individual and family strategies especially in the context of changes that might threaten privileges and powers'. The power of individual actions, therefore, is crucial in resisting state policies to reduce inequalities.[14] Thus, it was argued, empirical research on these theoretical ideas should 'move down from the level of macro-sociological relationships to study more immediately the social processes that are involved in class mobility or immobility': namely, how middle-class individuals draw on and apply family resources across generations in the reproduction of advantage. Within this remit, a place for case study research that could unravel 'the actual narrative structure of individuals' mobility trajectories' was acknowledged. Again, I was greatly taken by the elaboration of this micro-sociological theory and especially the methodological implications flowing from it.

As a qualitative researcher in the field of class analysis, I became increasingly interested in the idea of doing in-depth research on how parents mobilise their resources in the education of their children. After all, educational qualifications are the main requirements for entry into most middle-class occupations. Interestingly, the theory of middle-class reproduction was subsequently expanded by Goldthorpe with specific reference to explaining class differentials in educational attainment: namely, why middle-class children are still far more likely to pursue higher education and attain higher levels of credentials than are working-class children.[15] In a critique of Bourdieu's 'culturalist' explanation of class reproduction, he drew on Boudon's use of rational action theory (RAT) and, more specifically, the effects of various choices at different branching points in the education system, to explain persisting class differentials in attainment. Choices are determined by evaluations of the costs and benefits of different courses of action. Class – as in differential resources, opportunities and constraints – influences these costs and benefits and, by implication, the evaluations, decisions and strategies of people in different class positions. Thus, disadvantaged families require greater assurance of benefits for more costly courses of action to be pursued in comparison to advantaged families. This is why class differentials have stayed the same despite an expansion of educational opportunities. These opportunities may have grown but there are still constraints on working-class children going to university that middle-class kids do not have to confront.

While I remained enthusiastic about doing research on education and the middle class, I was disappointed with the development of this theory for various reasons, as I have argued elsewhere. First, although I share some misgivings about Bourdieu's theory of social reproduction, I thought it a shame that Goldthorpe now dismissed the role of cultural resources in the processes of class mobility and immobility. Indeed, it seemed that the mobilisation of social resources had also dropped from view, as had the possibility of exploring the interconnections between the different types of resources. Second, social class was discussed only in terms of economic resources and income derived from employment at that. I was always taught that social class was more than income.[16] I also wondered whether income levels alone could explain class differentials in education since it is important to consider the demands on that income (the number of children to be educated, for example) and choices about how it is spent (holidays might be preferred over education, after all). Third, I was not overly keen on the use of RAT to examine family (rather than individual) practices. While I have always believed in the importance of human agency, that people exercise choices and make decisions, I have never liked the economistic and often brutal sounding nature of cost–benefit analysis. Social life – especially family life – has always seemed much richer than that to me.[17] In sum, it was my view that much has been lost in the explicit development of a theory of middle-class reproduction.

Keeping up with theoretical developments

My dissatisfaction did not stop me embarking on empirical research and, indeed, theory construction has continued unabated. In his most recent collection of essays, for example, Goldthorpe elaborates on his theory of social mobility (as it is now called) where he pays close attention to mobility strategies and the 'causal narratives' that underpin them. The economic resources associated with different classes shape mobility strategies, including goals and aspirations. While members of all social classes may wish to maintain their position and avoid downward mobility, the priority attached to upward mobility via, say, higher education, might vary. In the context of class competition in which the advantaged middle class and disadvantaged working class are engaged, Goldthorpe distinguishes between strategies 'from below' and strategies 'from above'.[18] Strategies from below involve difficult choices with limited resources. There is a conflict between modest mobility into skilled manual employment, for example, which requires vocational qualifications, and the more ambitious aspiration of upward mobility into non-manual employment via higher education. It is rational for those in working-class positions to opt for the more modest route. This choice is reinforced by economic constraints as the opportunity costs of remaining outside the labour market still apply and continuing in education requires some parental economic support. These constraints influence the time frame by which choices are evaluated, pushing towards an early rather than late pay off. This is why members of less-advantaged classes have not pursued opportunities for higher education. Cultural and social resources are also directed towards the more modest goal of class stability.

Turning to mobility strategies 'from above', Goldthorpe suggests that the choices facing advantaged families are relatively straightforward. The obvious goal is to maintain their advantaged position via higher education. Thus, middle-class parents encourage and support their children in the pursuit of higher levels of educational attainment. That explains why they have been so ready to take up the opportunities presented by educational expansion. This choice is not constrained by inadequate economic resources, for middle-class parents enjoy high level and stable incomes which are at their highest as their children pursue higher education, thereby encouraging long-term investment. The costs are few to their standard of living and, indeed, they can pursue various options including buying homes in high-status areas with good quality state schools, paying for private tuition and buying a private education altogether. The resources and choices give 'children from more advantaged backgrounds a clear competitive edge in, supposedly, "meritocratic competition"'. This is why children from advantaged families are pushed to their academic limits and, where failure occurs, further investments are made. Ascriptive processes come into play here as social networks and social skills are mobilised. Goldthorpe concluded, 'In sum, while those pursuing strategies from below may show some reluctance to participate in meritocratic competition, those following strategies from above do so far more readily, even aggressively and on terms that are clearly weighted in their favour.'[19]

Overall, therefore, class structural constraints determine the rational adaptive mobility strategies of people in different classes that explain the relative stability of class across time and space. This is how the constraints of the mobility regime are reinforced and perpetuated. Without doubt, Goldthorpe's theory of social mobility is an elegant and sophisticated explanation of stable rates of mobility across time and space. Arguably, it is an example, *par excellence*, of 'middle-range' theory construction. It is, I think, highly convincing. As an abstract theory, of course, the analytic explanation is outlined in a very general rather than specific way so that it is not located in real time or space. It is context free in this respect. It needs to be subjected to empirical research that is located in specific temporal and social contexts. It is easy to imagine how empirical research would throw up problems with such a neat theory. Indeed, it is not hard to think about problems with the theory at an initial discursive level.[20] It certainly fits the statistics in a *post hoc* way but whether it is a plausible account of class mobility strategies in itself is another matter. To me, the characterisation of the working class and the middle class sounds like the classes of the first half of the twentieth century rather than those of the second half and the beginning of the twenty-first century. Arguably, the theory is too tight (a criticism Goldthorpe levelled against Bourdieu of course!) in seeking to explain continuity and does not give due acknowledgement to changes regarding the expansion of educational opportunities while also explaining continuity.[21]

These last points can be demonstrated with reference to the concept of 'strategies from below'. It is a wonder that anyone from the working class – including my sister and me – ever pursued higher education. To be sure, my parents were very keen for all of us to do well at school and go on as far as we could. Of critical importance, however, was the fact that I was able to go to a college of further education and then on to university, as was my sister, because we received state maintenance grants that were available in Britain in the 1970s and 1980s.[22] Thus, I am not convinced that members of the working class would see their first priority as to maintain their class position and seek upward mobility only as a secondary option. Securing a disadvantaged position is not the same as securing an advantaged position after all. That members of the working class shy away from higher education because the risk of failure threatens the maintenance of their class position sounds unconvincing too. It is hard to imagine the risk is high when children of disadvantaged families have had to demonstrate ability to a greater extent than their advantaged counterparts in any case. It is easier to imagine someone dropping out of college or getting poor grades finding themselves in low-level clerical work than low-level manual work (especially as this is fast disappearing in any case).[23] The discussion of the advantages of vocational training for employment in the trades applies much more to young men than young women. The description of 'strategies from below' does not explain how some members of the working class exploited the increased educational opportunities that became available in the second half of the twentieth century.

Similar kinds of remarks can be made about the characterisation of mobility 'strategies from above'. I am not so sure that things are now as easy and as straightforward for the middle class in the supposedly merito-cractic competition for good qualifications and good jobs as Goldthorpe suggests. My middle-class siblings and friends with children tell me other-wise, especially when their children struggle academically. Again, the portrayal of the advantaged middle class sounds like the middle class of the first half of the twentieth century and not the expanded, hetero-geneous middle class to be found in Britain and America today. To be sure, those in the top professional and managerial positions – in medicine, law, accountancy, high-level management – probably have a relatively easy time of it as they did in the past. Whether those in middle and lower-level non-manual occupations such as teaching, social work, mid-dle management, various administrative positions and so on are able to generate and sustain their positions over generations is open to question.[24] Moreover, one can imagine that many new members of the middle class – of working-class origin, of which there are many – would be unable to draw on resources, held over generations, compared with established middle-class families. When this heterogeneity is borne in mind, it seems more likely that the description of 'strategies from above' applies to its upper echelons and not all of the middle class. Families new to the middle class do not, I suspect, have a clear edge in the meritocratic competition. They feel anxious about helping their children do well in school.

These thoughts have sprung to mind as I have begun to draw on how my family and friends are now helping their children through school so that they get good jobs. Again, from my academic studies, I sense that middle-class reproduction is not easy or straightforward in America where there is much 'fear of falling': namely, concerns about downward mobility across generations.[25] It is not hard to imagine, therefore, that American sociologists would find the theory of middle-class reproduction problem-atic. After all, since the end of the post-war boom, income inequalities have grown in the UK and the USA. Tax cuts in both countries have led to a retrenchment in social welfare provision including educational opportunities. Members of the working class have experienced unemployment while members of the middle class have confronted job insecurity. It would not be wildly speculative to wonder if mobility into the middle class and stability within the middle class are both now much harder to attain than they were.[26] It is in this riskier economic and political climate that the meritocratic competition for educational credentials to secure entry into high-level jobs has become more important – and the source of much anxiety – for middle- and working-class families in Britain and America. Such anxieties are not merely private troubles. They are public issues that raise difficult questions about public policy – as to what governments can and cannot do – to create open and meritocratic societies. This is why the study of social mobility is so significant.[27]

The empirical research in Britain and America

My motive for research, therefore, was to explore how middle-class parents mobilise their resources to help their children through the education system and into good jobs. I was keen, in particular, to examine whether it is a straightforward process in the harsher economic and political climate that has prevailed since the end of the post-war boom in the mid 1970s. I also wanted to do comparative research between Britain and America. Having enjoyed a short spell in the USA doing secondary research for a textbook on class inequalities in the two nations, I now aspired to do some empirical research in America too. There are good intellectual reasons for comparing middle-class reproduction strategies of course. As I discussed earlier, they have broadly similar patterns and trends in social mobility and, as I have just noted, they have experienced very similar economic and political currents in recent years. Be that as it may, British and American parents help their children through quite different school systems. Different institutional and administrative arrangements – such as the public funding of education and the extent of educational opportunities – prevail.[28] An interesting issue to consider, therefore, is how do middle-class parents help their children through particular education systems and, importantly, how do they resist or circumvent national and local institutional or administrative arrangements that might undermine their ability to help their children succeed in school? Are middle-class mobility strategies easier to pursue successfully in one nation over another? Again, if so, what are the implications for public policy?

Accordingly, I undertook intensive interviews with middle-class parents in Manchester in the UK and Boston, Massachusetts in the USA. I did the fieldwork in Manchester during 1996–97 and in Boston during 1998–99. In total, I talked to 86 parents who had 116 children between

Table 1.1 *The sample of British and American interviewees*

	Interviewees	Number of children
British doctors	12	
British partners	12	33
British teachers	12	
British partners	9	28
American physicians	12	
American partners	9	27
American educators	12	
American partners	8	28
Total	86	116

them (see Table 1.1. See also Appendix A). Knowing that the middle class is heterogeneous, I decided to interview people from two middle-class professions – medicine and teaching – and their partners, who, of course, were in a wide range of other occupations. Doctors, or physicians as they are more likely to be called in the USA, were chosen as an example of an established profession known for its high level of occupation inheritance and social closure. In the recent past, it was a very male-dominated profession too. My interviewees occupied a range of positions in hospital settings in both nations, in General Practices in Britain and Community Health Centers in the USA. Some of them were married to fellow medics although I also spoke to husbands and wives who were social workers, engineers, opticians, teachers and so on.[29] Teachers, or educators as Americans sometimes say, were chosen as an example of a less established semi-profession known to welcome women. It remains female dominated.[30] I spoke to teachers in state or public schools, in private schools in Britain and in charter schools in America. Again, some of them were married to fellow teachers although I also spoke to partners who were bank lending officers, customer service supervisors, accountants and journalists.

The interviews were conducted either at the interviewees' home or at their workplace. They lasted, on average, about 2 hours. They took the form of life history interviews in that I asked the interviewees about their family and childhood, their educational experiences and their work histories. Then we went on to talk about their children and their education and, where applicable, work histories. I did not, in other words, formally operationalise the concept of resources in my *aide mémoire*. Rather, it was in the subsequent analysis of their narratives that I looked for the mobilisation of economic, cultural and social resources. By talking to the interviewees about their early lives first of all, I was able to get a sense of how they had *drawn* on family resources before they entered the labour market. The interviewees were, in effect, 'children' in these stories reflecting back on how their parents had helped them do well in the education system and enter good jobs in the labour market. I thought it important to hear about their experiences of education and employment first and how various opportunities and constraints had shaped their lives. I felt sure their experiences would influence, in some way, how they now assisted their children. The interviewees then became 'parents' as they described how they were *applying* their resources to help their children navigate their way through the school system into employment. In other words, the life history interviews captured, as far as humanly possible within 2 hours, the transmission of resources from one generation to the next.

The eighty-six people I interviewed in Britain and America were a diverse group of men and women. Most of the British interviewees were born in Britain although there were also first-generation migrants from Ireland, Jamaica, India and South Africa. Some of them were the second or third generation of families from Ireland, Russia and former East European countries like Hungary. It also became apparent during the interviews that a number of the informants were Catholic or Jewish. Most of the American informants were also born in the USA including four African Americans. The sample also included first-generation immigrants from Puerto Rica, Japan, Sri Lanka and Britain. Some of the interviewees were second or third generation of families from Ireland and (former) East European countries. Again, many of the American interviewees were Catholic or Jewish. They were, in other words, quite an ethnically and racially diverse group of people.[31] They were also diverse in their class backgrounds. Some came from long-established middle-class families whose grandparents, it seemed, were also middle class. Other interviewees came from families new to the middle class in that their parents had enjoyed upward mobility from the working class into professional and managerial jobs. Still others were from working-class backgrounds that had enjoyed long-range social mobility into medicine, teaching and various other occupations. The heterogeneity of the middle class, noted in nationally representative quantitative research, was certainly to be found here.[32]

The interviewees had 116 children between them. Most of the families I spoke to comprised two or three children. The sixty-one British children ranged in age between 1 and 34 years although each interviewee had at least one child making their way through the education system. Most of the interviewees' children were still working their way through the school system. They were to be found in state or private primary schools, secondary schools, sixth form colleges, colleges of further education and universities. The fifty-five American children ranged in age between 6 months and 29 years and, again, each interviewee had at least one child currently making their way through the education system. Thus, they were attending public or private elementary schools, middle schools, high schools, universities, liberal arts colleges and local community colleges. In both countries, some of the older children were trying to establish themselves in the labour market while others were already well established in their careers. There were examples of young people who were in high-level professions like medicine, law, accountancy and so forth. There were others in lower-level non-manual jobs like youth workers, hotel managers, athletics trainers, travel agents and billboard designers. Some of the interviewees' children – often the sons and daughters of medics and their partners – were already in the higher echelons of the middle class. Other young people, invariably the sons and daughters of teachers and their partners, were in the lower levels of the middle class.

Finally, since economic resources have been identified as the key to the transmission of middle-class privileges and power across generations, either in themselves (the emphasis from Goldthorpe) or in terms of their conversion to cultural capital (as discussed by Bourdieu), I want to make brief reference here to the interviewees' economic resources. Some of the interviewees referred to monies derived from family inheritance, other businesses, investments in stocks and shares and so on. Still, it seemed that salaries drawn from their jobs were the main source of family finance.[33] Most of the interviewees happily told me their salaries. Focusing on joint salaries, these varied considerably depending on whether (usually women) partners worked full time, part time or stayed at home or whether husbands and wives were now retired (early or otherwise).[34] Thus, the joint salary of British doctors and their partners ranged from £45,000 (a GP and a retired nurse) to £168,000 (two hospital consultants). The joint salary of the British teachers ranged from £28,000 (a secondary school teacher and former teacher retired early on medical grounds) to £67,000 (a secondary school teacher and head teacher). The joint salary of the American physicians ranged from $111,000 (a late entrant to medicine still on a low intern's salary married to a nurse practitioner) to $400,000 (two hospital physicians). The joint salaries of the American educators ranged from $93,000 (a teacher and insurance broker) to $208,000 (a high-school teacher and principal of a high school). The medics and their partners were certainly more affluent than the teachers and their partners although the range among the doctors and teachers and the overlap between them are worthy of note.

Plan of the book

I have organised the rest of this book around a discussion of the mobilisation of economic, cultural and social resources in the reproduction of advantage in that order. The chapters come 'in pairs' so to speak. First of all, I draw on the interviewees' accounts of how their parents mobilised a particular resource on their behalf when they were children. These accounts, of course, come from a sample with diverse social class origins including those from upper-middle-class and middle-class backgrounds maintaining (at least) the position of their parents and those from lower-middle-class and working-class backgrounds who have improved upon their parents' class location.[35] Most of the interviewees were growing up in the benign economic and political climate of the 1950s, 1960s and early 1970s. Then, I consider how the interviewees, all now middle-class parents, are mobilising these three resources on behalf of their children as they make their way through the school system and into the labour market. The interviewees' children were being educated in the 1980s and 1990s and, of course, in a very different economic and political context – arguably, a much harsher climate – as, I hope, will become readily apparent.

Chapter 2 draws on the interviewees' reflections on how their parents used their wealth and income to ensure educational success. Those from advantaged backgrounds enjoyed a high-quality education in private schools or the best public schools. In America, it was secured in affluent white communities thereby avoiding school desegregation and, in Britain, at the best grammar schools under the tripartite system.[36] They enjoyed financial support from parents through higher education although there were tales of financial hardship in meeting college fees in the USA. Those from more modest backgrounds enjoyed an ordinary public or state school education although parents found ways of circumventing risks. Academic success propelled the interviewees into higher education. Parents gave some financial support but financial constraints were felt, especially in the USA. Chapter 3 considers how the interviewees, now all middle-class parents, were mobilising their economic resources to secure their children's educational success. Against the backdrop of the decline in the public/state school system, money was used to buy the best education. In America and Britain, the most affluent paid for a private education or lived in exclusive, predominately white communities while the more modestly paid sought out the best public/state schools. In the context of spiralling college tuition fees, the affluent American parents were saving to support their children's higher education while the less affluent expected their children to draw on loans. In Britain, the affluent parents were untroubled by student fees while the more modestly paid were anxious about paying fees and living expenses.[37]

Chapter 4 focuses on how the interviewees' parents' educational aspirations and occupational horizons facilitated their success. In America and Britain, those from advantaged backgrounds spoke of high expectations regarding exam success and the pursuit of higher education. Similarly, parents had high occupational horizons, especially for sons. Medicine was viewed as a desirable career while teaching was viewed as a good job for women.[38] The interviewees of more modest class backgrounds also spoke of their parents' high aspirations although they more cautiously hoped for rather than expected academic success. In America and Britain, parents wanted their children to get good jobs but occupational horizons were lower. Teaching was a desirable job for men and women. Chapter 5 explores how the interviewees, as parents, were mobilising their cultural resources to the advantage of their children. In both countries, my informants clearly wanted their children to do well at school and go into higher education. Those who went to the top universities and colleges themselves expected their children to do so too while those with more modest educational experiences did not have such high expectations. Again, in both America and Britain, the interviewees did not have specific occupational aspirations for their children. They were less gendered than in the past. All of them wanted their children to derive satisfaction from their jobs. The affluent interviewees envisaged financially supporting their children if those jobs were low paid while financial independence was important to the more modestly paid interviewees.[39]

Chapter 6 considers how the interviewees' parents employed their social networks to their children's advantage. In both countries, those from advantaged backgrounds spoke of how people in their local communities shaped their educational aspirations and expectations. They spoke of the effect of their own contacts, made at school, college and beyond, on their careers, in helping them secure prestigious positions in medicine or teaching. At the same time, those with more modest class backgrounds also talked of how people around them, other academically able children and teachers, provided a supportive environment.[40] Contacts were also important for their career advancement although they were not necessarily high-level contacts providing information and advice on prestigious positions. Chapter 7 focuses on the interviewees as parents using their social networks to facilitate their children's advancement. Across the two countries, the interviewees drew on their contacts for trustworthy information and advice about the most academically reputable schools.[41] This process was especially pronounced in the USA given that the public school system is of more variable quality than the British state system although the difference is one of degree and not of kind. All parents wanted their children to mix with (invariably white) children of parents sharing similar aspirations. Parents' local interpersonal relations and their children's emerging social networks were shaping the course of their lives in circumventing setbacks in education and easing entry into the labour market.

In the Conclusion, I consider the key findings of the research and the implications for public policy. Talking to the interviewees as children from a diverse range of social origins, it was obvious that those whose parents occupied privileged positions utilised their available resources on their children's behalf. More importantly, however, I spoke to people whose parents did not have such resources to mobilise to their advantage and yet they were still successful. Their educational and occupational success has to be placed firmly in the context in which they were growing up, i.e. the benign economic and political climate that prevailed in the 1950s and 1960s that allowed them to exploit new opportunities for higher education and good jobs. The favourable economic climate was very important but so, too, were political interventions, in facilitating the take-up of such opportunities by disadvantaged groups. Politics made a difference then and it still matters now. Talking to the interviewees as adult parents, it was also readily apparent that they were using their resources to help their children do well in school and beyond. In the less favourable economic and political climate of the 1980s and 1990s, however, the reproduction of advantage was not easy, the desired outcomes were not assured and a level of indeterminacy prevailed. The difficulties of trying to ensure their children matched or bettered their social position left many unhappy with current educational provision. Arguably, these concerns are not just middle-class preoccupations, they concern all parents whose children are currently in school. They are especially pressing issues for the disadvantaged. Thus, there are political allegiances to be forged pushing for change which could replicate the important political interventions of earlier eras.

2   Material help with education and training

In the Introduction, I outlined Goldthorpe's theory about the mobilisation of different types of resources – economic, cultural and social – in the reproduction of advantage. I noted how Goldthorpe emphasised the crucial importance of economic resources – wealth, income and other forms of capital – in this process because they are exclusive goods (i.e. they are not owned by others) that can be easily transmitted from one generation to another.[1] Thus, with respect to education, middle-class parents with high and stable incomes use their economic resources to buy the best education for their children, especially in the acquisition of educational credentials. Armed with good qualifications, their children are then in the position to apply for high-level jobs that demand the very educational credentials they have bought. Without such economic resources, working-class parents cannot buy the best education for their children so they cannot ensure that their children do well at school and achieve the educational qualifications required for entry into good jobs. Economic resources are the key, therefore, for middle-class and, for that matter, working-class reproduction. The theory, of course, makes the processes of class reproduction sound deceptively simple and straightforward. What about the different demands on income such as the number of children to be educated? What about different choices about how money is spent, including holidays, for example, over education? How can a lack of economic resources be circumvented? How might other sources of economic capital be mobilised?[2]

This chapter draws on the interviewees' accounts of their childhood and experiences of education and how their parents mobilised their economic resources to ensure their educational and occupational success. To be sure, my interviewees had to reflect back on a process about which they may have been only partially aware.[3] I am sure there was much they could not or did not tell me. Nevertheless, as I hope to show in the course of this chapter, they revealed a great deal about how their parents helped them through school and college into 'good jobs'. They did so, fortunately for me, by situating their lives in the times when they were growing up: namely, the decades following the Second World War, from the initial austerity of the post-war period of the late 1940s and early 1950s, through the 'long boom' of the late 1950s and 1960s until the early 1970s when economic uncertainty started to increase again. My sample, as I noted in the Introduction, included people from middle-class backgrounds as well as those from lower-middle-class families (as Americans would say) and those from working-class origins (as the British might say). I heard stories of parents, therefore, who commanded considerable economic resources and those who had few to their name. This diversity allowed me to explore the processes by which affluent parents mobilised their economic resources for the benefit of their children and how parents in more modest circumstances found ways of securing their children's future without them.

I focus on the way the interviewees' parents used their wealth and income to secure the best education for their children thereby increasing the probability of academic success. I will show how, in the USA, the interviewees from affluent backgrounds enjoyed a wholly private education paid for by their parents directly and how it was especially important for circumventing the perceived risks posed by school desegregation in the 1950s and 1960s, or poor academic performance.[4] Alternatively, they lived in wealthy, invariably white, communities with the best public schools chosen by their parents for this reason specifically, thereby mobilising their economic resources indirectly. The interviewees from more modest lower-middle-class families, with limited wealth and income, attended a mix of good and bad regular schools. Be that as it may, they enjoyed academic success and the risks and constraints posed by school desegregation had to be avoided by other means. Similarly, the interviewees from affluent middle-class families enjoyed continued financial support at college as their parents met fees and living expenses, although a few middle-class parents, it seemed, struggled to pay these costs with other children to support too. Some of those from lower-middle-class origins did not face economic constraints as their parents, who enjoyed secure employment during the long boom, could support them through college. Others, however, clearly felt them when their studies were interrupted or limited to local community colleges. For the medics of modest backgrounds, however, soft money in the form of scholarships and loans eased their passage through medical school, as did the financial support of partners.

Like their American counterparts, the British interviewees from the most affluent middle-class families enjoyed a private education paid for by their parents. There were some interviewees from less affluent middle-class families who also enjoyed a private education albeit free of charge as academically able students who had won state scholarships to private schools.[5] Most of the interviewees, whether of middle-class or working-class origin, however, enjoyed a high-quality state education in grammar schools having passed the eleven plus exam under the old tripartite system. Some of the interviewees of working-class origin left school at 16 although it was not direct financial pressures that pushed them into employment. The majority, however, experienced no financial pressures to leave school and, as academically successful students, continued with their studies. Unlike their American counterparts, the British interviewees did not have to pay university fees under the auspices of a free state education system. The interviewees of middle-class origin had to rely on their parents for living expenses. Few spoke of parents experiencing financial difficulties with such expenses although family circumstances, notably the presence of younger children at home, sometimes meant that money was hard to come by. The interviewees of working-class origin enjoyed maximum grants from the state so they did not have to rely on parental support be they completing medical degrees, university degree courses or teacher training courses. Interestingly, state support was still available when academic success was not always forthcoming. A comparison of the mobilisation of economic resources in pursuit of educational success in America and Britain is considered in the Conclusion.

Economic resources and American education

Coming from diverse social backgrounds, my American interviewees told very different stories about their childhood, their families' standard of living and their educational experiences. Consequently, they recounted various ways in which their parents mobilised economic resources to ensure their educational and occupational success. Only two interviewees spoke of how their parents directly paid for a wholly private education from elementary school onwards. The son of a lawyer turned university professor and a clinical psychologist, Nikos Yacoby, and his three siblings, were educated at a small private school run on the principles of John Stuart Mill.[6] Living in a big city known for its poor public school system, especially large classes, his parents paid for an education that embraced a 'high level of individual attention'. Similarly, the only son of a successful businessman, Michael Reed, attended a small fee-paying Quaker school from the start. His parents, he recalled, had assumed he would attend the good local public school in the affluent neighbourhood in which they lived. He was redirected to another school by the local school authority as part of the desegregation of schools and bussing in the 1960s. Unhappy with their son going to a school with lower academic standards, poorer facilities, fewer resources and, specifically, large classes, they elected to send him to a fee-paying school with a strong academic reputation and a focus, once again, on 'individual expression and creativity'. Examples of parents paying for a wholly private education for their children, therefore, were rare indeed although, as I will show, the reasons why they did so frequently influenced how other interviewees' parents mobilised economic resources on their children's behalf.

Thus, even though many of the interviewees came from secure upper-middle-class and middle-class backgrounds, their parents were not sufficiently affluent, or inclined, to pay for a wholly private education for their children. That said, there were numerous examples of how parents mobilised their economic resources to pay for a private education selectively and strategically when circumstances demanded it. That is to say, there were some interviewees who moved between the public state system and the private school system in their elementary years. Such movement occurred when there was an element of risk in securing educational success in the public school system.[7] The risky situation, once again, was that of desegregation and bussing that was under way in America in the 1950s and 1960s. Growing up in a wealthy upper-middle-class family in the South, for example, Patrick Dutton's parents, a lawyer and a teacher, moved him and his siblings to a private school during the period of change. As he explained,

I actually attended three different elementary schools. At the time in the early 1960s, the American education system was going through endless turmoil with integration, melding poor social economic classes with higher economic social classes and although my family were, for their time and place very liberal, they realised that disrupted education was not the best for their children. I then went to a private school for two years and then went back to a state-funded education system until I was in ninth grade . . . This little town had a reasonable school system and, as a matter of fact, integration came very smoothly to [F] . . . Having said that, there were issues that arose with highly increasing class sizes, inadequate numbers of teachers for that time and I think that my parents felt that it wasn't probably appropriate for me to go through those sorts of issues at the time.

Patrick's parents, therefore, mobilised their economic resources when they feared changes in the education system could threaten the academic success of their son and his siblings.

A number of the interviewees also spoke of how their parents transferred them from public elementary schools in their local community schools to private high school. They mobilised their economic resources to secure the best education possible for their children. Thus, like those parents who wholly educated their children privately, they chose schools known for their academic reputation with good facilities, high-calibre teachers and, most important of all, small classes where their children could enjoy high levels of individual attention. These were the conditions that were seen to facilitate educational success. Jack Poole, for example, recalled how his parents, both MDs, applied to four private high schools on his behalf and he eventually boarded at a highly prestigious boys' academy where a high proportion of young men went to Ivy League schools. Similarly, Paula Bailey, the daughter of a highly successful businessman was sent to a 'very exclusive well-known girls' school' with a very high academic reputation. The academic record of such schools, in other words, was all-important. At the other end of the scale, other interviewees – like Kerri Clegg and Patricia Walker – were sent to small Catholic high schools where some fees were charged.[8] Kerri Clegg recalled how her mother, a single parent, worked very long hours as a hospital secretary to pay for her school fees. As Kerri explained, 'she would often take me in with her and so I often spent many hours there after school and weekends and things like that'. Considerable sacrifices were made to secure economic resources to ensure that Kerri had the best education possible.

Without doubt, these interviewees' parents mobilised their economic resources to increase the probability of their children's educational success and they were invariably successful in this objective. Many of these interviewees, as I will discuss later, went to Ivy League schools or other good colleges in which they completed four-year degrees. The direct use of economic resources to secure educational success, therefore, was obvious. It was also very important in circumventing failure (or only modest success). David Neale, for example, was the son of a very successful engineer, whose parents transferred him to a private high school in tenth grade. Again, there was a situation of risk although, in this instance, it was David himself who was 'the problem', as he readily acknowledged:

When I was in public school, I wasn't struggling but I did do badly in a couple of classes. I think so that they wouldn't have to be repeated, my Mom put me in a private school. I think tenth grade I didn't do very well. [The school] was big and there were a lot of distractions so I failed geometry and my Mom made me do summer school in geometry. And then I had been tested for the private school and been accepted and so then I went to the private school for eleventh and twelfth grade because I would have never, probably never, have graduated. I wasn't studious at all. I wasn't being bad but just doing whatever I wanted to do.

The private school, a school for the gifted and talented, had small classes and fewer rules and regulations and David eventually settled down to his studies.[9] The mobilisation of economic resources, therefore, was crucial in overcoming David's modest academic achievements in the public school system.

Most of the interviewees went to public high schools although it was evident from the interviews that some of them went to very good public high schools – known especially for their academic achievements – while others did not. Some of the interviewees lived in affluent suburban communities and they knew their parents had bought houses in particular localities for their good schools. In these instances, the interviewees' parents used their economic resources indirectly to increase the likelihood of their children's academic success. One of seven children, Rachel Gilbert was sure that her father, a highly successful businessman, 'picked the town because of the school system. My father was very involved in that. They knew and liked that system.' Similarly, George Marshall spoke of how,

[N] had a very good school system and I'm sure that was a major consideration of [my parents] when they moved there. I grew up the first twelve years of my life on a post-world war II housing development where there were very small five-room single family houses and then we ended up moving when I was 12 or 13 to a more upper-middle-class type area.

George followed his father, a medical scientist, to Harvard although, interestingly, it was a radical experience for him as he became involved in the anti-Vietnam War effort that shaped his subsequent socio-political beliefs and values. Reflecting back critically on his privileged background, he recalled how it was a very 'insular community' with 'little racial or economic diversity'. It was, in other words, all white and upper middle class. The racial dimension of his parents' decisions about where to live for the best schools did not go unnoticed.[10]

Not surprisingly, the interviewees from more modest backgrounds did not live in such affluent communities and neither did they go to such good public schools. Their parents did not have the economic resources to secure the best education possible either directly or indirectly. Be that as it may, many of these interviewees emphasised that their educational experiences in 'regular' public high schools were good. Almost invariably, they described how they attended large urban public schools. These were schools with lots of tracks to cater for academic and vocational careers and young people usually went on to college, although they attended local community colleges more often than not.[11] Bob Farrell, the son of a painting contractor, spoke of how his regular high school 'certainly had strong standards academically and behaviourally'. In the top academic track, as many of them were, these interviewees spoke of how they enjoyed good teachers who pushed them and other academically able students to succeed. Anna Gray was of the view that she got the education she needed. As she explained, 'I think if you are a self-starter, it doesn't matter where you are as long as you have access.' Interestingly, Mary Moran spoke of how she won a scholarship, via tests, to a private school. The daughter of a longshoreman, 'there was no question' that she had to get a scholarship as there was no money to pay school fees. She and her parents decided, however, that she should go to the local public school. As she explained,

I really always liked science and math and this was a girls' school and I don't think they were strong on science or math. My high school had 2,000 kids in it so they could afford to have a decent physics teacher. These other teachers who were at the smaller private school did not have the facilities no matter how much money you paid. It was too small.

There were others, however, who were more critical of the local public schools they attended. Ken Bailey, the son of an engineer, suggested the 'school system was actually pretty lousy'. Having enjoyed a good education in a North-eastern state, he then experienced a very poor public school system in a Southern state.[12] A low proportion of students went to college, standardised test scores were poor, academic expectations among the teachers were low and most kids were not academically orientated and went to community college or into modest jobs 'packing groceries' and so on. Ken admitted that it was only in the tenth grade that he took his studies seriously with a view to going to college, and he did well academically. Those from more modest backgrounds told similar stories. Ray Chapman, the son of a police lieutenant and a school secretary, explained that he attended a very ordinary school where most kids went into the trades and the aspirations of a largely homogeneous white working-class community were 'fairly limited'. He excelled in the academic track, however, and enjoyed the support of family and teachers. Similarly, Yuko Yacoby, who lived with her mother, an immigrant seamstress, and her sister when she was growing up, described her education as 'dismal' in comparison to her husband's private school experiences. It did not matter, however, she said, 'as I was always a studious student'. While she enjoyed teacher support, she stressed 'I've always been my own director. I have had teachers that were supportive *because* I was an A student and I always did very well.' Yuko felt that support only came with proof of ability and she was aware that it was not automatically forthcoming for all students at her school regardless of ability.

Despite the lack of parental economic resources and their sometimes 'mediocre' experience of public school education, the interviewees from more modest social backgrounds still succeeded in elementary and high school. To be sure, their academic ability and effort was a crucial component of their academic success. What was also important, however, was their parents' desire for educational success and how they circumvented risk without economic resources.[13] This was most evident among the African American informants of my sample. Roy Morgan, for example, was the son of an automobile mechanic and a nurse and they were political activists 'spearheading the effort to desegregate schools so that minority kids could be exposed to the better schools'. He explained:

> There was one school in particular, my junior high school, where my parents actually gave another address than our own address. They wanted me to start at the junior high school that was reputed to be of high academic standards and I'm glad they did because the neighbourhood school was a very, very troubled school. My parents did not want me to go there.

It was under 'these false pretences', as Roy put it, that he was able to go to a good public school and later a prestigious examination school. Similarly, Susan Rogers spoke of how her parents helped her secure a scholarship into a private school at the time of desegregation in Boston in the 1960s because they were 'very worried about me leaving the neighbourhood and having to go to another neighbourhood as it was very violent'. Not wanting to leave her school friends, however, she explained that, 'I just accelerated my programme and finished school a year earlier so I wasn't involved in the whole Boston thing.' As an A student, she could do so. In this risky situation, Susan's parents found other means of securing their daughter's academic success.

Overall, it was evident that the middle-class interviewees' parents mobilised their economic resources, directly and indirectly, to ensure that their children enjoyed the best education possible either in private schools or in the public school system. They sent their children to schools with excellent facilities where they enjoyed a high level of individual attention from high-calibre teachers. Such conditions increased the probability of educational success, reducing risks such as those posed by the desegregation of public schools in the 1960s and modest achievements in the public school system.[14] Thus, many of my interviewees of upper-middle-class and middle-class origin were very academically successful. The interviewees from more modest social backgrounds – from lower-middle-class and blue-collar origins – invariably attended regular public high schools. As academically able students, however, they were exposed to good teaching in the top tracks that also facilitated educational success. A lack of parental economic resources, therefore, did not hold these able interviewees back although the parents of my African American interviewees, without economic resources at their command, had to find various ways of ensuring that their children received a good public school education which would facilitate educational success in the context of desegregation and bussing in the 1960s. This was how the interviewees' affluent parents mobilised their economic resources for the benefit of their children and how parents in more modest circumstances found ways of securing their children's future without them.

Economic resources, higher education and beyond

With one exception, all of my interviewees continued with their education past high school, going to a variety of different institutions including Ivy League schools, private liberal arts colleges, state universities and local community colleges. The tuition fees of these establishments, of course, varied widely and the interviewees described how their parents helped them financially and how they obtained soft money including federal aid, scholarships, government subsidised (low-interest) and other loans. It was not surprising to find that those interviewees from upper-middle-class backgrounds, who had enjoyed an exclusive private education for all or part of their early life, went on to enjoy substantial economic support from their parents. Parents' earlier economic investments in private schools usually paid off in that their sons and daughters were, more often than not, very academically successful and they went to Ivy League schools or other reputable universities and colleges.[15] Jack Poole, for example, spoke of how about two thirds of his cohort applied to Ivy League schools and a third of them were successful in getting into these top schools. Indeed, he explained, 'the college officers tried to get people to apply to other places. They didn't want people to be disappointed.' Similarly, the other male interviewees who were wholly privately educated also enjoyed considerable academic success, and went on to Ivy League schools. Their parents supported them financially by paying all of their tuition fees and their board and living expenses. These interviewees did not have to take out any loans to finance their higher education and pay them back later. Parental financial support, in other words, was total.

Substantial investments of this kind were not always confined to the direct payment of college fees. Economic resources were very important, yet again, when educational success was in jeopardy. Paula Bailey, for example, became pregnant in her first year at college when she was 19.[16] She married her husband, a student in his fourth year of study, and had her second child at 21. Anxious that she continue with her degree programme, her wealthy parents continued to pay her college fees and contributed to her and her family's living expenses. Paula had planned to go to medical school and they indicated that financial support would be forthcoming, but she decided against such a demanding programme at a time when she was bringing up young children. Instead, they financed her through a graduate progamme in social work at a time when her husband was in medical school. As she explained:

They paid for my college and my graduate school. Ken was on a scholarship and he got a scholarship which paid for his tuition and the school gave us a small stipend each year so we lived on that stipend and then money my parents gave us, living expenses that they gave us. They bought a condominium when we moved as they have a lot of assets.

Arguably, in supporting their daughter in this way, they had also allowed their son-in-law to continue with his medical career rather than be under financial pressure to seek employment and support a young family in his early twenties. Ken acknowledged this help although he somewhat downplayed the extent of that assistance when he said, 'My in-laws helped us as because at that time we had my daughter. I was married in college and so we had financial assistance from them just for living expenses. You know they would help us out, just to help us get by.'

Such high levels of financial investment, however, were rare and most of the interviewees spoke of how they enjoyed some financial support from their parents while they contributed to tuition fees and/or living expenses by obtaining scholarships, taking out low-interest loans and working in the summer and sometimes in term time during their college years. For some, these packages were easy to assemble but, on the whole, they were not – even for those from middle-class families. A highly successful student at public high school, Anna Gray went to an Ivy League school. Although her parents were middle class in that her father became a successful businessman during her teens, they had come from more humble origins and her mother, for example, was fearful about college expenses. As she explained:

My Mom was raised during the Depression so everything was really financial and when I applied to colleges from high school, she thought I should go to the junior college right near our home town because it could save a lot of money as opposed to going to [S] and getting in there. My father said do whatever you can, do the best that you can and we will support you, which was a little different.[17]

Anna's parents paid her tuition fees, although it left them 'strapped' with four younger children still at home, and she took out loans and worked in the summer to meet her living expenses. Advanced Placement (AP) courses completed at high school counted as credits that reduced costs and she graduated early which 'saved my folks two or three thousand dollars'. She was cognisant of how her experience of college life was rather different from other 'prep school kids' at her Ivy League school for in the summer 'everyone was out having trips to Europe with their parents but [work] was what I had to do'.

Descriptions of such financial packages were not always so very different between the middle-class interviewees like Anna Gray and those from lower-middle-class backgrounds. They varied in the degree of direct financial support from parents but not in kind. Take, for example, Mary Moran, the daughter of a longshoreman who enjoyed financial support from her parents when she went to college. Born in the Depression, her parents had high levels of anxiety about money and 'they were very tight'. She said, 'They were never debt collectors or anything and they always had a lot of money in the bank but the reason they had that was they didn't spend any money.'[18] Their anxiety levels were high even though her father was 'reasonably well paid. It was just after the Second World War so it was a good time to be in America. You didn't have to be very educated to make a reasonable amount of money.' Given the high cost of university applications, Mary was limited to four and her choices had to be local to avoid additional travel costs etc. Nevertheless, she enjoyed parental financial support and it was 'an honour, almost a status thing' to use their retirement funds to contribute to tuition fees. Susan Rogers, the daughter of a machinist and a sales clerk, enjoyed a college scholarship, government loans and a little financial support from her parents. She was able, she said, 'to live on campus and get a full college experience because that's another way poor people who are not able to afford college tuition, they stayed at home. My parents encouraged me to do that. They thought that that was the total sort of experience.'

For other interviewees from more humble backgrounds, however, financing a college education was much tougher and there were fewer opportunities or choices. Substantial loans were taken out to pay for tuition fees for reputable if expensive colleges and were still being repaid. Others, however, were confined to their local community college.[19] Bob Farrell was the son of a painting contractor whose income was very seasonal. As he explained:

My father's income was very much lower middle class and because they had a mortgage on the home and five children, there wasn't a lot of money left. I was accepted to three schools and [S] community college was the cheapest of the three to go to and that pretty much determined that I was going to go there. I also got a scholarship in the first year that paid for my tuition so my first year and last year at [S] were free on scholarship and the middle two years the family paid for.

The scholarships were won 'on the recommendation of teachers and grade performance'. As one of the older interviewees, Bob lived at home and he explained how savings were made:

Commuting back and forth from home to [S] was somewhat expensive but when you commute you can pay for it as you go rather than whereas if you live there you have to pay for that upfront, plus I worked part time whilst I was going to school to earn some money that I needed to commute back and forth. It was kind of a hand to mouth thing.

Thus, there were variations in levels of financial constraint among those from lower-middle-class backgrounds. While Mary Moran's father enjoyed a secure and good wage as a longshoreman, Bob Farrell's father's seasonal work meant that financial constraints were more keenly felt.

It was those from modest backgrounds who also experienced interruptions in their higher education. That said, it was my African American and first-generation immigrants who described the harshest ordeals. Yuko Yacoby's parents divorced soon after they immigrated to America and Yuko, as the eldest daughter, felt greatly responsible for her mother and younger sister. She dropped out of college for three years and worked so that they could move to better accommodation and she taught her mother to drive and helped her get a job, so 'I made her as independent as possible then I felt more comfortable going back to school.' Going to college in the late 1960s, Roy Morgan recalled how 'the political times were such that scholarships became available to us'. Issues of racial inequality were high on the agenda and he explained how African American students found that 'universities were literally waving fist-fulls of dollars to have us go'. Roy was able to attend a prestigious college that paid for the first three years of his studies. However, 'the bottom fell out of the programme' in his final year and he had to leave, find work and return the following year.[20] He also recalled: 'I got a job at university working for support services which is kind of ironic, which basically meant a white man with a big stick stood on the side and I would drive back and forth to the physical plant bringing paper over for the duplicating centre.' It was not surprising to find that it was a woman of colour, Bernice Hughes, who never made it to college because of economic constraints in her youth. As she explained:

I could have gone but I didn't go. In twelfth grade, I had been accepted but I didn't know what was next once I had gotten accepted and they sent the bill and it was like 'Oh my goodness, now what do I do' so I didn't go. I don't know how to acquire the money because it was something new to me.

Experiences of higher education, therefore, were very different depending on the interviewees' socio-economic background and family circumstances as it influenced the type of institution that they attended and the extent to which they worked through college and/or took out loans to be repaid later. For most of the American educators, their full-time education finished with a college degree at 21. They often acquired Masters' qualifications later on which they paid for themselves. For the physi-cians, there was still a lot more education to be undertaken. In their early twenties, they embarked on four-year and sometimes seven-year courses if doing a combined M.D./Ph.D. programme.[21] There was less financial support from parents although it varied along similar lines to before. Most of the medics took out low-interest loans and obtained scholarships from the medical schools to finance their studies and every-day living. Not surprisingly, those from the very affluent backgrounds continued to enjoy some financial assistance from their parents. They finished medical school relatively free of debt although not all of the medics of upper-middle-class origin did so. David Neale's early indiffer-ence to education made his life somewhat more complicated later on. He gained entry to medical school on his third attempt when he was in his early thirties with stepchildren and children to support. Now in his early forties, he was still on a low intern's salary and it was his wife, Sarah, a nurse practitioner who was the main breadwinner. With outstanding loans of $160,000, David planned to move to a cheaper state and pursue a lucrative clinical, rather than research, career once he had completed his training.

Loans, it seemed, were readily available to the medics as 'good risks'. Ken Bailey explained how the banks operated when he said, 'If they think you are a good risk, they won't give you money, they'll shove it down your throat because they want you to take it so you'll pay them the interest.' Such loans were available to all medical students irrespec-tive of their socio-economic background. It was not straightforwardly the case, however, that those from more humble backgrounds were the most saddled with debt. While she lived very frugally as a medical student, Judy Kennedy took out the maximum in loans that her father, a TV engi-neer, invested in the stock market in the 1980s. Monies made reduced her debts considerably. As she explained:

I think he always was savvy but he didn't have any money to do anything because of all the kids. I think, finally, when we all got out from underneath him, they were very frugal and he was saving all along as best he could but, at that time, he realised very quickly that the way to make money was to put it in the stock market.[22]

The other women doctors, of modest origins, often enjoyed good scholar-ships from medical schools keen to attract women and women of colour. As young people in their twenties, many of my interviewees married while studying and the financial support of partners was often very important too. Directed into teaching at high school, Susan Rogers went to college and then embarked on a teaching career. She later enrolled in graduate school and obtained the all-important pre-med qualifications. Armed with a scholarship, she also enjoyed the financial support of her husband, an engineer, through medical school and, later, on a low intern's salary. Many ways and means of doing medicine were found without relying on the financial support of parents.

Overall, the interviewees from upper-middle-class backgrounds frequently enjoyed a smooth transition into higher education as they moved from top private or public schools to the most reputable universities and colleges. Their parents gave them considerable direct financial support in paying tuition fees and living expenses and other forms of indirect financial support, especially when academic success was threatened once again. The interviewees from less affluent middle-class families could not draw on such financial support from their parents – especially if there were younger children at home – so they often worked and took out loans to finance their studies. Among the interviewees from middle-class families, therefore, there were quite different experiences of parental economic support through their years of higher education. The same can be said of the interviewees from lower-middle-class and blue-collar backgrounds. Some of the interviewees were able to go to colleges of their choice and their parents gave them important financial support. Enjoying relatively stable incomes in the affluent 1960s, while maintaining modest lifestyles, they were in a position to do so. Grants from government programmes and scholarships from colleges and other bodies were also important sources of economic support. That said, there were other interviewees who faced considerable financial constraints confining them, for example, to less prestigious local community colleges. Interruptions to studies due to financial pressures were not uncommon among these interviewees either. Consequently, their experiences of higher education were very different – i.e. much tougher – than for the more affluent interviewees.[23]

Economic resources and British education

Like their American counterparts, the British interviewees from the most affluent middle-class backgrounds usually enjoyed a wholly private school education at fee-paying schools. Once again, their parents' aim was to buy the best education – at schools with high academic reputations, extensive facilities that were the basis of a broad curriculum, high-calibre teachers and small class sizes so their children enjoyed a lot of individual attention – to facilitate educational success. Of course, some of these interviewees went to prestigious schools where they also boarded, that were very expensive, while others went to local independent schools where fees were lower. Be that as it may, all of them stressed the importance their parents attached to educational success and, quite simply, how money was used to buy the best education possible. Lawrence Foster and his three siblings, the children of a GP, all attended fee-paying boarding schools, and reflecting back he said, 'it was enormously expensive and there's the wrench of having your children away from you at a boarding school but I think they thought it was the way to get the best standards that they could for their children.' Echoing these sentiments, Edward Myers spoke of how his parents 'had a perception that the best they could do was to get an education that they would pay for', while Andrew Underwood stated, in a matter of fact way, that he was sent to a particular private school because 'it was known for its academic achievements and they could afford to pay'.[24]

It was very clear, therefore, that economic resources were mobilised to buy the best education possible thereby increasing the probability of academic success. While educational success was crucial for sons, parental investment in daughters' education was not so clearly directed towards this end, as two of my older women interviewees – married to doctors – explained. Both Margaret Brown, the daughter of a small businessman and Janet Jones, a GP's daughter, attended expensive fashionable ladies' colleges. Margaret was sent away because,

I think at that time it was possibly thought to be fashionable. I had an aunt who went there and certainly in her day it was fashionable. I always felt it was for young ladies, you know, which, in my aunt's generation was OK but the time I got there the girls had started to go to university.

Janet spoke of how she was expected to learn the appropriate social graces that would facilitate a marriage to an equally eligible young man. She recalled how,

My sister and I were both send away. My brother stayed at [S] grammar school. The boys' education in [S] was rather better than the girls'. I think we were expected to acquire some social graces. Education was more important for boys . . . [My brother] went to Cambridge whereas the girls were expected to marry well.

Janet's remarks also highlighted the importance attached to her brother's education although he did not go to private school. As she explained,

J. would have gone if he hadn't been so clever but he got a free place at a good school so they kept him at home. They thought he would get a good education. They would put the money into sending him to university and getting professional qualifications.

Indeed, he later became a top lawyer in London.[25]

Most of the interviewees, however, did not come from families with parents wealthy enough to afford this kind of exclusive education. There were examples, as in America, where some interviewees dipped in and out of private education to increase the probability of academic success. Some of the middle-class interviewees, for example, explained how their parents sent them to private primary schools to increase their chances of passing the eleven plus examination to grammar school. They were very keen to ensure that their children received the best state education possible. Ronald Watson's parents, for example, transferred their son to a private primary school between the ages of 9 and 11. As he recalled,

I can't remember the exact details but my parents decided to transfer me to [T] and took me on the train to school. I presume it was because they wanted me to go to a grammar school and they thought perhaps I would have a better chance at the eleven plus and you could perhaps get a scholarship. It was quite a successful outcome as I passed the eleven plus and I got a scholarship.[26]

Similarly, Sylvia Harris, the daughter of a small businessman, followed her older sister to a private primary school. They were educated privately since her sister was a 'slow developer' and 'my mum felt that she wouldn't be very well placed in a large group of thirty children'. Both daughters, however, passed the eleven plus examination and went to their local state grammar school. As Sylvia explained,

I think the fact that I passed the eleven plus seemed to be the key factor. I think possibly had I not, my dad was of the persuasion that perhaps I would have gone somewhere else and he would have found the money for me to do that.

These interviewees' parents, therefore, strategically mobilised their economic resources to ensure their children enjoyed a high quality state education that would facilitate academic success. They educated their children privately so as to increase their chances of passing the eleven plus examination which guaranteed entry into the well-regarded grammar schools under the tripartite system that operated in Britain from the mid 1940s to the mid 1970s. Indeed, a number of other middle-class interviewees enjoyed an elite education at fee-paying direct grant grammar schools although it was not their parents but the state that paid school fees. At the time they sat the eleven plus, these interviewees also sat the entrance exams for such schools in the hope of winning a scholarship. The scholarships covered the fees although parents were expected to make a contribution in the region of £50 per annum. Muriel Crisp, whose mother was a nurse and whose stepfather was a self-employed taxi driver, explained how, 'You took the eleven-plus and you also took an exam for the school. Manchester in those days gave out free places and so I got a free place. They couldn't have afforded for me to have gone private.' Susan Pearson offered an interesting perspective on these state scholarships to the effectively private schools. As she explained, 'They were just local based schools for middle class kids and they cost. There were ten scholarships a year and I took the exam and I was accepted for one of those scholarships. We couldn't haven't afforded for me to go but I went free.' It was the lower-middle-class parents, it seemed, who exploited this way of securing the best free state education for their children.[27]

This issue aside, most of the interviewees' parents did not have the economic resources to invest in their children's education. As academically able students, however, the majority of them, of middle-class and working-class origin, attended their local grammar schools. Interestingly, a number of the working-class interviewees referred back to their parents' education and how they had been thwarted from going to grammar school because of a lack of economic resources. They talked about how their parents had passed the eleven plus but had not been able to go because a grammar school education had to be paid for in the 1920s and 1930s. Sometimes coming from big families, they experienced economic pressures to seek employment at the earliest opportunity, usually at fourteen.[28] Others spoke of how their parents had had the opportunity to go to grammar school. Nevertheless, the expectation was to leave school and find paid work. Their experiences of economic constraint clearly shaped their aspirations for their children to enjoy the opportunities presented by the introduction of a free education system after the Second World War. These economic constraints fuelled a fierce desire for their children to enjoy mobility via education. It was a desire that was born, in part, out of resentment at how economic constraints had restricted their lives. It accounted for the ways in which everyday sacrifices – albeit of a smaller kind than in the past – were made for books and specially measured school uniforms that often cost, in the words of Susan Parry, 'an arm and a leg'.

Unlike their parents, none of these interviewees experienced financial pressures to leave school at the first available opportunity, at 15 or 16, in order to find paid work and contribute to family income. As in the USA, their fathers often enjoyed stable albeit relatively modest incomes in the post-war period of affluence and/or they came from small rather than large families so outgoings were not so high. Moreover, as academically able students, different expectations prevailed, for as Sheila Parker explained, 'If I hadn't have passed, I would have left at 16.' In the context of growing opportunities for higher education in the 1960s, parents were happy for their children to continue with their studies if they so wanted even if some financial sacrifices were required. That said, it was those interviewees of working-class origin who left school at 15 or 16, although it was unhappy experiences at school rather than direct economic pressures that propelled them into paid work. Pauline Lomax, in fact, offered a strong class slant to her account of why she left school at 16. The daughter of a miner, she had a strong sense of being looked down on at school, because of her family's working-class background. In so many words, she hinted that she did not have the required cultural capital even though she was an A stream student. Accordingly, she hated school and was anxious to leave at the first opportunity, and with good O level results she joined the civil service in a clerical position.[29] Her parents, she said, were 'delighted when I got O levels and left and went into the civil service, you know. It was a white-collar job. A big step up.'

Institutional arrangements, whereby academically able students went to grammar schools while the less able attended secondary modern schools, had a major impact on educational outcomes including expectations and the willingness to make economic sacrifices in pursuit of educational success. Interestingly, a small number of interviewees attended state secondary modern schools. The daughter of a small businessman, Celia Watson failed the eleven plus examination and attended her local secondary school and she said, there was 'never any question of my staying on for any kind of higher education'.[30] Her parents being quite comfortably middle class, however, she was sent on a one-year secretarial course at a reputable private college paid for by them so she would secure the better secretarial jobs available and eventually marry well. Arguably, their economic investment paid off in that she married a doctor. Graham Dowds, a computer systems manager, went to a secondary modern school and it 'didn't get any resources. All the resources went to the grammar school. It was secondary in all ways.' Nevertheless, the head teacher believed he had students with potential and, 'He decided to have a stream to do O Levels and sent letters out to the parents of those who were in the A stream and some parents didn't want anything to do with it but fortunately my parents said yes, we will sign a form to let him stay on until he's sixteen.' As an only son, there were no financial pressures on him to leave school at 15 and nor were there economic constraints propelling him into paid work. Graham did not transfer to the local grammar school, as he could have done, as he did not enjoy school. His parents were very happy when he found a secure office job with the local electricity board. His parents' attitudes, he said, came from 'the uncertainty of the war and the recession before the war and all that, and that's what they were looking for, for me to get a nice steady job'. His parents' experiences of past economic constraints shaped Graham's school career and his choices in subtle and complex ways.

Finally, only one interviewee, Bridget Underwood, went to a comprehensive school in the early 1970s since she lived in an area where the local education authority had abolished the old tripartite system and sent all children at the age of 11, regardless of academic ability, to one school. That said, her parents, a welder and a clerk, moved their only daughter from the state comprehensive to a private convent between the ages of 14 and 16 when, as Bridget acknowledged, her 'work started slipping off and I think my behaviour starting slipping off as well'. As she recalled, 'Basically, I got one report and they had a massive row with one of the teachers. I can't remember how it happened. I know there was a monumental row one Friday and on the Monday I was in the convent.' In the new school, her academic performance improved and so did her behaviour. However, the cost of sending Bridget to a private school was high and, on the advice of a teacher, her parents transferred her to a state sixth-form college at 16. Her mother, she recalled, 'needed to hear that because at that time Dad had lost his job so financially it was very hard to stay on at the convent. I think Mum was really relieved to hear of a non-fee-paying school that had a good reputation.' Bridget's parents mobilised their economic resources to circumvent their daughter's poor academic performance at a state school, although, with a modest income, they could only afford their daughter's convent school fees for a short period of time. The two years spent at the convent, however, were enough to facilitate Bridget's academic success, allowing her to pursue a medical career later on.[31]

As in the USA, therefore, it was readily apparent that the middle-class interviewees' parents mobilised their economic resources, both directly and indirectly, to ensure that their children enjoyed the best education possible either in private schools or in reputable state grammar schools. In Britain in particular, however, middle-class parents mobilised their economic resources to ensure that their children were academically successful enough to pass the eleven plus examination to secure entry into high quality grammar schools. They were well aware of how success or failure at the eleven plus dictated the quality of state education their children received and its implications for their children's academic success.[32] Above all else, therefore, they sought the best state education to increase the propensity of their children's academic success. As academically able students, the interviewees from more modest working-class backgrounds secured entry into grammar schools and, like their middle-class counterparts, they also enjoyed a high-quality state education free of charge. Unlike their parents, who had faced economic constraints in the 1920s and 1930s, they did not experience financial pressures to leave school at 15 or 16. That said, it was those from working-class backgrounds who left school – be it grammar school or secondary modern school – at the first available opportunity. Economic pressures did not push them into paid work directly but past experience of financial constraints shaped their parents' and their own decisions and choices in subtle and complex ways at that time.

Economic resources, higher education and beyond

As I noted above, few of the interviewees experienced any financial pressures to leave school at the first available opportunity, including those from modest working-class backgrounds. Accordingly, the move from compulsory to further education was smooth as the interviewees usually continued their studies at the same school.[33] The transition to higher education differed from that of their American counterparts because the future doctors embarked on a specialised (usually six-year) medical degree course at 18. Some of the medics attended the prestigious London medical schools while others attended Manchester University's medical school. Unlike in the USA, the interviewees' parents were not expected to pay university fees so there was no talk of an issue that so dominated the American interviewees' lives. Of course, the British interviewees' parents were expected to contribute to board and lodging. For the older interviewees going through medical school in the late 1950s and early 1960s, state scholarships were available on a competitive basis according to A level results. Thus, some of the interviewees from quite wealthy backgrounds enjoyed these scholarships as a result of examination success. Still, there were financial pressures to live at home so that parents would not have to meet additional living costs. Knowing that it was not a good thing to do, Edward Myers had no option but to attend the local medical school where his father taught because his parents 'were in no position to support me away from home', since his older sister was working her way through medical school while his parents were paying private fees for the younger sister still at school. Family circumstances, albeit affluent ones, dictated otherwise.

Doing a medical degree, therefore, was not a substantial financial burden for the British interviewees or their parents. Of course, the interviewees from affluent backgrounds still enjoyed financial support from their parents who contributed to their living expenses and they could often be generous in allowances to their children. Those from working-class backgrounds could not draw on such family resources but they had full maintenance grants from the state to support them. Economic support from the state, therefore, was crucial in facilitating their studies. Barbara Coombes, for example, spoke of how 'I was on a full grant because [my parents] had very little money.' In effect, she was financially independent from the age of 18 and she did not have to depend on her parents for financial support.[34] Medical schools often gave scholarships to the academically successful. Julia Dodd was one of three children of a manual worker and a housewife. Excelling at her local grammar school, she spoke warmly of how her headmistress encouraged her to do medicine. Her parents were greatly alarmed when she expressed this aspiration because they 'thought this would be absolutely impossible because they couldn't afford to buy me a practice but eventually, they, I think, saw the headmistress and she reassured them on that score'. The headmistress helped her with her medical school application and she was accepted at a prestigious medical school in London. She went on to say,

and then the headmistress got some notification of something else and she said 'would I like an entrance scholarship as well?' so I had another interview which everyone thought was a terrible waste of the fare to London but I ended up getting the major entrance scholarship to [M] which meant I had a hundred quid a year extra for all my time there on top of a full grant.

Although academically successful, there were plenty of stories of exams that were failed, finals that had to be re-sat and so forth. Consequently, some took longer to complete their courses than others, especially if they also did a specialist degree as part of their medical training, and needed additional economic resources. One medic, Peter Smith, failed his exams mid-way through the course and was forced to leave. One of the older interviewees, he completed two years of National Service and spent two unhappy years working as a drug rep. Anxious to complete his medical degree but unable to return to his former university, he completed the final three years of study abroad and lived away on a local education authority grant. At the time, he was married with a young son and his wife, Diane, explained how they managed financially:

I went back full time when Damien was about two and I worked full time until Peter finished his training and came back. I had a sister's post at the outpatients department at [C]. It wasn't bad. I wasn't being taxed. I had a child which I could claim tax relief on and Peter actually got a grant from Manchester. He managed on his grant and I managed on my income. We had to move from a nice comfortable flat but it paid off. We didn't look upon it as a sacrifice although other people did for us.

That said, she later spoke of how it was a difficult time when, effectively as a single parent, she had to work full time to secure the regular hours in hospital and the income was all important to support herself and her son, who attended a nursery full time, to her regret, from an early age. Her financial independence during this period, however, clearly allowed her husband to finish his studies unfettered by financial worries at this time.[35]

Having completed their medical degrees, these interviewees completed their pre-registration years, worked towards professional qualifications in hospital medicine or took the route into General Practice. Unlike their US counterparts, they enjoyed full salaries rather than nominal salaries during these periods of training. The path into a teaching career also was somewhat different in Britain in comparison to America. Some of my interviewees went to university and completed a three-year degree course and then undertook a one-year postgraduate certificate in education course (PGCE). Others went to teacher training colleges and gained either a Teaching Certificate that took three years or a degree in Education that took four. The route chosen was dictated by A level grades, in that those who were academically successful went to university and those who were less so went to college. The first route enjoyed a higher status than the second and was seen to lead to better careers in secondary rather than primary school teaching. Thus, it was not surprising to hear how Rosemary Hill's parents, a manager and a teacher, encouraged her to remain at home an extra year and retake her A levels with a view to improving her grades and going to university. They supported her financially during that year although she stressed, 'Money wasn't something that I had much of as a teenager at all. It wasn't considered to be appropriate. I had a very, very small allowance. I think it was sort of like half a crown that didn't get you very far even in those days.' Still, her parents did not apply any financial pressure to force her to go to teacher training college or find a job. They supported her financially into her late teens so that she could pursue the more attractive route into teaching via university.[36]

The interviewees from middle-class backgrounds did not usually get a state maintenance grant for living expenses since their parents' income was deemed too high for government support. It was parents, therefore, who paid for accommodation and day-to-day living. Few of these interviewees' parents had difficulties giving financial support to their children although, again, some found it tougher to find money when they had a number of dependent children at home to support. Those from less affluent, working-class backgrounds usually enjoyed a full maintenance grant from the state that covered their living expenses. Again, they were not reliant on parental financial support during their time at university for a state grant gave them financial independence at a relatively young age. It was the norm to go straight on to a PGCE course for which all of the interviewees, irrespective of parental income, enjoyed a statutory state grant. As with the British doctors, progress through higher education was not always straightforward. Rosemary Hill, for example, became pregnant in her first year at university. She married the father of her child and they returned home for a year. They then went back to her university town where her husband, David, started as a trainee accountant in local government and Rosemary resumed her studies with her son in the university nursery. During this two-year period, David Hill was the main provider. They had their second son during this time and Rosemary spent the next two years primarily looking after the children. She then completed a PGCE and they moved close to both sets of parents for support at a time when they had little money or time as a young family.[37]

Both coming from what they described as lower-middle-class families, each with two children, their parents were an important source of financial and other support in allowing them both to establish professional careers and to raise two children at a comparatively early age. To be sure, such stories were not confined to the interviewees of middle-class backgrounds. Norman Jones started a joint degree in maths and physics but was distracted by student politics and the good life. His failed his exams badly and was thrown out of university at the end of the second year of study. He recalled how 'I blew it. There's no two ways about it', and he spoke of how his parents were 'desperately disappointed'. He applied to a teacher training college which was happy to accept him, because of his specialist subjects, and allowed him to complete a three-year course in two. As the son of a manual worker, he had enjoyed a full student grant for two years at university from his local education authority and they paid a further two years of grant at teacher training college. Having enjoyed the maximum amount of state grant (four years), Norman was not in a financial position to do another year of study and obtain a degree in Education.[38] He married a fellow student at college, they had their first child at the end of their teaching course and there were financial pressures to work. As he said, 'The child was born thirteen months after we were married in the August, which was the August after we'd both finished so with a child, living with parents, the financial situation, there wasn't very much choice.'

The role of state maintenance grants in facilitating less than straightforward careers should also be noted in the case of Pauline Lomax who, as I described earlier, left grammar school at the first available opportunity, with good O level results, to join the civil service in a clerical position. After three years in the civil service, she moved on to other low-level non-manual jobs but found herself redundant in the mid 1970s as the end of the long boom, especially in a declining region of the country, was increasingly felt. Returning to live with her parents, she worked in a succession of casual jobs and went to night school in the hope, initially at least, of securing A levels to get a better job. Enjoying success in her studies, however, she was encouraged to go to university. She recalled that it was a 'negative choice' at the time. As she explained,

> it was well, what's going to happen? Am I going to scratch around looking for a new job, possibly be unemployed again? You could actually get a grant then, full grant, so why not go to university on a full grant, you know? I'd got nothing to lose really.

In her early twenties, therefore, Pauline was able to go to university with a full grant to cover maintenance costs since her parents were not in a position to support her financially to any great extent. She completed a three-year degree followed by a PGCE. A teaching career was not her first choice but in her late twenties, she felt unable to forge a financial career in London when she wanted a family too. Her 'lost six years' as she saw it seriously curtailed her career options as a mature student later on which, as I noted earlier, she very much saw through the lens of class.[39]

Like those at university, those who went to teacher training college either relied on their parents to cover board and living expenses, or had a mix of parental support and grant money, or they enjoyed a maximum grant from the state. Such arrangements depended on their parents' economic status. There was only one reference to any financial hardship. Susan Parry's mother refused to give her financial support to do drama at university and persuaded her to do teaching training. Although Susan's father was a manual worker in local government, she did not receive a maximum grant since 'by that time Mum was working as a secretary so there was too much money'. That said, money was extremely tight because 'they'd sent my sister to a private school so we weren't better off at that stage but that wasn't taken into account on grants'. Her mother, in other words, had a lot of clout because of this financial situation. With one exception, these interviewees opted to complete their studies after three years. In their early twenties, they were anxious to find work and earn money and, indeed, as job opportunities in teaching tightened in the early 1970s, they were encouraged to take a job. Sheila Myers, who left school at 16, entered a career in teaching quite soon afterwards. After two years working in a laboratory, she worked as an unqualified teacher for three years at a time of teacher shortages. At 21, she went to teacher training college and enjoyed a grant and the financial support of her parents as she still lived at home. She married her husband, a newly qualified doctor, in her second year and also enjoyed his financial support while she completed her studies. The financial support of partners, therefore, came into play once again.[40]

As in the USA, once again, the British interviewees from affluent middle-class backgrounds experienced a smooth transition into higher education as they moved from their private schools or state grammar schools to highly reputable medical schools and universities. Unlike America, of course, their parents did not have to pay tuition fees so financial support was confined to living expenses. Sending their children into higher education in Britain, therefore, was not an expensive undertaking for most of these parents at all. The difficulties encountered by the less affluent middle-class interviewees in the USA were absent in Britain. The UK interviewees from less affluent working-class families could not draw on the financial support of their parents to the same extent although their parents, with relatively stable and secure incomes in the 1960s, could support them in various albeit modest ways. However, parents did not need to be the main source of financial support for living expenses. Rather, these interviewees enjoyed full maintenance grants from their local education authority that effectively made them financially independent at 18.[41] Government support, therefore, was important in meeting the indirect costs of higher education. It meant that economic constraints did not limit university choices or interrupt studies as was evident in the USA. Some of the harsher experiences to be found in the USA were absent in Britain.

Conclusion

This chapter has explored the processes by which the interviewees' parents mobilised their economic resources to secure their children's educational and subsequent occupational success. It has relied on the interviewees' reflections on their childhood and educational experiences and their thoughts regarding the financial support of their parents. Their narratives are told from their perspective as children and as the recipients of economic investment. Partial as their stories may be, the empirical material revealed much about the ways in which affluent upper-middle-class and middle-class parents used their financial assets to secure the best education possible for their children – whether it was in private schools or good public schools in affluent communities in the USA or in private schools and highly esteemed state grammar schools in the UK. Different institutional arrangements in America and Britain, of course, meant that middle-class parents mobilised their economic resources in different ways to increase the probability of their children's academic success and, crucially, to circumvent the different risks that might undermine such success. In America, however, some of the interviewees from less affluent middle-class families, whose parents had younger dependent children to support, experienced economic constraints as they sought to meet the financial costs of higher education via college fees. In Britain, arguably, the middle-class interviewees' parents did not have to make substantial financial contributions to their children's higher education under the auspices of a welfare state embracing a free education system.[42]

The empirical material, therefore, certainly confirms Goldthorpe's theory of middle-class reproduction although his emphasis on the ease with which this is achieved applies less well to the American data than the Britain findings. What, then, of those interviewees from modest class backgrounds without such economic resources? How did they succeed? In both the USA and the UK, the interviewees from such backgrounds were academically able students who enjoyed a good education in the top tracks of the large urban public schools in America or in grammar schools in Britain. The successful acquisition of educational credentials allowed them to pursue higher education. Against the backdrop of the period of post-war affluence in the 1950s and 1960s in both counties, their parents, who often enjoyed stable and rising incomes, could offer them financial support or, at the very least, they did not expect their children to contribute to family income.[43] Of considerable importance, however, were other sources of economic support beyond the family, in the form of federal grants, college scholarships and other sources of financial aid in the USA and state maintenance grants in the UK. It was in these circumstances that the interviewees could overcome their lack of parental resources and go on to enjoy educational and occupational success in medicine and teaching although the American interviewees still experienced economic constraints in meeting college fees in a way their British counterparts did not. For some working-class families therefore, a lack of family economic resources did not inhibit educational and occupational success as Goldthorpe's overly tight theory of working-class reproduction might have led us to expect.

3   Financial choices and sacrifices for children

The mobilisation of economic resources by parents certainly helped my American and British interviewees from affluent backgrounds in the pursuit of educational and occupational success as Goldthorpe's theory led me to expect. They were especially useful in risky situations that might jeopardise advancement. A lack of economic resources, however, did not hold back the interviewees from more modest class backgrounds in either country, somewhat contrary to Goldthorpe's theory. Academic success was, of course, crucial and soft money from various sources made up for the absence of financial assistance from parents not in a position to help out. In other words, the mobilisation of resources increased the probability of academic success although a lack of economic resources did not necessarily limit educational and occupational advancement. That said, the experience of competition for good jobs was much easier for the more affluent and far harsher for those from modest backgrounds.[1] These are the key findings of Chapter 2. This chapter focuses on the interviewees as parents and their accounts of how they were applying or had applied their economic resources to help their kids do well in school and get good jobs. Despite their diverse class backgrounds, the interviewees are now, of course, all in middle-class jobs in medicine and teaching although diversity persists in that the medics would be described as upper middle class by Americans and middle class by the British and the teachers would be described as middle class by Americans and lower middle class by the British.

The American and British interviewees were raising their children in different times. They had made their way through the school system in the 1980s or were still making their way through it in the 1990s.[2] In this chapter, I will show how some of the affluent American interviewees paid for their children's private education in its entirety. Most of the affluent physicians lived in expensive white communities chosen for their good public schools. Still, many expected to transfer their children to private high schools rejecting public high schools as too risky. The more modestly paid educators and their partners lived usually in less exclusive communities with ordinary schools albeit outside Boston. They shared similar concerns about public high schools but they were not in a financial position to circumvent this risk. Consequently, they had to monitor their children's progress very closely. All of the American interviewees wanted their children to go to college and they expected to support them financially although there was widespread anxiety about spiralling college fees. The most affluent physicians were in a position to save and they could expect support from their parents too. The less affluent teachers were very conscious of sacrifices still to be made and deeply concerned about the loans their children would take out. Some of the educators with older children had not experienced financial difficulties in helping their children. Those now sending their children through college, however, were feeling the strain, especially if they had younger children at home.

Again, the most affluent British interviewees and their partners paid for their children's education from the start. The remaining medics, however, transferred their children to private school at 11 so they could experience an old-style grammar school education, as they themselves had, rather than risk the local state comprehensive school.[3] The less affluent teachers and their partners were more likely to educate their children in the state system. Those who lived in Manchester's outer suburbs and beyond were happy with their children's state education in local schools. It was those in the city who had to think explicitly about the impact of residence on securing access to the best state schools. The affluent doctors continued to pay for their children's further education at private schools and further financial investments were made if educational success was not immediately forthcoming. They did not report financial difficulties supporting their children through university and those with younger children were not perturbed by the introduction of tuition fees or the abolition of student grants. The more modestly paid teachers and their partners also supported their children's further education in state schools and continued to do so despite setbacks. While the teachers with older children had not encountered financial difficulties supporting their children through university, those with younger children were greatly worried by new costs and they were adjusting their career plans and lifestyles according to the changed circumstances. The conclusion will take up the comparative findings regarding the mobilisation of economic resources in America and Britain.

Economic resources and American education

The direct use of economic resources to pay for a private elementary school education was found among only a minority of the more affluent

American physicians and their families. They elected to pay to secure the best education available. Michael Reed, as I described in Chapter 2, had enjoyed an elite education and he automatically sent his only son, Simon, to a private school. Even though he lived in a Boston suburb with one of the best public school systems, he said:

Both the public schools in our neighbourhood are very good but a lot of the extra curriculars that public schools used to have aren't there any more. People have tried to cut back on property taxes and have eliminated a lot of the sports and the arts, music and so we decided to send him to private school which is right near our house but which is able to offer a lot more of those resources.[4]

Michael enthused about the advantages of his son's private school where he enjoyed very high levels of individual attention across a range of subjects. Mary Moran and her husband sent their eldest son, Joseph, to private school after a very short period in a public elementary school. She explained:

We lived in a reasonably nice town where people are nice or they are not violent at least and some little kid smashed into him and the mother called up because the child had been sent to the Principal. It was almost like I could understand how this other kid could do that to my child because he would stand on the edge of the playground oblivious to the other kids around him and you could see how it would be so tempting to another aggressive kid just to give him a shove. So he needs smaller classrooms or whatever so we put him in private school for first grade and he has been there every since.

A preoccupation with small classes, where their children would enjoy individual nurturing and attention, was evident once again.

Given his own elite education, Michael Reed was entirely comfortable with sending his son to private school – what he was doing and why he was doing so. Other physicians made decisions about private education that were more anguished. Although he came from an upper-middle-class family and was educated in an affluent suburb of Boston, George Marshall now loathed his white suburban upbringing and both he and Judy, from a lower-middle-class family, were anxious to live in Boston so their three sons could enjoy the diversity of their mixed race neighbourhood. This diversity was very highly valued. The disadvantage of the city, however, was the Boston school system. There was a lot of violence in the schools, resources were poor, the quality of teaching uneven and so on. Moreover, both parents, as physicians, stressed that time pressures meant they could not monitor their kids' progress in the public school system.[5] As Judy explained, 'George was still pushing when Matthew was young to go through the whole public school system. I said there was no way. We don't have the time in the day to make sure things are going all right and he realised that. There was a lot of discussion though.' Consequently, they sent their children to a private school in the city although, as George explained:

It's not as diverse as we would like. I think they are very good in terms of teaching the kids about diversity and they have a real priority in hiring teachers who are from different ethnicities but it certainly is predominantly white. It doesn't have a big endowment so it doesn't have a lot of money for scholarships so there is some ethnic diversity. There is no economic diversity. There is not a lot of scholarship so it tends to be more middle class.

George and Judy were the only white physicians who lived in the city. Similar dilemmas confronted two African American women physicians and their families. As Susan Rogers explained:

We made the conscious decision to raise our children in a pretty diverse setting. However, in order to get any diversity you really have to remain in the city and in remaining in the city you make choices because not many parts of the city are affluent and people also envisage doctors and professionals, if you will, leaving the city and moving out to the suburbs where it's more affluent. My husband and I decided that that really was not the way to go. We enjoy the city. We believe the city, being a diverse environment, has a lot to offer our children so we decided to do that but with some consequences. Basically, the Boston system is lousy now although I'm a product of that public school system.

A sense of its decline, therefore, led Susan and her husband to send their three sons to expensive private schools. Interestingly, Kerri Clegg, who had had a private Catholic school education in the South, was involved in trying to increase the diversity of her son's private school. As she said:

Anyone can send in an application and I am pretty sure they are going to get a fair deal getting into the school but can you honestly say you want colour when you know what the average income is of people of colour and yet tuition is so outrageous. It's kind of built into the system where it's just not set up for certain people to participate.

These black middle-class families used their economic resources to pay for the best education although it was a white education.[6]

Most of the American interviewees, however, sent their children to public schools in the suburbs and small towns encircling the city of Boston much like their parents. The most affluent physicians and their families were heavily concentrated in communities with the most reputable public schools and they stated very explicitly that their choice of residence was influenced, first and foremost, by the local school system. On moving to Boston, they had talked to colleagues at work and other contacts (i.e. mobilised their social networks) about the best public schools, and they had sought out information that was available on a whole variety of issues including SAT scores, teacher–pupil ratios, teachers' salaries and so forth.[7] Houses in such areas were usually expensive to buy – in the $300,000 plus range – and expensive to maintain in the sense that the interviewees had to pay high property taxes as well. It seemed they could afford both. Even so, many of them talked about how they could have (and would have preferred) to move to suburbs and towns with far cheaper properties and property taxes but they were prepared to take on this 'burden' and make these 'sacrifices' for the sake of their children's education. Effectively, they were mobilising their economic resources indirectly to secure the best education for their children against the backdrop of a variable national education system As David Neale suggested, 'We are paying for the school one way or the other so if you don't pick the right school then you are going to hurt yourself, there is no question about that. It's definitely an advantage to go to a good public school.'

Like the physicians who sent their children to public schools, the less affluent teachers and their partners also sought to live in communities with good local public schools. Thus, while many of the teachers worked for the Boston school system (like the doctors who worked in the city hospitals), they invariable lived in the white suburbs and towns circling the city. Some of them lived in the more affluent suburbs of Boston although they frequently discussed the financial difficulties of doing so. Ray Chapman, an associate professor at a small college, conceded that he and his wife 'had struggled to live in a community which is expensive', with a high mortgage and high property taxes to pay, as well as meet the instalments on their own student loans. Rachel Garrett, a teacher, and her husband, Alan, a customer services supervisor, had rented in the community in which they lived for many years. They had moved to an expensive suburb when Alan was relocated to Boston as part of his job and they could afford to do so because the company paid for their house rental for the first two years. When the deal was up, they wanted to stay for their children's education but could not afford to buy. As Alan explained:

I came close to buying a house at one point but financial circumstances weren't right so we held off. I would like to buy a house but at this point I'm not looking, and saying when the kids are out of school we don't need to stay in this community. For now, we need to remain [here] for their sake really, for the continuity of them finishing school, their friends.

The Garrett family anticipated that they would only be able to buy a property in their fifties and then they would move to a cheaper community.[8]

Most of the teachers and their partners, however, lived in the less select suburbs and towns surrounding Boston. Only one family lived in Boston.

Again, as an African American family, Bernice Hughes and her husband preferred to live in a diverse community within the city. Nevertheless, Bernice's children were being educated in a white suburb under the auspices of an old bussing system.[9] Her neighbour introduced her to the programme when she expressed her unhappiness about her stepdaughter's schooling in Boston. She went through the programme and Bernice then signed up her own three girls when they were young. She described the programme in these terms:

> It is a special bussing programme called [M] and [M] was established basically over 20 years ago. It was initially set up to help desegregate. It was sort of private. It wasn't really mandated by the state or anything but someone thought it up that children from Boston would be bussed out, basically black children at first, to predominantly white suburbs to the schools there and some suburban school communities picked up the programme and they wanted to participate in that programme and that's how, and now it's basically Blacks, Spanish and Asian children who participate in and go out to the suburban schools who want to participate in it.

While the African American doctors and their families could afford to pay for a private education in Boston, this African American teacher did not have such resources but relied on a free bussing programme instead. In the absence of sufficient resources to send them to a private school, Bernice had to find other ways of securing a good education for her daughters.

While the interviewees, as parents, valued the local public elementary schools for the way in which they integrated their children into the local community, they had mixed views about public middle schools and high schools. Some physicians and their partners were planning to transfer their children to private high schools. Jack Poole's three children were currently in a public elementary school in one of the most select suburbs outside Boston and he was happy with their education so far. Even so, he was going to transfer them to private high schools so that they would enjoy the education he had experienced in a private school. As he explained, 'I think there's a lot more variability and so we just don't feel that there would be enough consistent school education through all the grades and especially high school.' When it came to the all-important high-school education when their children had to perform well in tests, these interviewees intended to exploit their economic resources directly in this way. Although his wife Jane was very anxious about the tuition costs, they expected to cut back on their standard of living for the sake of their children's education. The families that anticipated opting for a private high-school education usually included one interviewee – often husbands – who had been privately educated themselves. There were other physicians and their families, however, who were happy with their children's high-school education. First-generation immigrants from India, Charles and Nadia Khan, were largely content with Sukhdeep's education in one of the best school systems in one of the most select Boston suburbs. They had achieved what they had hoped for in emigrating.[10]

Many of the teachers and their partners shared similar concerns about high schools. Roy Morgan's daughter, Tina, was about to start at one of the best high schools in Massachusetts but he had reservations about its size with over 2,000 students since 'there is so much bigness there that she may get caught up in the social aspects of things'. Similarly, Elisabeth Danson's eldest son was about to take an entrance test for a parochial Catholic high school. As she explained, 'It's a matter of size. Socially, Nathan is not a butterfly. He would just rather sit with two or three friends and let the world pass him by. He needs to be pushed, go see what this is doing, go check out this club.' Parents, therefore, were often concerned that their children would be 'lost in the crowd' and not enjoy the individual push required to fulfill their academic potential. For the Dansons, however, financial considerations loomed large. As she said,

The question is how are we going to pay for it? We can pay today but in three years I'm going to have three kids at college at the same time. Do we want to start doing this now? We have to look at the big picture and how we're going to pay for college. It's a big issue. We've nothing saved. We're the typical American family.

Families without the economic resources to send their children to private schools, therefore, were worried about the public school system, the kind of education their children would receive and the extent to which they would be academically successful. They did not think the large public schools provided the right environment for academic success or, at least, there were many risks, which were difficult to monitor, control and circumvent. Circumstances demanded they keep a very watchful eye over their children's education.[11]

In remarkably similar ways to their parents, the interviewees were mobilising their economic resources to increase the chances of their children enjoying educational success. The most affluent physicians and their partners did so directly by buying the best private education possible or, indirectly, by living in the most exclusive and, of course, predominately white, communities on the outskirts of Boston known for their highly reputable public school systems. Those who preferred the diversity of Boston felt compelled to send their children to private schools and even some of those living in the most exclusive communities envisaged sending their children to a private high school. The backdrop to these investments was the perceived decline of the public school system due to a lack of investment. The interviewees were not happy with the quality of educational provision, or with the environment – with concerns about school violence and so forth – in which their children were expected to learn.[12] Accordingly, they took their children out of a system that posed a risk to academic success. Very similar concerns preoccupied the less affluent educators and their partners. They, too, sought to live in areas with good public school systems and some were able to do so by making financial sacrifices while others had to live in less expensive areas with less reputable public schools. Greatly concerned about their children's academic success, they closely monitored their progress through school, aware of the risks and their limited power to escape or circumvent them through the mobilisation of economic resources.

Economic resources, higher education and beyond

All of my interviewees expected their children to go to college and some of them expressed their hope that they would be successful in gaining entry to Ivy League schools, other reputable universities and colleges and, indeed, that they would go on to graduate school as well. Like their parents, there was no question that they would meet the financial costs of sending their children through higher education. It was often perceived as their responsibility as parents to do so. It was an 'absolute'. That said, many of the interviewees were incredibly anxious about tuition fees that had risen substantially since their time at college. Referring to media reports, for example, Jane Bennett spoke of how 'when I hear reports about what people speculate about the costs of going to college, I just, I am totally aghast, the numbers are so astronomical I can't quite comprehend them'. Such media projections, it seemed, made many parents, especially those with younger children, fearful of whether they could meet the financial burden of tuition fees.[13] Even the most affluent physicians and their partners expressed these fears although some of them were in a financial position to plan for the future. They were saving specifically for their children's college education with various savings plans, investments and so forth. Anna Gray, hoped her only daughter Amy, 6 years old, would go to an Ivy League school as she and her husband had done, 'if they could afford it'. She said, 'We have a savings plan. Everything gets taken out every month. We had a financial planner come in when she was about a year old and set things up. The cost is so much more now than it used to be.'

Anna was in a financial position to save for college fees since both she and her husband were physicians and they had only one child. Their financial position empowered them to plan for future education costs. Others had less sense of control although they envisaged ways of dealing

with the situation. With three children close in age who would be attending college in quick succession, Jane Bennett hoped that 'we'll get to the
point where we'll have fewer expenditures and I can obviously go back to
work full time'. There were other physicians and their families who had
not been in a position to save but they could rely on their parents to help
them out financially. Ken and Paula Bailey had not saved any money for
the two teenage children's college fees. Ken spoke of how he was ready to
remortgage his home, take out loans and so forth 'without hesitation' as
his parents had done for him. Again, however, Paula gave a different slant
to the issue. As young parents of teenage children, they had no savings as
Ken 'has only been out of training for two years and we bought this house
and so a lot of our resources have gone into this'. Still, she expected her
wealthy parents would help them out.[14] As she explained:

A number of years ago, maybe seven or eight years ago, they said something to
me about having a trust fund for the kids for their education but [they] wanted
to make sure they weren't offending Ken because [he would want to] feel like he
provides for his family or whatever. At the time, he said 'No, I can provide.' Now
reality is setting in so I'm not so sure. That's one of the questions that we have to
try and figure out soon.

The less affluent interviewees were also greatly worried about college
fees. They, of course, were also prepared to make sacrifices for their
children's education and they wanted them to be able to go to a college of
their choice. Despite the additional expense, many hoped and anticipated
that their children would go to small liberal arts colleges rather than huge
state schools where, again, they would enjoy individual attention and
excel, rather than be lost in the crowd and fail to fulfill their true potential.
They wanted their children to go to college straight from school, to have
the full college experience of living in dorms and maybe go on to graduate
school. Elisabeth and Don Danson, whom I referred to earlier, had three
sons of 13, 12 and 11. They expected their children to go to college,
like themselves. As Don said, 'I am very conscious of how much college
costs nowadays but one way or the other, they've got to go to college.'
They had started to seek advice from friends about remortgaging their
home, taking out loans and exploring the different scholarship options
in the hope that their children 'are smart enough or good enough to get
a scholarship'. Remembering financial pressures in the past, Elisabeth
hoped,

We don't want them to even have a hint that it's causing a hardship. They will
know it's costing big money and they will have to pull their end of it as far as
having some little part-time job and doing well but I don't want them in any way
to think that this is taking our livelihood away.

Don had additional concerns. He said,

I mean, I would hate to see them graduate from college with a big bill because I don't know, honestly, how much of it I would be able to pay towards their education. We don't have money saved up right now, that's for sure. It's coming up fast, four years.[15]

These interviewees with children currently exploring college options felt these tensions most keenly. Ray Chapman admitted that he and his wife had been 'like ostriches' who had not been in a position to plan ahead. As he said, 'We live from pay check to pay check in spite of having two professional careers. We have saved virtually nothing for college education and I have no idea how we are going to finance that.' From a modest working-class background, he had taken out loans to finance his own higher education and 'it was a large set of loans that got folded into a home equity loan that we will be paying for until the end of my days'. Without wealthy parents to help them out, the financial sacrifices involved in helping his children would be felt.[16] He did not envisage either of his children, Aileen or John, enjoying athletic scholarships and he conceded that 'my daughter's not an intellectual superstar, she won't get courted in that way'. Similarly, Rachel Garrett spoke of how she and her husband, Alan, had spent all their money living in a community with reputable schools to ensure a good education for their two children, leaving little for college fees. They could not shield their daughter, Chloe, from financial concerns as she herself would have to take out substantial loans. Chloe wanted to be a social worker and the consequences of an expensive school and then a low-paid profession – namely, paying big loans for many years to come – had been discussed. Alan also spoke of how his daughter 'is aware of her financial situation and she will have to get loans for herself and pay them back. It's going to definitely be difficult – this whole thing.' The debts they and their children would incur were of great concern.

Some of the interviewees' children had embarked on their college careers while others had completed their studies. One of the physicians' children had started college and financial considerations had been uppermost in the mind of David and Sarah Neale. He was still on a low intern's salary and Sarah was the major provider. Regretfully, Sarah explained:

Katy didn't apply to any Ivy League schools because they don't give money bursaries and I knew that Katy probably had the potential. I knew she did [have the potential] academically to get into an Ivy League school but they don't give much support and we just couldn't do it. We make enough money but we couldn't borrow money or if we did borrow money we would have had to start paying it back right away and we can't do that. We are trying to pay our loans. We can't pay her loan, so that definitely was a financial consideration.

Similarly, David emphasised that he did not want his daughter to carry debt from her undergraduate studies although he could foresee that and he expected her to come out of graduate school with debts. Taking a more upbeat and critical view, however, he said:

I'm from the mid-West and I think she had a great opportunity at [K] and she had some good opportunities that were reasonably priced so I think she is better off where she is . . . I don't know if you ever see those rankings where they rank the value of the school . . . They rank the values of the schools and you'll never see the best schools up there because they are not good value.

As it turned out, Katy was scouted for a full athletics scholarship that was a source of great relief given their financial concerns.[17]

A number of teachers' children had completed their college courses or were making their way through the system at the time of interview. They had attended or were attending a variety of colleges, choice being determined, most importantly, by academic performance. Financial costs, of course, varied and the interviewees spoke of the different packages they had assembled to pay for their children's education. Carole Gedicks described the way in which she financed her two daughters, Beverley and Hester, now in their early twenties, through private colleges:

Here, you remortgage your house. That's what you do. That's what I did. Well, the way I did it, it's called a credit line, and I was approved for so much money that I could borrow and so every time a bill came in I wrote out a check and the bank would pay for it and they would just up how much money I owed them so that's the way it worked. Now the girls also ended up [with loans] because you can borrow from the government but you have to pay it back; it's not until after you have graduated. So they have loans too. They owe about $15,000.

Both daughters returned home, where they were not expected to pay 'board and room', while trying to establish themselves in the labour market. Similarly, the Rothmans estimated that they had spent over £140,000 educating their three children in both expensive and inexpensive colleges. All three had remained in Massachusetts to avoid travel expenses and higher school fees although they had all boarded at college and completed their studies free of loans. The Rothmans had remortgaged their home and made sacrifices in their own standard of living about which they were very proud.[18]

Other interviewees, however, recalled the difficulties of financing their children's higher education. Despite coming from a wealthy family in the Caribbean Islands, Al Lopez had a very chequered career history, with experiences of redundancy, and his teaching career had begun only late in life.[19] It was Martha Lopez, with an uninterrupted teaching career, who had provided a stable salary. When the private college sought to reduce the amount of scholarship their daughter enjoyed in her second year of study, Martha explained:

> We weren't going to be able to send her but she found a way. She went in and spoke to them and said, 'I'm not going to be able to come back,' and the person in the financial aid office told her to have us write up what comes in and goes out and she got additional money. It was still very difficult. We were able to pay monthly instead but it was very difficult. By the time she finished, the fees were up to $21,000 and by that time we had our son in college as well.

Other interviewees told very similar stories. Patricia and Joel Walker, with four children aged between 13 and 20, spoke of the financial difficulties in sending their eldest daughter to college. Joel was sure that tuition fees had risen much faster than salaries when he considered college expenses in his day. He had hoped for more financial aid from federal programmes but 'with the income level that we have we don't get that much financial aid, so it's a big strain'. He suggested, 'Compared to your salary, it's definitely a lot to have to pay and everyone does the same thing. The middle classes are the ones that get the squeeze. The rich can do it because they have the money, the poor can do it because they don't have anything.' Despite two teachers' salaries, their financial strains were worrisome.

To be sure, not all of the interviewees' children had enjoyed straight-forward academic success. Nevertheless, as parents, the interviewees still supported them financially in the pursuit of educational qualifications. Barry Waite's two sons from his first marriage dropped out of college and he and his first wife had been very fearful about the consequences 'because of the decisions they had made'.[20] After a number of years working as a cook, the oldest son, Lee, had given up his job, returned home and enrolled on an IT certification programme at his local community college. Despite winning a full scholarship to a good university on the basis of high SAT scores, their second son, Anthony, dropped out, worked for a year as a ski-lift operator and then spent two years in 'his room not doing much of anything except reading and doing computer things'. Now in his twenties, he had been coaxed back into education also via a computing programme at the local college. Both sons, then, were living at home with their father and his second wife, Wendy, and their young daughter, Ellen. Supporting both sons directly with college fees and indirectly by having them live at home remained important to Simon who indicated, whatever the outcome, 'our commitment remains'. Similarly, Marion Chaves' only daughter, Jessica, dropped out early in her college career. Initially indifferent to returning, she now wanted to resume her studies and Marion and her husband were ready to help her do so financially if she was able to put her plans into practice. For these interviewees, financial support was an 'absolute' despite setbacks and disappointments.

Overall, it was clear that the American interviewees expected to or had already mobilised their economic resources to help their children through college, university and beyond. The main costs, obviously, were tuition fees which were the source of much anxiety to both the affluent physicians and the less affluent teachers although, of course, many of the former expected their children to attend the most expensive institutions while the latter did not. The most affluent interviewees were in a financial position to plan for anticipated costs through savings plans or they envisaged increasing their hours of work. The financial support of their parents could also be called upon to help the grandchildren. Even so, it was still apparent that financial considerations shaped the decisions and choices of the physicians and their partners regarding their children's higher education. The less affluent educators and their partners were very aware of the financial sacrifices they would have to make for their children's education by adding more loans to their own and so forth. Economic considerations were already affecting their children's choice of institution at which to study, whether they expected to work or not, and their overall experiences of college life. While some of the older American interviewees had successfully navigated this path, others had experienced financial difficulties, and anxieties about such difficulties loomed large amongst those with younger children yet to make their way through the system.[21] Ensuring their children's educational success, it seemed, was neither easy nor straightforward.

Economic resources and British education

Like their American counterparts, some of the British parents used their economic resources to pay directly for a child's early education. Again, it was the more affluent interviewees – the doctors rather than teachers – who educated their children wholly through the private school system, so their children effectively enjoyed an elite education. The common theme, once again, was the desire to get the best education possible for their children. For the parents who had been privately educated themselves, their explanation was extremely simple. As Bruce Brown said of his two children, 'Well, I never thought of anything else. We were both privately educated so neither of us has any experience of any form of state education.' Lawrence Foster, also privately educated, elaborated by saying in relation to his own two children:

Yeah, well, it's a chapter of private education isn't it? I think we discounted the state education system where we were. That was the first thing, not being good enough, and presumably our decision was exactly the same as my parents' decision before me and that was to send them to the best education you could get for them.

There were other interviewees, of course, who had not had a private education themselves but elected to send their children to private schools from an early age. A success in the state system, Barbara Coombes suggested that her decision to send her two daughters to fee-paying schools was the result of 'snobbery, I suppose, initially and advice from colleagues who had children, saying what were good schools. I did want them to do well.' Indeed, she had had high hopes that they would follow her into medicine and a private education was perceived as the best way of ensuring educational and occupational success.[22]

There were less affluent interviewees who dipped in and out of the private school system, using their economic resources, to circumvent their concerns with the local state schools in the localities in which they lived. Living in less select areas, they judged the local schools to be of poor quality, often voicing their concerns, heard many times before, about class size. Anxious that their children obtain a good education, they were prepared to pay for it and make any sacrifices necessary. Susan Parry was very unhappy with her son Luke's playgroup and the bad influence of some boys on her son. Even though he was due to go to the best infant school in the area, she was not happy that these other young boys were going to go too. She explained:

I decided I wasn't very happy about this. Then when I did a little bit more research, their reception class had something like thirty-two children in it and I wasn't very happy about that either. So put the two things together and I thought I'd better look round and see if I can give him a better grounding so I sent him to [A] because the classes in them [had] the maximum of fifteen; through the whole of the infants, a maximum of sixteen children and I quite liked the discipline in the school and the fact that he was wearing a uniform and children were not encouraged to say F-off.[23]

Sandra and Eric Booth also spoke of how they had spent 'thousands' on educating their four children privately on various occasions because they regarded their local schools as 'horrendous'.

The majority of parents, however, sent their children to their local state primary school, again emphasising the considerable importance they attached to them being part of a local community. Bridget Underwood, for example, was delighted with her two young daughters' small Catholic primary school and the fact that she was able to send them to a 'nice local school'. Most interviewees sent their children to the nearest school while some talked of sending their children to particular primary schools locally. The former acknowledged that they lived in select areas where the schools were mostly good. David Hill, who lived in a town outside Manchester, for example, said, 'It was the nearest school and in fact, it's a nice area, quite a genteel middle-class area and quite a good school.' The latter group, most notably those living in Manchester and its closest suburbs, were more anxious to send their children to particular primary schools with good academic reputations. Sylvia Harrison delayed her house move, for example, so that her children could go to the frequently cited and highly regarded primary school. As she explained,

In fact we didn't move to this house until after my daughter started school because the house was out of the area and we weren't allowed for her to go to [B] school from this house. The zone was at the end of the road where the traffic lights are so we didn't actually move although we could have done. Otherwise she wouldn't have been allowed to start.

As in the USA, albeit in a less pronounced fashion, choice of residence influenced access to good schools in the city of Manchester. The indirect use of economic resources, via decisions about where to live in the city, was required to secure a good education.[24]

Invariably, the more affluent interviewees transferred their children to the private sector for their secondary school education. Unhappy with the state system, they elected to send their children to fee-paying schools. Indeed, all of the British doctors sent their children – bar one – to fee-paying schools that were former direct-grant grammar schools that had become independent with the abolition of the tripartite system in the 1970s. They were highly reputable schools with some of the best academic results in the country. They sought to buy the kind of education, namely a single-sex grammar school education, in which they themselves had been successful. As selective schools, however, the parents had to ensure their children passed the entrance examination to gain entry into the school. A number of interviewees described how they paid for additional private tuition to ensure their children passed the selective entrance examinations.[25] More often than not, they were successful in this strategy and only one doctor's child, the Hunters' daughter, Teresa, had not gone to such a school. As Rod Hunter explained:

In order for them to get to a better secondary school, we had to tutor them in the last year they went there [the local primary school]. It was extra tuition from a private tutor but, in the end, my daughter [has] gone to a comprehensive. She wasn't really up to it. We weren't going to force her, at the age of ten or eleven, to do something which she patently wasn't able to do. She's of average, I'd say, average education ability . . . so we decided to drop the tuition after about six months so she didn't try for any eleven pluses.

Her secondary school, however, was very reputable. Her younger brother, Scott, went private.

Again, some of the interviewees never had any intention of sending their children to state secondary schools. Their decision to send their children to state primary schools had been a strategic one of delaying the substantial cost of private education until later. Janet Jones readily conceded that as someone who has enjoyed a wholly privately education, she was very worried about 'failing her children' if she had chosen differently. A product of the state system, Janet's husband Gerald was less anxious, although he believed that 'you don't know where your children are going to end up in life and I have the feeling that you have no option but the private sector'. Mr and Mrs Jones were entirely certain private education was best for their children. Others, however, were uncomfortable with the decision to educate their children privately but felt compelled to do so to ensure their children enjoyed the same education as they had done. Peter Smith said:

I was more interested I suppose in the best foot up the ladder I suppose. If they went to an established grammar school and these schools really had gone independent, that's why they still existed, they wouldn't get caught up in the turmoil of the comprehensive argument that was going on, still goes on actually.

He went on to explain:

my own feeling is we should either have a complete comprehensive system or the old system. We haven't got a true comprehensive system because there are still independent grammar schools that can take out of the pool, if you can see my point. The only true comprehensive schools we have, in my view, are the local primary schools.[26]

Institutional arrangements, namely, the existence of private schools that could siphon off able (middle-class) children thereby reducing the pool of talent in the comprehensive schools, seemingly forced Peter Smith's hand. Again, others expressed anxiety about the risks of sending children to a local comprehensive school even if it had a good academic reputation. The mobilisation of economic resources allowed parents to circumvent these perceived risks. Such worries, it seemed, were acute for those interviewees who experienced the changes in the education system as they were happening. Rosemary Hill was greatly concerned with the organisational upheaval when she visited the comprehensive school that her sons, Nickolas and Mark, were to attend. As she explained, 'I went to visit the place and I wasn't happy at all. I thought "Oh God, this is awful." In fact it turned out very well but it was a case of do I risk my child's future on something that may or may not turn out very well so it was a very traumatic time actually.' The private school offered 'better security and prospects'. Similarly, Stephen and Julia Dodd lived in an affluent suburb of Manchester that would have allowed their two children to go to the best comprehensive in the city. Stephen emphasised the benefits of a private education, however, even over a good state education. He said, 'even though my wife is a paid up member of the Labour Party, like Tony Blair or whatever, the private school offers a bit more in terms of education. Although [P] is good for those who are good, I'm not sure it's so good for those who aren't.' They were not prepared to take the risk, especially if their children were not academically able, of using the state system.[27]

Most of the less affluent teachers and their partners sent their children to state secondary schools. Some parents considered the private school option – which implies that they could have afforded to pay for it – but eventually sent their children to the local comprehensive. Jill and Graham Dowds' eldest daughter, Claire, for example, passed the entrance exam to go to a selective grammar school. Jill, however, had disliked her own single-sex education at a grammar school and did not wish the same experience for her daughter. A visit to the school left them unimpressed while they had been impressed when they visited the local comprehensive that 'had good academic results as well'.[28] She also went on to say, 'I've got to say my father was devastated. My dad wanted her to go to [B] because he thought it was the best school. She'd get better results than she would if she went to the comprehensive school, but she couldn't have got any better results.' Similarly, Hilary and Ken Butler considered the private school option and, as Ken explained, 'There is no doubt that kids that went to [K] and [Q] school did extremely well.' Nevertheless, they were entirely happy with the local comprehensive school. As an informed teacher, Mr Butler said, 'It was the sort of school that unless you were disastrous, the nature of the intake, the success, it was very much like a grammar school. It was a selective school by catchment. It was almost selective by property.' They did not have to worry about academic success here either and their two children did well.

Distaste for the private sector and a commitment to the state school system shaped other parental choices. As Norman Jones suggested, 'My mother-in-law was quite prepared to pay for them to go to [B] grammar. That was not acceptable, the whole grammar school thing, as a principle.' Similarly, Sylvia Harrison said her husband Roger, whom she described as a staunch socialist, 'wasn't that keen on them going there. He thought [P] was perfectly adequate.'[29] Sylvia agreed even despite having attended a selective grammar school herself. As she explained:

You've got to have enough money, not just to pay for the education but you've got to have enough money for the lifestyle that goes with it, and I know that I didn't have the life-style when I was a child so I always felt at a disadvantage and I felt it was far better if we had extra money to improve our lifestyle as opposed to just paying for the education, 'cos she was going to get just as good an education at [P].

The majority, therefore, were largely satisfied with their children's state education although it must be said that all but one of the interviewees attended the best schools in the Manchester suburbs and beyond by dint of affording houses in the more expensive areas. Economic resources, therefore, had this indirect effect. Only one couple, Pauline Lomax and Martin Webb, sent their daughter, Kathryn, to a city school that did not have a high academic reputation. Again, Pauline expressed her unease at how middle-class parents made sure their children got into the best schools in Manchester. Of her two children, she said, 'They don't need to stand on somebody else's head to get even more, you know.' That said, the decision required that she be very vigilant about her daughter's academic progress through a school without a high academic reputation.

The British interviewees, as parents, were now mobilising their economic resources to increase the probability of their children's educational success. Some of the most affluent doctors and their partners, often privately educated themselves, paid for a private education for their children in its entirety. They wanted the best that money could buy. Other, less affluent parents dipped in and out of the private system at primary level as a result of their unhappiness with local state provision. Most of the interviewees' children attended state primary schools. With one exception, however, all the physicians transferred their children to the private sector for their secondary school education. They paid for private tuition to ensure that their children were successful in the selective entrance examination and paid high fees to schools with some of the best academic results in the country.[30] Academic success, without doubt, was all-important. They mobilised their economic resources in this way so that their children could experience the kind of high-quality grammar school education in which they had been successful. Furthermore, they were not prepared to risk a comprehensive education, fearing that if their children were not academically able, it would not serve them well. The less affluent teachers sent their children to state secondary schools and were often satisfied with their children's education. As they readily acknowledged, however, they lived in areas with good schools, in the towns surrounding Manchester or in the city's better suburbs. Mobilising their more modest economic resources indirectly in this way, they had also circumvented risks that might undermine the pursuit of credential success.

Economic resources, higher education and beyond

Virtually all of the interviewees' children who attended fee-paying schools were highly successful in acquiring educational credentials – O levels/ GCSEs – at 16 and most of them continued with their A levels at the same private schools. In this respect, the most affluent interviewees got what they paid for: namely, their children's academic success. Very keen to have their children continue with their studies, there were certainly no financial pressures to leave school at 16. The investment of economic resources in private education continued almost without question. Some of the interviewees' children transferred from private schools to free state colleges of further education to pursue their studies. The Lambs' daughter, Molly, moved from one private school to another at 14 because, 'she was finding the academic pressure, even at that stage, very high and I feel terrible about people pushing children academically when they are not academic'. At 16, she expressed a desire to go to a state college for her A levels. Ian Lamb said:

I wasn't positive about it. I thought she should stay at [C] and I wasn't impressed by her arguments but she persisted and she was very clever about it because she found out about the [J] college, which I had never heard about. She found information on the outcome of education at [J] which was very impressive so she pushed it but she pushed it in a most mature kind of way.

Ian gave in to his daughter's wish, knowing from previous experience that forcing his daughter through a rigorous academic programme would not be good for her. Interestingly, he and his wife Pamela withheld their economic resources although they took some comfort from the fact that their daughter's choice of college had a reasonable academic reputation.[31]

There were other circumstances when the interviewees' children transferred from the private sector into the state system at 16 to complete their academic studies – working towards A levels – with a view to going to university. It came as no surprise, for example, that the Hills' two sons did not like their private school – very much like their parents – and transferred to a local college of further education at 16. Nor was it a surprise to find that David Hill was very laid back about the issue especially as the sixth-form college was now well established. As he said, 'It was no problem. Saved on the fees!' In less favourable circumstances, the Booths' third child, Juliet, transferred from a private girls' school to the state mixed Further Education college at 16. Malik Booth was a self-employed businessman and his business at the time was not doing very well. As Sandra Booth explained, 'I think we had the café bar then and it was starting to lose money so I was worried really about financially keeping her on in the sixth form.' Financial considerations aside, however, she was anxious for her second daughter to experience the freedom of college life before university since their oldest daughter, Kirsten, had gone 'wild' in her first year of university. As she said:

I thought if she went to [P] which had a good reputation, it was more of a university environment than the school was, and I thought it would help prepare Juliet for university but she made the decision and she found it very hard to make but in the end she decided to go to [P] and she said that that was the best decision she made.

Arguably, Sandra was adept at making a virtue out of necessity and she had to help her daughter think along these lines too![32]

Most of the interviewees' children who attended state schools also did well in their examinations at 16 allowing them to continue with their academic studies and plan for university. Again, there were no financial pressures for any child to find paid employment at 16 and, without a doubt, the interviewees were keen to financially underwrite their children through further education. Only one child – the Crisps' second daughter, Bella – was expecting to go out to work at 16. Financial considerations did not play a part in this decision, as Bella, able but not academically inclined, was anxious to leave school and establish a career in hotel and catering. Some of the interviewees' children were less academically successful, whether they were educated in the private or the public sector. Even so, their parents continued to invest in their children's education, albeit of a vocational kind. The Willis' adopted son, Mark, was never academically successful at school and he was on a hotel and catering course at a local state college.[33] Without fees to pay, his parents supported him living at home with absolutely no hesitation whatsoever. In a not dissimilar fashion, Edward Myers explained that his son Robert was 'certainly not as bright as his sisters and like all boys, he is not as assiduous either'. Struggling with his A levels at private school, he transferred to a BTEC course at a state college. This vocational route still allowed Robert to go to university where he was currently completing a degree in computing. There was no question that investment was conditional on educational success and, indeed, economic resources were mobilised to secure the best education possible in the circumstances.

The interviewees' investment in their children's education, therefore, was not dependent upon academic success. Additional financial investment, for example, was made when children did not do as well as they hoped in their A levels. Interestingly, many of the interviewees' children did reasonably well but not well enough to pursue their aspirations unconditionally. Parents, therefore, invested more so that their children could pursue their preferred option. Neither of the Lambs' sons, Geoff or Ian, obtained the necessary grades to gain entry into medical school as they had hoped. Their parents paid for them to attend a private 'crammer' with a view to retaking the exams and improving their grades. As Pamela Lamb explained simply, 'there was no reason why we couldn't manage it'. The additional financial input secured academic success and both sons obtained better A level grades that allowed them into medical school. Financial support of both a direct and indirect kind had been forthcoming to secure their entry into the medical profession. Similarly, Amy Dodd did well enough in two A levels but dropped a grade in one subject that meant, in the words of her mother, Julia, that 'it didn't actually give her that many options'. She also went to a fee-paying 'crammer' and re-sat the subject and 'stayed at home, working in a pub . . . and applied to university and got in there'. Her parents supported her financially, therefore, through the fee-paying crammer to ensure she went to the university of her choice, and supported her indirectly by letting her live at home for another year without making any financial contributions.[34]

Of course, there were examples of parents whose children attended the state sector who did not do well either. Again, parents invariably gave their children additional financial support to secure educational success. The Hills' youngest son failed his A levels twice after staying on an additional year at college. They supported him in staying on for the second attempt, as David Hill explained, 'Obviously, he was disappointed when he didn't get them the first time. We said, look, we're your mum and dad. We will support you. If you seriously think you can do it, go back and do it all again and he did but I think it was just an excuse not to look for a job.' On failing again, their son left home and lived with friends locally, then moved away and worked part time but eventually returned to college part time also. Doing well, he then embarked on a two-year diploma course at the local college that allowed him to do an additional year of study for a degree. Again, his parents supported him financially. Reflecting on this continuing support David said:

My Mum and Dad were modern, forward-looking people. They didn't have children as possessions. They were there to support. I've said to my kids, I owe my parents nothing because I didn't ask to be born but I owe you my children everything because you didn't ask to be born. I decided you were going to be born. That doesn't say that I don't love my Mum because I do very much and I'll do anything for her but really you've got to do things for your kids. You've got to be there to support your kids.

Financial investment continued, in other words, until children found their way through the education system, irrespective of failure and, it seemed, however long it took to succeed.[35]

A number of interviewees' children enjoyed straightforward academic success at A levels and proceeded to university. Some doctors' daughters, for example, attended the elite universities of Oxford and Cambridge, having obtained top grades and enjoyed additional tuition for entrance exams at their private schools. Others, especially those from affluent backgrounds, went to other reputable universities. Unlike their American counterparts, there was no talk of college fees as many of the interviewees' children had made their way through the university system when it was free. As affluent families, they were rarely eligible for state maintenance grants. Parents, therefore, were expected to support their children's accommodation and living expenses. Few of the more affluent doctors reported any difficulty in supporting their children financially in this way. Gerald Jones spoke of how he supported his daughters at Oxbridge colleges, revealing the affluent lives they enjoyed. As he said,

They're all good managers with money. I've never had problems with them at university, you know. I've given them a reasonable allowance and they always managed. They've always worked in the holidays if they wanted to do something special. They all travelled widely abroad and generally they've funded themselves.

Indeed, all three daughters had travelled extensively to places like South America during their student days and pursued expensive hobbies like scuba diving (thereby increasing their cultural capital of course). Barbara Coombes bought a house for her two daughters while they were at university and suggested that their lifestyle was 'totally unrecognisable' when compared to her own youth, revealing, 'I mean, my kids have never been on public transport!'[36]

None of the more affluent interviewees with children yet to embark on a university education were perturbed by the introduction of student fees (at a nominal figure of £1,000) and the abolition of student grants, which did not affect them in any case. This was not the case among the less affluent teachers and their partners with children still making their way through the education system. The Parkers' son, Jonathan, was awaiting his A level results with a view to going to university. His father, Dennis, said,

Higher education is expensive and is probably at the moment about £4,000 for my daughter and it'll cost us another £4,000 a year for Jonathan if he goes, so next year is going to be a very difficult year for us, which we don't mind paying at all.

There was some trepidation about his results and whether he would apply himself. It was important, Dennis stressed, that his son 'realize that if he doesn't work then he has to do something that's going to give him some money'. Other parents spoke of how retirement plans were being influenced by the introduction of student fees. They envisaged staying in employment longer than originally anticipated. As Graham Dowds said of his own career plans, 'What I'm aiming to do is keep going until Rebecca finishes university. I'll be about 55 and then hopefully take, if possible, early retirement or voluntary redundancy. Then probably I'll go on contract.' Similarly, Sandra Booth said 'there's pressure to work until Alex gets through university'. Earlier plans to reduce her working hours had been cancelled. The teachers with younger children still assumed they would go to university although greater sacrifices would have to be made to meet fees and living expenses.[37]

Financial support after university was also evident with additional assistance during further study as children embarked on their different careers. Economic support was especially useful while exploring different options in the labour market. Sarah Jones sought a career in horticulture and she was currently working in a labouring job in a nursery to 'get her hands dirty' before embarking on a masters degree. As her mother, Janet, explained, 'She [is] earning about three pounds an hour. Of course, she wants to put extra money aside for her MSc but we have said we'll support her if she doesn't get funding.' Sarah's parents were supporting her in *ad hoc* ways while she worked in a poorly paid job and they envisaged supporting her later in an industry where even management jobs are poorly paid. Financial support also opened up avenues for the Browns' son, James, who had not yet settled in a career. He set up his own business after university, then trained as an accountant, travelled around the world for a year and had returned home to set up his own business again. Asked if he helped his son financially, Bruce Brown said:

No, I never have. No, I mean they were both helped a bit by their grandfather. Their grandfather, my wife's father, invested in a unit trust when they were born so they got about sixty thousand or so when they were twenty one so James [has] been using that in part. I mean James only reads the *Financial Times*. I don't know what he's done with his but I suspect it's increased in that respect.

The money had given James the space to try out these options and he still hoped, without having 'settled' to a profession or business, to be a millionaire before he was 30![38]

Having numerous branching points allowed young people to pursue different educational options – as well as leave the education system altogether. In this context, it was interesting to see how the British parents mobilised their economic resources on their children's behalf in a variety of ways.[39] All of the interviewees, as parents, supported their children as they pursued further education whether it was directly by continuing to pay private school fees or indirectly by supporting them at state schools and colleges of further education. Interestingly, many of the interviewees' children experienced setbacks at this juncture but additional financial support was often forthcoming. Fees were paid at 'crammers' to improve on exam grades, for example, so that better options could be pursued, rather than just making do. Unlike the American counterparts, few of the interviewees, especially the affluent doctors and their partners with older children, spoke of financial difficulties in supporting their children through university. On the contrary, many of them supported their children's high standard of living at university – allowing them to enjoy travel, pursue expensive hobbies and so on. Neither the introduction of nominal university tuition fees, nor the abolition of state maintenance grants greatly troubled them. Some of the less affluent teachers and their partners, however, were increasingly concerned about the financial costs – tuition fees and living expenses – that they would incur in the future, shelving plans to reduce their working hours or retire early. Economic considerations, in other words, were rising in importance for these British middle-class parents.

Conclusion

In this chapter I have explored the processes by which my interviewees, now all middle-class parents, used their economic assets to help their children succeed in school and beyond. They encountered different institutional arrangements, of course, as their children made their way through the school system in the 1980s and 1990s. For example, tracking in the American public schools had mostly gone as had grammar schools in Britain. Most importantly, however, both the American and British interviewees had to confront a poorer and more variable public or state education system. Seemingly, the risks to academic success were greater than in their own day and, arguably, the importance of economic resources to increase the probability of academic success.[40] That said, the most affluent interviewees in both countries simply opted out of the public or state system by paying for a high-quality private education that would facilitate their children's acquisition of educational credentials. With regard to higher education, however, even the affluent physicians and their partners in America were increasingly anxious about the spiralling costs of college fees, especially, of course, to the more academically reputable institutions. Their decisions and choices were not unfettered by economic considerations. The affluent doctors and their partners in Britain, however, remained untroubled by the introduction of nominal tuition fees and the abolition of maintenance grants. Once again, therefore, the empirical material has confirmed Goldthorpe's theory about middle-class reproduction although my interviewees' narratives suggest that it is not so easily secured in America as in Britain.

At the same time, Goldthorpe's theory of middle-class reproduction does not capture the experiences of a less-affluent middle class who do not, for example, command the economic resources to pay high private school fees or live in exclusive residential communities. Instead, they confront a variable public or state system where lack of investment and poor facilities do not appear to them to be conducive to academic success. They are also confronted, as in America, with huge college fees, so that financial considerations loom large in the choices and the decisions they can make about their children's higher education. Such financial worries about the cost of higher education are increasingly perplexing British middle-class parents. Again, the difficulties of securing their children's future were expressed more forcefully in the USA than in Britain.[41] Middle-class reproduction, therefore, felt neither easy, nor straightforward, especially when the mobilisation of economic resources could only increase the propensity for academic success. It could not guarantee success in the acquisition of educational credentials so important for entry into good jobs. Much has been said in this chapter and the previous one about the high value placed on educational success and how it shaped the interviewees' parents and the interviewees themselves, as parents, and their decisions and choices. It is appropriate, therefore, that attention now turns to the mobilisation of cultural resources in the reproduction of middle-class privilege and power.

4   Expectations and hopes for educational success

This chapter and Chapter 5 focus on the mobilisation of cultural resources in the reproduction of advantage. In the introduction, I noted how Goldthorpe initially equated his notion of cultural resources to Bourdieu's concept of cultural capital to refer to the value attached to education within families. He also included issues of occupational inheritance and traditions of self-employment within families. Later, however, he rejected Bourdieu's culturalist explanation of class stability because of its inability to explain change: namely, the increasing participation of *both* middle-class and working-class children in higher education in the 1950s and 1960s. He also directed hostile criticism at Bourdieu's characterisation of a working class seemingly lacking in cultural capital and suffering from a 'poverty of aspirations'. Now, as I have argued elsewhere, it is one thing to identify the shortcomings of Bourdieu's theory and another to deny the importance of cultural dispositions and practices in the reproduction of advantage altogether. Despite some of the problems with Bourdieu's work, which plenty of others besides Goldthorpe have noted, I think his ideas about the importance of cultural capital in the reproduction of privilege and power are worth considering further.[1] After all, the previous two chapters illustrated how parents convert their economic capital into cultural capital by investing in a good education for their children so that they acquire the necessary credentials to gain access to desirable jobs. That they invested their financial resources in this way was influenced by the value attached to educational success.

Critics of Bourdieu have long been frustrated by the elusive character of 'cultural capital' and how the embodiment of cultural dispositions seems to embrace so many things including verbal facilities, general cultural awareness, aesthetic preferences, information about the school system and so on. It is only in his later work that Bourdieu sought to distance the notion of cultural capital from an appreciation of high culture and how the concept should be equated with informational capital: namely, an awareness of how the system works.[2] I focus in this chapter and the next on how parents socialise their children and seek to subtly inculcate in them their own values and practices to promote educational and occupational success. Special attention is devoted to educational dispositions with respect to expectations and aspirations regarding academic success and horizons and hopes about occupational success. This chapter returns to the interviewees' accounts of their childhood and, as in Chapter 2, draws on their retrospective accounts of how their parents supported and encouraged them in school. Again, it will be remembered that the interviewees came from a variety of class backgrounds: from the upper middle class/middle class and lower middle class/working class. This diversity allows me to explore the ways in which those parents with cultural capital helped the interviewees enjoy academic success, and those parents supposedly without cultural capital also helped their children to succeed in school and beyond.

All of the American interviewees, as I will show, spoke of how their parents valued educational success highly and wanted them to go as far as possible in the education system. While the interviewees from well-established upper-middle-class families talked about 'high' cultural activities, the others spoke of how their parents thought education was important for getting a good job. Accordingly, parents stressed the virtues of hard work and discipline and these values shaped family lifestyles. While some parents were pushy, most of the interviewees spoke of subtle forms of parental support and encouragement. The interviewees' parents who were college educated very much anticipated that they would go to college. Those parents without college degrees did not presume but hoped that their children would enjoy a college education, exploiting the growing opportunities in the 1960s that had been unavailable in earlier decades.[3] The parents of interviewees from well-established middle-class backgrounds had high occupational expectations, often expecting sons to follow them into medicine. For others, medicine was a highly desirable career associated with status and power. Those interviewees' parents of modest means did not always have such high occupational horizons. They did not stop the interviewees pursing a medical career given their academic success in the sciences. Irrespective of class background, many of the interviewees' parents viewed teaching as a highly desirable job for women and they were directed into teaching for this reason. Teaching was also a desirable career for men from modest social backgrounds as it represented an improvement on blue-collar work.

All of the British interviewees' parents placed a high premium on educational success too. Again, it seemed that the interviewees from established middle-class backgrounds expected their children to do well. Others of middle-class origin spoke of how their parents had been very keen for them to succeed and, once more, promoted the virtues of discipline and hard work in their everyday family lives. The expectation was that these interviewees would go on to university just as their parents before them. The interviewees from modest working-class backgrounds also spoke of how their parents valued educational success and how the same values translated into everyday family practices.[4] They also hoped that their children would go to university in the 1950s and 1960s as they themselves had been unable to do. Turning to the interviewees' parents' occupational horizons, it was evident that fathers in medical positions expected their sons to follow in their footsteps. A medical career was also seen as a highly desirable career by other middle-class and working-class parents. Again, it seemed that working-class parents did not limit their children's occupational aspirations if academic success in the natural sciences was leading them into a medical career. As in the USA, many of the interviewees' parents viewed teaching as a good job for a woman and, irrespective of class background, many were directed into this career. Parental aspirations were highly gendered. Teaching was also considered desirable among the working-class parents of the male teachers although there were pressures from their schools to do more prestigious jobs.

American educational dispositions

Almost all of the interviewees said their parents had placed a high premium on educational success. They wanted them to do well in school and to go as far as possible in the education system. How they did so, however, manifested itself in different ways depending on their parents' socio-economic background and education. Some of the interviewees, whose parents (and sometimes grandparents) were highly educated spoke about their parents' high level of cultural capital. Their parents, it seemed, appreciated the experiences derived from travel, they enjoyed (mostly classical) music and they were widely read people interested and engaged in the world around them. This was the family environment in which some interviewees grew up and they themselves were expected to appreciate the joys of music and reading.[5] Rachel Garrett, the daughter of a public relations executive who had been educated at Harvard, spoke of how she came from a 'musical, literate family'. Patrick Dutton described how reading was highly valued by his father, a lawyer, and his mother, a university professor:

To give you some idea, when I was four years old, I remember very distantly driving to the post office to pick up my edition of the World Book Encyclopaedia. So, for my fourth birthday, I received a full set of encyclopaedias. I read them from A to Z and that was the ethos of the family. We did not have a television or, if we did, it didn't work or it wasn't turned on so for a lot of my childhood there was no television but we all read voraciously. Education was very, very valued by both parents.

These values shaped the kinds of lifestyles they led.

It was the interviewees from seemingly long-established upper-middle-class families who stressed high levels of cultural capital in the family. Most of the interviewees, however, spoke of how their parents saw educational success as the key to occupational success in a more instrumental fashion. Ken Bailey was the son of a professional engineer, originally from a 'poor family', who had struggled to get an education. He said:

My Dad, I wouldn't say he enjoyed school. He approached it as this is what you need to do if you want to make something out of yourself in life. You've got to work your tail off. You've got to go to school at night. You've got to work two jobs and this wasn't fun. This wasn't something you look forward to. You bite the bullet and grind your teeth.

His father, he said, 'was completely self-motivated and he expected the same out of me'. The work ethic was key. Other interviewees from modest backgrounds made the same point, adding that education was the key to a job where they could support themselves and be financially independent. Judy Kennedy, the daughter of a TV engineer, who went to college after a period in the armed services, said, 'To him, education to get a job was important. It wasn't education for education's sake. It was education to find work.' Her father vetoed her sister's desire to go to art college because it was not 'practicable'.[6] Jane Bennett completed the necessary pre-med courses to get to medical school although she had majored in art history. Although her parents never asked her to change courses, she 'knew that they wondered would I be able to support myself'.

Again, this disposition towards education, with the emphasis on the need to work hard to succeed both educationally and occupationally, shaped the interviewees' early lives. The interviewees spoke of how their parents were strong on discipline, some relating these practices to their religious beliefs and rejection of consumer culture. They had 'structured days' and the overriding expectation was that homework had to be completed before any sort of play. Parents, it seemed, wanted their children – the interviewees – to work hard, to perform to the best of their ability and get good grades at school. Asked if her parents valued education, Linda Chapman said, 'Absolutely. Yes. It was very important to our family. I think my homework was always expected to be done. Every day my parents would ask me how I was doing at school. It was just assumed that I would be doing well and working hard.' Similarly, Bernice Hughes recalled the powerful influence of her mother even though she died when Bernice was 10. She said, 'I can always remember my mother, she always had the message of "You can give out but you don't give up". You know, that sort of thing. So, perseverance was something that we were always taught. That was very important to her.' It was a message that her aunt continued to reinforce and, interestingly, Bernice spoke of how these expectations acted as 'external pressures' that she internalised. Such family expectations left her with 'no choice' but to excel at school. The interviewees, therefore, frequently described how their parents inculcated in them the values of discipline and hard work.[7]

Some of the interviewees acknowledged that their parents were 'very directive'. It was expected and, indeed, assumed that they would excel and there was no question of being rewarded for academic success. Reflecting back on this ethos, Patrick Dutton recalled with sadness that 'my father never gave the impression he was satisfied. We never did quite enough.' Like Ken Bailey, Anna Gray spoke of how her father, a Jewish immigrant from Eastern Europe, was raised in abject poverty and how he managed to secure a college education through the Navy. He was, she said, 'an achiever' and 'he was incredibly bright'. His experiences meant that 'his sense of what he wanted to do for his kids was to send them as far as they could go, as far as they wanted to go'. Mary Moran also spoke of how her mother was very ambitious for her. She said, 'I was the oldest child and by far the most dutiful and I think she lived through my scholarly pursuits a little bit more than was actually healthy for her.' Missing an opportunity to go to college herself made her even more anxious, Mary believed, for her children succeed educationally. As she explained:

Right around the time she was thinking about college, her father died and she was the oldest of six and at that point, although she was offered to go to a four-year college she just kind of copped out and it was not strictly just a matter of money. I think the attitude was, if I can't go to a great school then I'm not going to any school. It may have been that she was very depressed about her father dying but I look back on it and think, boy, that wasn't a very mature thing to do.

Consequently, her mother was desperate for her children to go to college.[8]

It was far more common, however, for the interviewees to stress that their parents were not 'pushy' parents, even though in saying this the importance of education was still obvious. Importantly, the interviewees did not feel pushed because they were, by and large, successful students. As George Marshall said: 'They were not in any way pushy parents when

I was younger. I did well at school so it was easier for them but my sister did less well and my father spent a lot more time with her, with what she needed. I guess I didn't need that.' Similarly, Daniel Lewis was not interrogated on a day-to-day level about school activities. He said:

I grew up studying with the television and the radio on at the same time as I studied. Early on my Mom was concerned, but I did well that way so she was like, you know, 'That's how you study. Why do I care?' So, day-to-day things, there wasn't much pressure but the long-term goal was quite obvious. You are going to college. That's what's expected.

The inculcation of the value of educational success was quite subtle. Interviewees from more modest backgrounds made similar remarks. Judy Kennedy said her parents 'never drove me. They put their foot down here and there over specific instances but I never felt personally driven by them.' That said, she acknowledged that she 'enjoyed school and I applied myself and I liked it so, in terms of being a student, I wasn't a problem for anybody'. In the context of academic success, parents were rarely 'aggressive' or needed to be. Echoing the sentiments of many others, Joel Walker stressed how his parents 'were very supportive and always encouraged us to do our best'.[9]

In the context of this parental support and encouragement, many of the interviewees acknowledged they were diligent students. As Anna Gray said, 'I was kind of a nerd so I never did anything that got me in major trouble. My sisters and brothers had a lot more fun but I didn't!' There were others, often the male interviewees, who did not always stay 'motivated' and 'on track' as the case of David Neale, discussed in Chapter 1, testifies. Be that as it may, all of the interviewees stressed that their parents wanted them to go to college and, in some instances, beyond, to graduate school. The interviewees from upper-middle or middle-class families, whose parents were highly educated and in high-level jobs, spoke of how it was assumed that they would go to college like their parents and their older siblings. Al Lopez was the son of a college-educated high-level businessman from the Caribbean who sent Al and his four sisters to American universities. As he explained, 'When we were growing up, especially in high school, the question wasn't "are we going to college?" It was "where are we going to college?"' Those interviewees from more modest backgrounds who had at least one parent who enjoyed a college education made the same point. Roy Morgan's father went to a technical institute before becoming a mechanic while his mother went to college and then on to a nursing programme. Originating from an upper-middle-class family, she was unusual, as an African American woman, in going to college in the 1950s. On the matter of going to college, he said, 'My mother made it a matter of tradition. "I went to college. I expect you to go to college."'[10]

The interviewees whose parents had not been to college did not share the same assumptions but they had similar aspirations nevertheless. They did not expect but they hoped that their children would be in a position to take opportunities that had been denied to them. Both of Susan Rogers' parents, a machinist and a sales clerk, finished high school and went straight out to work. She said of her mother, 'She did aspire for us to go ahead even though that wasn't her experience or [that of] other people in my family. It wasn't their experience either.' Indeed, many of the interviewees spoke of how their parents, coming from large families and growing up during the Depression before the Second World War, were under financial pressures to find employment at the earliest opportunity.[11] They wanted something better for their children. Carol Gedicks' parents started work when they were young. Her mother worked in a store while her father started on the factory floor of a paper mill and made his way up to the laboratory. Their expectations for Carol and her sister included college. As she explained,

They didn't push. They were not pushers but they did hope that we would do well and they certainly always talked about us going on to higher education and that was sort of the goal that they had for us because I think in part they wanted it but had never been able to in their family.

Similarly, Ray Chapman spoke of how his parents were 'Depression era children' subsequently affected by the war. Ray's father enjoyed success working in the police and then the FBI but 'he grew to realize that he had hit a ceiling for his own advancement' and 'regretted not having a college education'.

In their different ways, therefore, the interviewees from diverse socio-economic backgrounds spoke of how their parents valued education highly and how their dispositions shaped their lifestyles. The family environment of support and encouragement was conducive to educational success, as almost all of the interviewees went on to complete four-year college degrees. It did not guarantee success, however. Despite strong pressure to do well at school in her early life, economic constraints and family circumstances meant that Bernice Hughes left high school and went to work rather than college although opportunities, in her twenties, allowed her to go to college part time and eventually to pursue a career in teaching. It was a tough road to travel. Marion Chaves was the only interviewee who explicitly suggested that her parents did not value education. Like other interviewees, she spoke of the impact of the Depression and the Second World War on her parents' lives. She explained that her father 'had to stop school. School wasn't important because survival was. So they were sent to work at a very early age, so they had to find their own way. It was just the way of life.' They were keen for her to finish high school since 'that was the given expectation in my generation, you are talking the sixties', and delighted when she, as the first member of the family, graduated with an associates degree from her local community college. Her parents were keen for her to take a clerical position at the factory where her father worked but she took up a clerical post in a medical practice instead, working for nearly twenty years before going to college and pursing a career in teaching with the support of her husband who was a fellow educator.[12]

With few exceptions, therefore, the majority of the interviewees spoke of how their parents placed a high premium on educational success. Some of the interviewees, usually from long-established middle-class families, spoke of their parents' high cultural tastes. Most of the interviewees of middle-class and lower-middle-class origin, however, spoke of a more instrumental approach; namely, educational success was important to get a good job and, important for parents of modest means, to be financially independent. Accordingly, these interviewees spoke of how their parents' values translated into lifestyle practices that facilitated educational success. While some of the interviewees spoke of their parents being pushy, most spoke of more general encouragement and support as they did well in school. It was evident that the interviewees from middle-class backgrounds, whose parents enjoyed an (often reputable) college education, presumed their children would go to college too. Some parents, in lower-middle-class occupations, had also enjoyed a (more modest) college education and they also expected their children to follow in their footsteps. Those interviewees whose parents did not have a higher education, however, wanted their children to go to college too.[13] Notably, they hoped rather than presumed that their children would do well enough at school to continue with their studies. These hopes were very much shaped by their own experiences of limited opportunities in the 1930s and 1940s and a desire for their children, if academically able, to exploit the opportunities for higher education that expanded in the post-war period of prosperity in 1950s and 1960s America.

American occupational horizons

I also talked to my interviewees about their parents' occupational dispositions, the kinds of occupations they considered desirable and held in high esteem and the extent to which their parents directed them into medicine or teaching. The conversations revealed more about the cultural capital of the interviewees' families. A number of the interviewees' parents were physicians. Both of Jack Poole's parents were physicians and, indeed, two of his three siblings also became medics like himself. His father, he said, 'definitely' wanted him to follow him into medicine while, he said, 'My mother was more interested in [me] going into research, scientific research but they both definitely had expectations that really I would do something in the sciences . . . I guess because they had both studied biology and they had done research.' An interest in the sciences, therefore, was passed down the generations. Charles Kahn, whose father and grandfather both had been doctors in India recalled the medical environment in which he grew up as his father and his father's friends studied at home. He explained, 'I would see these people come and all the skeletons would come out and all these books around the place and they are things that I would say had a very, very important impact on the formative years of my life.' An important component of this occupational inheritance was the close relationship between fathers and sons. George Marshall's father was a medical research scientist and he said, 'I was very interested in a lot of the stuff my father did. I was very close to him.'[14] He spoke of how it was 'logical' to follow his father to Harvard and into medicine although he later switched from research into family medicine that suited his own socio-political proclivities.

There were other men who were directed into medicine even though neither parent was a medic. Michael Reed, whose father was a businessman and mother was a dental hygienist, recalled that they wanted him to go into medicine. As he explained, 'It was perceived as being a good job, as stable, as prestigious, as interesting. All the things that medicine used to be perceived as being good for.' His father did not find his own job interesting so he hoped that his son would find medicine rewarding. More often than not, the interviewees stressed that their parents did not explicitly direct them into medicine. That said, the influence of fathers on sons was evident again. When he was young, Ken Bailey envisaged that he would be an engineer like his father. A growing interest in research in biochemistry led him to consider medical research as a potential career and set him on the path to becoming a medic. Similarly, David Neale was the son of an engineer and his brother became an engineering professor and one of his sisters a physician. After eventually obtaining a degree in chemistry, he went to work as a chemist in a laboratory for six years. He recalled how,

I just thought I was going to get a job and go to work for a company and do what my Dad did, try to work hard and show up every day, do well and make a living. I don't think my parents really cared about what I was going to do. My Dad just wanted me to be productive.

Once in employment, however, he found those ahead of him had advanced degrees and he decided to do a Ph.D. in chemistry and then study medicine as a secure occupation in which he could also pursue his research interests.[15]

None of the American women medics came from medical families where they were directed into medicine. Be that as it may, some of them recalled how their parents' views of medicine as a high-status job influenced their own aspirations. Growing up in India, Nadia Khan recalled, 'I think they always wanted me to be a doctor. In India, if you are a doctor, you are looked up to a lot and it's considered to be a good job.' Mary Moran recalls that her mother pushed her towards medicine as a job with high status and also, importantly, control.[16] Of her mother she said, 'She feels very disenfranchised. She feels not powerful. She perceives that I am powerful but I don't think so at all. I think she somehow thinks that people look at doctors and aren't as patronizing or whatever and I say "No, that is not the case."' She saw them as people 'who [are] in control of their own destiny to a certain extent'. More subtly, Kerri Clegg recalled how her aspirations to be a doctor were formed by the fact that she spent many hours with her mother, a secretary, at work at the weekends in a hospital. Other interviewees recalled that their parents did not push them in any particular direction. Their interests in the sciences led them towards medicine. When Anna Gray's love of science led her to decide on a medical career, she said her parents 'thought it was pretty cool. That made up for the fact that I didn't go to [military] college.' Others also spoke of how their inclinations towards the sciences led them to do the necessary premedical qualifications at college. Judy Kennedy recalled how she knew she was 'going to head into the sciences' and thought 'about veterinary school but that's even more competitive than medical school because there aren't that many of them'.

Parents, and most notably those from modest backgrounds, did not direct their children, implicitly or explicitly, into medicine. Other influences were important. Yuko Yacoby recalled a careers talk organised at her local community centre and how 'they had on the panel a physician and I was very focused on that one person. I was about nine and a half and I made my mind up at that time.' Interestingly, Susan Rogers recalled how she was directed into teaching at school when she expressed an interest in working with children. She majored in education at college, taught for a year and then returned to graduate school with a view to becoming a scientist until she was encouraged by teaching staff to complete the necessary pre-med qualifications and apply to medical school. Looking back, she wondered if her teacher's advice reflected a 'sexist view of education or limited aspirations'. She recalled also how she was not exposed to such ideas from her parents or other family members because, 'There were no physicians in my family and physicians were looked at as the really upwardly mobile people. It was such a closed society so it was never something that I was exposed to, that I could never reach for then.'[17] However, her parents, a factory machinist and a postal clerk, supported her decision to pursue a medical career in her mid-twenties, and she laughed when she recalled:

When my husband asked my father if he could marry me, I remember my father saying 'Yes but not until she finishes school.' I mean at this point I was twenty-four years old! It was like, 'Oh, okay.' And he still had that sort of view that we're not going to let anything interfere with her. She now wants to be a doctor so you can have her but wait until she fulfills her aspirations and don't let that interfere.

Unlike their medical counterparts, a number of the women educators spoke of how they were strongly directed into teaching as a respectable professional career for a woman. The influence of gendered aspirations was obvious here especially for those women making their way though school and college in the early 1960s.[18] Gillian Wolkowitz desperately wanted to follow her best friend to law school. She recalled, however, how,

My junior year when I was looking at applying for a six-year law programme, I was living at school and [my mother] called me every night and had a fight with me that I had to be a teacher. My grandmother and she had worked this hard for me to be a teacher. I absolutely could not go to law school. Nobody would marry me if I went to law school.

Given the value placed on education, teaching was a very respectable career. If she had gone to law school, she would have been overeducated and, it seemed, an unattractive option in the marriage market. Linda Chapman recalled also how her parents

Always told me I was going to be a teacher. I think they thought it was the best job one could have. You get your summer off. It was always something you can fall back on. That concept that you could always fall back on it was very much engrained in me. It was a great job for a women. It's not a job where you are getting your hands dirty. No physical labour.

They rejected her aspiration to go into theatre and acting as 'way too competitive' and 'insecure'. Similarly, Rachel Garrett laughed when she recalled that she had wanted to be 'a musician or some sort of poet' in her teenage years. She recalled how she was 'always told that you can do anything, be anything', although as college drew near she was pushed into teaching despite her own reluctance.

Other women educators spoke more positively of going into teaching, although they emphasised the limited choices they had. Joanna Rothman recalled, 'At that time, women were expected to be either nurses, teachers or secretaries. My mother was a secretary and really didn't want that for me and she knew I wasn't the nursing candidate and that left teaching.' Of her mother's aspirations, she said, 'I think that she thought that she could have done something else had she been given the opportunity to and so since I was going to be given the opportunity for education that I should do something else.' It was in this climate that she 'chose' to go into teaching. In the sample there was only one women educator, who was the daughter of a schoolteacher. Elisabeth Danson's father became a teacher after the Second World War when teacher shortages opened 'doorways' in Boston for industrial labourers who had the opportunity to teach and acquire a teaching qualification at the same time. He and Elisabeth's mother, a nurse, were very pleased when she decided on a teaching career. However, she also recalled her father's concern. As she explained, 'He knew times were changing, with the demand for hiring minorities and bussing going on, forced bussing in Boston. He knew it was going to be very tough and I was one of millions coming out of college for teaching jobs.'[19] Indeed, unable to secure a permanent job in teaching, she worked in the insurance industry for seven years before she had a family, did day care which led to substitute teaching and finally a secure teaching position many years later.

Some men educators remembered how their parents hoped they would pursue medical careers. Al Lopez recalled that his father wanted him to go to medical school because medicine was a 'prestigious career' where you could be independent, with your own practice. He followed his father into the business world instead, however, as an engineer (and only much later went into teaching). Barry Waite also recalled how his mother, a nurse, would have liked him to become a doctor. As he explained:

I think she loved medicine and loved the involvement and that and would like to have seen me be part of that. It's something we would talk about at dinner, talk about what was going on at the hospital, what was going on with this doctor and that doctor, but nothing more obvious than that.

His father, a postal worker, wanted 'whatever it was my sister and I wanted' and both parents were happy, in fact, that he chose teaching, being inclined towards the arts rather than sciences. Roy Morgan spoke of how both parents wanted him to go to college and how his father wanted him to do something in business. As he explained:

When I first went to college, my father was one of those guys, nobody goes to college except to go into business. Why else would you go to college? So he convinced me that I needed to take math, statistics and business and all this stuff. I hated it and so I changed from Business to English with a minor in secondary education. I remember calling him and telling him and breaking into a cold sweat. 'Dad, I've changed my major.' He said, 'Oh. Very good. You are going into education. Let me ask you a question? Are there any other boys who've done that?' I couldn't believe what he'd said. My mother was more supportive than he was.[20]

Gendered dispositions about good jobs for women and men, therefore, clearly shaped the occupational destinations of my interviewees. Bob Farrell recalled exactly how his parents thought in these terms, although, from a modest background, teaching was seen as an attractive career for a man. He recalled how his parents, although not college educated themselves, attached considerable importance to him going to college, although not his sisters. As he said:

It was very important to them. I think my father's economic situation seemed unstable to them. It was important to them that mine be stable and so it was always expected that I was going to college. However, that was not the case for the girls. That was an aspect at that time. An incorrect aspect and a poor aspect but one of the time and the locality and that type of thing.

The expectation was that he would be a family breadwinner in the future.[21] As Bob suggested:

My father was constantly mentioning the fact that he thought teaching was a good secure profession which would allow you time off because we have the summer months when the school doesn't meet and there are vacation periods during the year or three one-week vacations through the school year. He felt that this would provide a minimum level of security financially, and that you could do other things in that time that we had off to supplement the lower income, but it was something that you could count on and he kept saying, 'Oh I really like how a friend of theirs, the fact that things are going well for them and they don't seem to have these up and down periods that we have', and that particular person was a teacher.

Given his father's job insecurity as a painting contractor, the security of teaching was an attractive option for his son.

Overall, the discussions on parents' occupational aspirations revealed the considerable impact of gendered views about good jobs and the somewhat lesser effect of class background on occupational dispositions on the interviewee's early lives. The male middle-class medics spoke of how they followed their fathers into medicine or imagined they would follow them into scientific occupations. Their parents valued high-level occupations like their own jobs so a class effect was apparent. All the women medics were from modest class backgrounds. They certainly recalled their parents' high regard for medicine. It appeared, however, that their academic success in the sciences propelled them into medicine although the ability even to consider a medical career came late to some. The effects of class on occupational aspirations were there although also overcome. Many of the women educators from middle-class families recalled the limited occupational choices they had had. Educational success did not necessarily translate into high-level occupational success, as a good job was one that allowed them to combine work and family commitment. This was why teaching was more highly esteemed than a high-level career in, say, law. A career in teaching, however, was highly regarded in itself by those parents from modest social backgrounds, for women and men alike. In contrast to their jobs, it was seen as a well-regarded, reasonably well-paid occupation that, above all else, was secure. The interviewees' parents' modest class backgrounds, therefore, shaped their occupational aspirations – i.e. the height of those aspirations – for their children, that in turn, shaped the kinds of careers they considered desirable.[22]

British educational dispositions

Like their American counterparts, all of the British interviewees spoke of how their parents valued educational success. It was the key to occupational success and many things besides. How they spoke about these issues, of course, varied according to their experiences of education and their parents' socio-economic background and educational histories. Not surprisingly, the privately educated interviewees demonstrated their parents' educational dispositions by pointing to the fact that their parents had paid for the best education possible for them. Their parents' cultural predispositions dictated how they mobilised their economic resources to ensure their educational success.[23] Some of these interviewees spoke at length of their parents' high academic expectations and how they were expected to follow in their footsteps. Edward Myers recalled that the 'Protestant work ethic' was 'utterly crucially important' to his father who had been a highly educated hospital consultant too. He explained, 'Well, he was a bit of a stern man my father, and he had very high expectations. He saw education as a fundamental stepping-stone to a fulfilled life and obviously a life where you were able to maximize your potential experience. Obviously, income, I'm sure, was part of that.' The son of two GPs, Andrew Underwood also recalled how, 'Father was very much of the view that you went to school to learn. He always used to read my school reports and tell me off when they weren't right or they weren't very good.' These men were in no doubt as to what was expected of them either at home or at school.

At the same time, many of these interviewees spoke of how they knew and sometimes felt the weight of their parents' academic expectations in more implicit and subtle ways. Speaking of his mother, also a GP, Andrew Underwood said, 'I don't know that she ever doubted that I would do very well. It was unspoken that I was going to do very well. I don't know what her aspirations were but I presume she wanted me to do well but she never really discussed it because I was always going to.' Bruce Brown recalled that his parents wanted him and his sister to 'have some sort of decent education and we'd end up doing something they'd think was suitable but they didn't really talk about'. For both of them, a 'decent' private education led into 'suitable' careers in medicine. As Bruce stressed, 'I mean they never sort of said anything but, you know, apart from failing physics at A level, I didn't have any problems at school, you know. They weren't really rushing around saying you must do better or anything.' Similarly, Stephen Dodd recalled that his parents, both pharmacists who paid for his minor public school education, 'weren't too pushy about it. I suppose in some ways, I didn't find school too difficult so I just ambled along.' Thus, those interviewees' parents who sent their children to private schools seemed to assume their children would be academically successful as they had been. Educational success was what they had paid for after all and, for the most part, what they got. They could almost assume that their children would be academically successful, thereby facilitating occupational success.[24]

To be sure, the parental dispositions of those interviewees from middle-class backgrounds who did not have an elite education and who went to state grammar schools after passing the eleven plus examination were not so very different. These interviewees also spoke of how their parents placed a high premium on educational success although such expectations were, more often than not, left unspoken, as if the importance of educational success did not have to be vocalised to any great extent. The inculcation of values from one generation to the next was a subtle one. These interviewees implicitly knew what their parents expected of them. Gerald Jones, for example, attended the grammar school where his father taught. His mother had been a teacher before she married and had children. His parents valued educational success in that 'there was an expectation that I would go to university', although he very much stressed, 'I never felt particularly oppressed.' There were some interviewees from middle-class backgrounds, however, who acknowledged that their parents were 'pushy parents' when it came to educational matters. Often coming from modest backgrounds, their own educational and occupational success had not been easily obtained and it was these parents who expressed their educational ambitions for their children most keenly.[25] Peter Smith's father was an industrial chemist – a 'staff graded man' at a major chemical company – who had obtained a external degree from a university which he completed at night school. There was 'no two ways about it', he said, for his father emphasised the importance of 'education in this world' and 'knocked it into my head'.

Peter also spoke of how his family's educational dispositions shaped his early family life. His father's sister, an unmarried teacher, devoted a lot of time to him and constantly 'stressed the importance of reading and writing'. He recalled, 'I can remember regularly as a child going to [the] library and taking out, each week I took out four books, and I'd read those in that week.' Susan Pearson also spoke of how her parents were very keen that she do well and how this aspiration manifested itself in their daily lives. Her father, a teacher, came from a modest background and spent his early working life in the Navy and only experienced a college education in his thirties. She explained:

He, I think, felt very strongly that education was the key to success. In other words, there was no question, not even the consideration that I might not go to university. There was not really any question about what we were going to do and I can distinctly remember him saying, with respect to other things we did, it was always more important that we did well academically, in place of sports, in place of anything.

Her mother, a hospital receptionist, was also 'extremely well read' and 'intellectually capable'. She went on to say:

Our annual vacation was to a different part of Britain to look at museums and such. I think, as a child, I remember thinking 'not another art gallery' but that was the way we operated. We didn't go to the beach. We had an intellectual upbringing but I think it was pretty narrow in some ways. What my parents were into were old churches and art galleries and I think they did try and broaden it a little bit for us but I think there were times when my brother and I would have rather gone to the fair.[26]

On educational matters, the interviewees recalled how their parents were very keen for them to pass the eleven plus examination to gain entry into the good local grammar schools. They knew, in other words, how the education system worked and they were proactive in ensuring their children did also. Rosemary Hill recalled how her mother, a teacher,

brought home tests and things from the school where she was teaching and decided that I didn't know my tables properly and she sought to drive me if you like, made sure I was able to pass the eleven plus. Put it all down to my mother's influence, that particular thing, 'cos I didn't particularly want to. I wasn't interested really.

Once at such schools, parents could be fairly confident and trust that their children would do as well as and go as far as they could with their studies.[27] It seemed, indeed, that the interviewees were diligent students and many echoed the remarks made by Yvonne Johns when she said, 'I wanted to do well so I used to work hard.' Parents and teachers alike assumed that everyone would go into higher education. Mary Bull recalled how, 'There was definitely an expectation. I was on the conveyor belt. There was never any question that what followed O levels was A levels and what followed A levels was university. It was never questioned, never discussed. It was just an expectation.' Ken Butler spoke of the same 'assumptions' and how 'There was no question of doing anything else . . . It was just the norm rather than anything else. It was automatic.' Only Jill Dowds wanted to leave school at 16 and go to secretarial college and earn money but she was 'persuaded to stay on by my parents and although I found it very hard at the time, I appreciate it now'.

Those interviewees from more modest working-class backgrounds also spoke of how their parents attached considerable importance to educational success even though they were not highly educated themselves. In contrast to those interviewees from middle-class backgrounds, the parents' ambitions for their children were often fuelled by the fact that they had not had the opportunity for education themselves. Although they were not formally educated people, these interviewees spoke of their parents' intelligence and culture.[28] Often, they had passed the eleven plus examination to go to grammar school but lack of money prevented them from doing so. Family circumstances, the death of a parent at a young age and a large number of children, for example, frequently dictated that they seek employment in low-level jobs at the first available opportunity at 14 and 15. Diane Willis, for example, spoke of how her parents and extended kin 'were an intelligent family who hadn't had opportunities basically'. She explained:

My Dad was the thirteenth of fifteen children and my mother was one of eleven and my mother resented it. She resented it. My mother came from a very close family, a very loving family, but she still resented the fact that having come from such a big family and being so poor they had no choice in what they could do.

Her parents wanted a better life for their only daughter, including a good education and a good job. Similarly, Barbara Coombes recalled that her father, 'Was clever but he had not been able to go to a grammar school because in those days you had to pay so he was keen that I should have all the opportunities that he had missed.'

These interviewees' parents did not want their children to be thwarted as they had been, growing up in the economically depressed decades before the Second World War. They had high aspirations for their children and wanted them to enjoy the expanded educational opportunities available in the 1950s and 1960s. Many of the interviewees spoke of how their parents were 'overjoyed' when they passed the eleven plus exam and went to grammar school. Confirmation of their children's academic ability was crucial in sustaining their parents' early hopes.[29] John Willis, for example, recalled that his mother, in particular, was 'very keen that we should do well' and 'as soon as we demonstrated that we had the ability then the opportunity was created in the home and things were sacrificed so we could do it'. Like their middle-class counterparts, these interviewees spoke of their parents' continual support and encouragement. They also remembered their parents' adherence to a strong 'work ethic'. John's mother's view, he recalled, was that 'we were bright kids and we were going to have the motivation to succeed'. Barbara Coombes also recalled that her father's view was, 'It's a steady plodder that gets there.' Like a number of these interviewees, Barbara also stressed that her parents' religious beliefs were important in sustaining these values, 'They brought me up in a Christian environment and I think that was a big influence because a Christian morality is very much a middle-class morality and it taught me standards of behaviour – right and wrong – and I adhered to that morality.' This was the cultural environment of the families of the interviewees who enjoyed mobility from working-class origins into middle-class jobs in medicine and teaching.

What was distinctive about some of these interviewees, however, was that their parents did not automatically assume that they would stay on at school past 16 and continue with their A levels and go on to university. Those interviewees from middle-class backgrounds spoke of the one path ahead of them: namely, going to university as their parents desired and expected. While leaving school at 16 was not a desirable option for these interviewees, the parents of the interviewees from working-class backgrounds would have been quite happy for their children to leave school and go into office work. Hilary Butler recalled how, 'My father's ambition was to see me do well but then I think if I'd gone into the bank he would have been highly delighted, you know, that was the sort of thing that they would have been happy with but I'd always wanted to teach.' She also recalled:

When I got the grades to go to university, you know, my parents were quite happy about that although they'd always said, 'Well, you know, if you want to teach, we're happy for you to do so. Don't worry about university, just go to teachers' training college', but they were always behind me in whatever I decided.

The interviewees acknowledged that it was the wider encouragement of teachers at grammar schools coupled, of course, with their own academic success and motivation that propelled them into higher education. Crucially, it seemed, their parents never discouraged them from entering higher education. They often deferred to their children in the decisions they made about college, university and beyond.[30]

In sum, like the American interviewees from middle-class backgrounds, my British informants spoke of their parents' high expectations for academic success. Again, it was assumed that they would do well at school and this was reflected in their everyday lives. All of these middle-class parents, according to the interviewees, had clear expectations that their children would go as far as they could with their education, thereby attaining the highest level qualifications possible. Certainly, leaving school at 16 or even 18 and anything less than a professional or managerial job were considered highly undesirable and were not options worthy of consideration. Turning to the interviewees from working-class backgrounds, their parents had high aspirations fuelled by the fact that they had been thwarted in their early lives in the 1930s and 1940s. Again, however, they did not so much expect their children to do well but they very much hoped they would. These aspirations were sustained when their children passed the eleven plus examination for grammar school thereby demonstrating their academic ability to others.[31] Moreover, these interviewees' parents had more modest educational ambitions; they would have been happy for their children to leave school at 16 or 18 and enter clerical work which was well regarded as a secure, white-collar job. Thus, leaving school was not such an undesirable path to consider. For the working-class women and men of this study, however, academic success and parental support set them on a path to higher education and on to professional careers in medicine and teaching.

British occupational horizons

There were examples of occupational inheritance as a small number of the male doctors were the sons of doctors. Some clearly came from 'medical families' since their mothers were either nurses or, in one instance, a doctor too. Lawrence Foster very much downplayed the influence of his family – his father was a GP and his mother had been a nurse – on his decision to become a GP. He stressed, 'That was never foisted on us. The fact that two of us became doctors was just coincidental, I think. I think you tended to get that in medical families anyway. At least one or two went into medicine.' Interestingly, Lawrence emphasised the coincidence that he and his brother were both medics although he went on to acknowledge a tendency for medical families to produce more medics! Other interviewees talked explicitly of the pressures to follow their parents even when their preferences lay elsewhere. Edward Myers was the son of a hospital doctor and a former nurse and he recalled pressure from his father. As he explained:

Oh he always wanted me to be a doctor. That was pretty plain that he expected me to be a doctor and to go into the NHS. I had aspirations, I can remember in my early teens, I had a view that I would like to be architect but that wasn't quite fitting. I would not like you to get the impression that I regret becoming a doctor, because I don't regret that. At the time, I felt I might like to be an architect. I think I talked about it a bit but he was quite a dominant character, my father.[32]

Andrew Underwood's parents were both GPs and worked in the same practice and he said, 'I think it was always intended that I was going to be a GP, ever since I was born . . . I actually wanted to do architecture but I was discouraged from doing that on the grounds that there wasn't a secure job at the end of it.'

Pressures, therefore, of both a subtle and less subtle kind, led these men into medicine and, in the case of Andrew Underwood, into the family practice rather than hospital medicine. Of course, most of the male doctors did not come from medical families although they were encouraged, by parents and schools alike, towards the sciences and, almost inevitably, towards medicine if they did well enough academically. Peter Smith, for example, was the son of an industrial chemist who had obtained an external degree at night school. He recalled: 'I was a good all rounder at school. I was as good on the arts side as I was on the science side but my father was of the opinion that you'd do far better if you specialised on the science side rather than on the arts side. You'd come out as something on the science side.' Rod Hunt's father, a religious minister, was a classically trained musician in Russia before the Second World War and Rod suggested he was inclined towards music and languages like his father. However,

My school itself was very determined to steer people always from those sorts of subjects and to do the professions like law, accountancy, medicine, dentistry – those were the sorts of boys they liked to produce . . . So the headmaster took me aside and said, 'Look, you're very average at whatever you do so you might as well do something useful. Otherwise you'll be a frustrated teacher like me.' He was quite honest about it. He said, 'Do the sciences. You're quite capable of doing them', so I changed.

His father was 'quite relieved. I think anything that meant I had a steady income and, you know, solid foundation he found reassuring.'[33]

Medicine, therefore, was regarded as a highly reputable professional occupation for young men and it was in this environment that the interviewees' occupational dispositions were formed. Similar pressures were felt by some of the women medics. Bridget Underwood, for example, recalled that her father, a welder, was anxious that she do well at school but it was her mother, the more dominant personality, who had ideas about medicine. As she explained, 'I have to say that medicine did feature heavily in my mother's conversations. She used to work in the path lab at the hospital when she first got married and "it was such a lovely atmosphere and it was such a lovely job and medicine's such a lovely thing"'.[34] Being contrary, Bridget was going to do the opposite and read English at university when a cousin told her about pre-med courses for students with advanced qualifications in the arts. When he mentioned it, she said, 'I just suddenly thought what would I do with my life if I had an English degree', and she rang around at short notice and got accepted for medical school. Other women spoke of how they decided on medicine themselves although they counted on parental support too. After a spell in hospital, Barbara Coombes decided she wanted to be a doctor. She said, 'My father was supportive. The headmistress sent for him when I was in about the second year, when she asked me what I wanted to be, and so she sent for my father to tell him that I had aspirations beyond my capabilities.' Despite the fact that the school was discouraging, her father was 'keen that if I wanted to do something, he would not stand in my way'.

Although Barbara was discouraged by her school headmistress, she was determined to succeed and she recalled how, at 14, 'I started to realise that you just didn't get to where you wanted to be by messing around.' It was a belief generated and sustained at home. Schoolteachers, however, were incredibly surprised when she did very well in her A level examinations and went on to medical school, citing her many years later as an example 'of what you could do if you wanted to'. There were other women medics who enjoyed encouragement from schoolteachers, although it was not the norm. Coming from a modest background, such promotion was crucial for Julia Dodd. Her parents were quite fearful of their daughter's desire to do medicine, thinking that she would need money they did not have to give in order to buy a practice, as we saw in Chapter 2. It was her headmistress who reassured them and it was she who encouraged Julia to consider medicine. Most young women at her girls' grammar school, Julia explained, went into teaching and nursing and, for a while, she considered physiotherapy. The headmistress, she said,

Suggested to me that I should think about medicine. She was quite a remarkable woman when I think about it. She was quite devoted to her particular career and quite unselfish in her attitude to everybody although a bit of a cold fish! She had us all terrified of her but I think it's perfectly obvious, looking back on it, that she'd obviously spotted that I had potential that could be nurtured which, you know, I shall always be eternally grateful to her for her help.[35]

It was the norm, however, for most of the women interviewees, especially in the 1950s and 1960s, to be channelled into teaching. Even when they were able to go to university, teaching followed afterwards. Rosemary Hill described how her mother and her aunt went into teaching. She said:

My mother's mother, my grandmother, was determined that her daughters were not going to go into service and do the things she had to do. She took in washing and things and so both daughters became teachers because she decided they were going to. That was what they were going to do. They were told that was what they were going to do and that's what they did.[36]

Although she was not 'told what to do' by her mother, the expectation was that she and her sister would go into teaching after university, which, indeed, they both did! Sandra Booth remembered,

My father was very keen for me to teach. I don't know why. Perhaps then there was not a wide choice of careers for women. He thought teaching was the be-all and end-all. Of course it isn't like that now but in those days it was. It was a secure job for a woman who could get married and also have a family and teach.

She also recalled that her grammar school 'churned out teachers' and now wondered why it was so 'narrow'. Other interviewees also recalled how teaching was considered a 'good' job. The academic achievers were directed to university first while the less academically inclined went straight to teacher training college. Many had a sense that they had 'little choice'.

Gendered ideas about teaching as an appropriate job for a woman were also to be found among those from more modest backgrounds, although it was a desirable job in itself too. Sheila Myers' mother, a shirt machinist who worked full time while bringing up her two daughters alone, was very keen for her to go into teaching. She said, 'I think she thought it was a nice profession for a girl. I think she also saw it was one that could easily fit in with family, more easily than she had been able to.' Similarly, Susan Parry recalled how she wanted to be an actress, being heavily involved in drama. She spoke of how, 'My mother had no intention of letting me be an actress. Let's put it that way. She wanted me from the very beginning to be a teacher. I think it was a secure profession, good money for women.' Indeed, Susan's mother refused to let her go to university and do drama and she went to teacher training college instead. Again, schools also played a major role in directing women into teaching. Sheila Parker described how 'in the sixth form, the high achievers went to university and everyone else went to teacher training college. It was obvious that I would never reach the university standard so it was teacher-training college.' Her parents, she said, were very happy about the path their daughter subsequently followed. As she said, 'They wanted us to do well. They wanted us to climb upwards . . . We were sort of able to come out of the council house and the working-class background to having a secure job as our parents would have seen it, a good job, a professional job.' A secure professional job was highly sought after and teaching was such an occupation for bright middle-class and working-class women in the 1950s and 1960s.[37]

The male teachers were not directed into teaching in such a gendered way. Ken Butler recalled that while his parents were keen for him to succeed academically they did not have particular occupational aspirations. He drifted into teaching, since remaining at university, doing a PGCE, was better than looking for a job in the late 1960s! Teaching, however, was well regarded among parents from modest backgrounds. John Willis recalled how his parents' aspirations were for him to go as far as he could. He gave a moving account of how his father's views, shaped by his life as a manual worker, shifted over time. As he explained:

My father, now this is an interesting thing. My father and mother were different. My mother wanted us to go the whole way, as far as we could go. My father had no concept of what that meant, but to him, what he didn't want, he said, he didn't want his sons to go to work and come back with their hands dirty. He said he'd had all sorts of awful rough jobs in his time and he didn't want us to do that. He wanted us to get a good clean job, a steady job, a reliable job and his idea of good jobs was working in the offices at British Rail. Now, you know, when we were about eleven years old, he said, 'Well, you could do that sort of job.' Then, as you're going through school, you realize you're leaving that sort of job behind. So then he shared my mother's aspirations and our aspirations and we went as far as we could go.[38]

Indeed, John wanted to be an academic but his Ph.D. application was, for various reasons, unsuccessful, and that was a huge disappointment to him at the time. Needing a job and an income at short notice, he had the opportunity to go into teaching. He enjoyed it and went on to have a very successful career and his parents were very proud.

Interestingly, other men were actively discouraged from teaching, not by parents, but by schoolteachers. Norman Johns' school actively discouraged him from a teaching career even though his parents fully supported his desire to go into education. Norman wanted to teach because he thought he could do a better job than the teachers at his secondary modern school. His parents thought teaching was a good job too. As he explained, 'In those days, you know, it was secure and safe and, relatively [speaking] the money was good and it was a profession so it was certainly something they supported.' It certainly compared well with his father's job at the local water board where he spent most of his life as a general labourer. However, on transferring to grammar school at sixteen, Norman found quite contrasting views about the social standing of teaching as a career, especially for men. He recalled the 'culture shock' for 'there was only one thing they were interested in and that was university entrance'. He remembered that, 'Teaching was not the profession one went into. That was for failures. You came under a lot of pressure. You were effectively told "We're not going to work hard for you unless you go to university." That's what they were about.' His application to a redbrick university 'wasn't really approved of but it was better than going to teaching training'. Given that his parents 'couldn't advise me because they had no knowledge of the education system', the greater pressures of the school headmaster, preoccupied with rank and status, propelled him on to university. Teaching came later.[39]

Once more, parents' gendered views about good jobs were the dominant influence on the British interviewees' career aspirations, although the effects of class were also in evidence. As in the USA, there were examples of male medics who followed in the footsteps of their fathers. To do otherwise was not quite fitting! The high premium placed on academic success in the sciences rather than the arts, pushed by fathers and schoolteachers, also propelled other middle-class men into medicine. Again, all of the British women medics were from modest backgrounds although they were not thwarted in their aspirations to do medicine, especially as, being academic successfully in the sciences, schoolteachers sometimes reinforced these aspirations. Forging their careers in the 1950s and 1960s, however, it seemed that teaching was regarded as the only desirable job for young women of middle-class and working-class origins alike. It was assumed that women would have childcare responsibilities later in life, and thus, teaching was viewed as a good job in being compatible with family life. To be sure, for the women teachers of working-class origin, teaching was also a 'step up' from their parents' more modest jobs into a more economically secure profession. Working-class parents held similar views about teaching for their sons although it was not necessarily a message reinforced at school. Again, therefore, socio-economic background shaped occupational aspirations. It influenced the level of parental occupational aspirations that, in turn, shaped the interviewees' career paths.[40]

Conclusion

This chapter has focused on the mobilisation of cultural resources in the reproduction of advantage drawing on the interviewees' accounts of their parents' educational dispositions and occupational horizons. As in

Chapter 2, the interviewees were reflecting back on their youth and thinking about how their parents had supported and encouraged them in their
studies. They were recounting their childhood experiences and, therefore,
offering their perceptions of their parents' educational and occupational
dispositions. Their parents may have thought quite differently, of course,
although I think it unlikely that the interviewees would have presented
their parents' values and dispositions in ways completely at odds with reality. Arguably, their perceptions of their parents' expectations and hopes
were as important as, if not more important, than they might have been in
reality, for their perceptions clearly shaped their own values, dispositions
and so on. The empirical findings in this chapter clearly demonstrate that
all of the interviewees' parents had cultural capital in that they placed a
high premium on educational success and occupational advancement.
That is to say, both middle-class and working-class parents very much
wanted their children to do well in school and to go as far as they could in
the education system, attaining the highest level of credentials possible in
order to get good jobs. Almost all of the parents of modest backgrounds
wanted their children to do well precisely because they themselves had
been thwarted in their ambitions when they were young in the 1930s and
1940s. They wanted their children to take the opportunities for education, including higher education, that became available in the 1950s and
1960s.[41]

There was, then, no evidence of a 'poverty of aspirations' or any lack of
cultural capital among the lower-middle-class and working-class families.
In this respect, Goldthorpe is entirely correct to be critical of Bourdieu's
notion of cultural capital and its key place in his theory of social reproduction. However, I would argue that Bourdieu's concept of cultural capital does capture important class processes which Goldthorpe neglects.
It captures the way in which where people start out in life very much
shapes their educational and occupational horizons, what they would
like to do, how these hopes shape their thoughts and actions, and the
confidence with which they feel they can realise their dreams.[42] In both
America and Britain, for example, the middle-class interviewees talked
about their parents' (often unspoken) assumptions and expectations that
they would be academically able and that they would succeed. They did
not entertain or would not allow things to be otherwise. They were
confident in these views and knew what their children should do to
succeed. The interviewees from more modest class backgrounds spoke
about their parents' educational dispositions and aspirations somewhat
differently. They wanted their children to do well but they did not confidently assume they were academically able. They were cautiously hopeful and, thus, delighted when their children enjoyed academic success.

5   Fulfilling potential and securing happiness

As Bourdieu had led me to expect, the middle-class parents of my American and British interviewees mobilised their cultural resources to facilitate their children's educational and occupational advancement.[1] They assumed and expected that their children would do well in school and they held high occupational aspirations for them. These dispositions and values contributed to the interviewees' success in becoming doctors and teachers. That said, in both countries, the parents of my working-class interviewees did not lack cultural capital. They also placed a high premium on academic success although they hoped rather than assumed that their children would do well. Their occupational horizons were somewhat more modest than their middle-class counterparts but they did not seek to limit their children's aspirations as academic success propelled them onwards. They were keen, in other words, to take up educational opportunities that expanded in the post-war period of prosperity. In this chapter, I turn my attention to how the interviewees, now all middle-class parents, seek to mobilise their cultural resources to ensure their children's educational and occupational success. Most of the interviewees' children were still making their way through the education system although some of them, as young adults, were seeking to establish themselves in the labour market. Despite the diversity in their ages, all of them had been in education from the 1980s onwards when a harsher economic and political climate, including tax cuts reducing the quality of public and state educational provision, took hold. The interviewees' educational dispositions and occupational horizons for their children are considered in this context.

The American interviewees were keen for their children to start learning at an early age and for their intellectual curiosity and inquisitiveness to be satisfied and stimulated further at school. They monitored their children's academic performance closely with the aid of standardised tests.[2] Many anticipated that their children would do well and they expected teachers to challenge their children to fulfill their potential. Again, there was a strong emphasis on lifestyle practices as they sought to inculcate their children with the work ethic, although they wanted their children to enjoy education, to experience success and, in turn, increased confidence and empowerment. A high premium was placed on keeping adolescent children on track and avoiding the distractions posed by peer culture and the attractions of the opposite sex. All of the interviewees anticipated that their children would go to college because it was imperative for a good job. They wanted them to get into the best universities and, indeed, many of their children had expressed aspirations to go to the better schools. Mixed views were expressed on the desirability of medicine as a career, especially for young women, although it was still considered a good job overall. A degree of ambivalence was also expressed about teaching as a good career. All of the interviewees wanted their children to have intrinsically rewarding jobs that they would find enjoyable and challenging. The more affluent physicians hoped they could support their children financially if need be while the less affluent educators stressed the importance of financial independence as well.

The British interviewees shared similar educational dispositions. They wanted their children to learn from an early age and their inquisitiveness to be stimulated at school. They too found comfort in standardised tests confirming their children's intellectual development and took action if they fell behind. They sought to inculcate in their children the importance of succeeding at school although they wanted them to enjoy education so they would be increasingly self-motivated. Even so, they monitored their adolescent children so that they stayed on track. Most of the interviewees could report on their children's academic success although there were examples of struggles between parents and children who did not value education highly. Some of the interviewees' children were planning to leave school at 16 although parents were anxious that they seek jobs with training opportunities and career prospects.[3] Some of them had been distracted during their further education and parents still hoped they would get decent jobs. The majority continued into higher education, often attending very prestigious institutions. There were mixed views about the desirability of a medical career, especially for women, although it was still highly regarded. Occupational inheritance was evident. A high level of ambivalence was expressed about a teaching career that was no longer well regarded. Like the Americans, the British rarely had specific occupational aspirations, hoping their children would choose fulfilling careers themselves, the most affluent doctors placing a high premium on this over financial independence which was valued by the more modestly paid teachers.

American educational dispositions

The American interviewees' children spanned a wide age range so that some children were in kindergarden while others had completed graduate school and were establishing themselves as young adults in the labour market. Not surprisingly, the way in which the interviewees spoke about their children's education was related to where they were in the school system. The interviewees with young children, for example, talked about what they had looked for when choosing pre-schools in ways that revealed much about their educational dispositions. Without doubt, the interviewees attached a lot of importance to their children making friends, learning social skills in terms of interacting with other children and enjoying their time in a 'nurturing environment'. They had sent their young children to pre-schools where, they claimed, they enjoyed the 'right balance' between play and work rather than to overly rigid schools preoccupied with preparation for school. Be that as it may, many of the interviewees acknowledged they were keen for their children to start learning in a formally structured setting. A number of doctors and their partners, for example, had sent their children to (often very expensive) Montessori pre-schools known for their formal curriculum albeit one tempered by a philosophy of individual expression and learning.[4] Jack Poole and Jane Bennett sent their three children to Montessori schools, and Jack explained, 'Both my wife and I felt that there was a definite advantage to having the children in a classroom type structure early on . . . We both felt that they would get more accomplished in a formal setting.'

To varying degrees, therefore, the interviewees were keen for their children to start learning early, which would stand them in good stead when they started elementary school. These same issues preoccupied parents as their children transferred to kindergarten and then to elementary school. To be sure, they were keen for their children to be happy and settled in a secure environment and to be with friends from their local community, as I noted before. Many parents wanted their children to have friends from diverse ethnic and cultural backgrounds so they could appreciate the diversity of the wider world and be culturally sensitive. Educational success, in this respect, was only part of the story. Nevertheless, the interviewees were anxious that their children continue to learn, to be inquisitive and, most importantly, to enjoy and embrace learning. Parents placed a very high premium on reading and they very much encouraged it at home. Daniel was clearly delighted that his young daughter, Amy, was on, 'The cusp of reading . . . She has a lot of books and she can read them by just knowing exactly what comes next but she is extremely eager to read and usually we will do a book together where I will do a few words and she will do a few more. So I think she is enjoying it.' The development of linguistic abilities including verbal skills, a growing vocabulary, different styles of expression and so forth was seen as crucial to children's intellectual development and their ability to acquire further knowledge in the future.[5]

Parents were highly attuned to their children's continuing intellectual development as shown by their keen interest in their performance in standardised tests, project work and the like at school. On his young son's early performance, Michael Reed suggested 'he seems very verbal and his reading skills seem better than most of the kids in his class'. Often involved in their children's school, they spoke about their children's education demonstrating a considerable knowledge of curriculum developments in general and how their own children were performing, in particular. Their progress was monitored closely. Gillian Wolkowitz and Roy Morgan, both educators with considerable expertise, were closely involved in their daughter's schooling and Roy talked about how he knew, 'That the curriculum is being implemented effectively and I know she is learning what she is supposed to learn and the standardised test results are off the chart with all grade A.' Test results, therefore, assured parents that their children's educational advancement was appropriate for their age. If not, they could take action to improve the situation. Elisabeth Danson spoke of how her eldest son, Nathan, was diagnosed with Attention Deficient Disorder (ADD). As she explained, 'I picked it up. I always knew it but I was able to hold off on the medication until third grade. When his reading scores started to fail and he was unable to focus in the classroom, I had to have him formally diagnosed and he just sailed right up from there.'[6] The interviewees, therefore, paid very close attention to their children's intellectual development and found comfort in the fact that they were performing according to their age as set by external standards.

Many of the interviewees, especially the highly educated physicians from established upper-middle-class backgrounds, anticipated that their children would do well. They were very confident of their children's academic abilities. What was crucially important, therefore, was that their children be intellectually challenged and that teachers succeed in getting them to perform to the best of their abilities. It was for this reason that they attached great importance to high-calibre teachers and to the fact that their children enjoy as much individual attention as possible. Most of the interviewees were happy with their children's elementary school (and middle-school) teachers. Of course, many of the physicians and their partners had sent their children to the best private schools or public schools which had attracted highly respected teachers with good pay who remained with the schools for a number of years. Constant monitoring left some less satisfied however. Yuko Yacoby's two daughters, Natalie and Nancy, were advanced in reading age yet Yuko was seriously concerned about her elder daughter's education. As she explained, 'She had had the worst teachers at each grade level . . . and because she had been ignored and not been challenged, she will say, Mom, I'm bored. I'm finishing my homework in five minutes.'[7] Similarly, irrespective of the high reputation of the elementary school his children attended, Ray Chapman felt that the quality of teaching was not consistent across all years. Despite being very involved as a member of his children's school council, his children had 'encountered some bad teaching' which had been 'personally frustrating' not least when his interventions helped future generations but had 'less impact on your own kids'.

The interviewees as parents, therefore, possessed 'cultural capital' in the sense that they understood the education system well, having experienced it themselves, and they knew how their children should perform to succeed in the school system. They utilised this 'cultural capital' to the advantage of their children. They were also critically aware of their role as parents in facilitating their children's success. Like their parents, the interviewees spoke of how their role was to encourage and support their children in fulfilling their potential and making the very best of their emerging talents and abilities. Interestingly, however, they rarely discussed the ways in which they helped their children acquire 'cultural capital' in terms of participation in elite cultural activities such as attending museums, theatres, concerts and so on although I am sure many of them undertook these activities. What they emphasised was the way in which the value they placed on educational success shaped their lifestyle practices, including the use of leisure time, in a much more mundane way. They talked, for example, about the importance of homework being completed after school before all other activities and how television viewing was restricted both in terms of the amount of time spent watching TV and the content of what was watched, and how playing with friends, sporting activities and so forth, were always secondary in the evenings.[8] As George Marshall suggested in relation to his three sons, 'Clearly, we place a lot of value on academics. We don't let them watch TV very much. After homework, they can mostly do what they want, creating things, art stuff, playing on the computer but not that much, and reading. Reading is top of the list and they like it.'

It was these everyday cultural practices, therefore, which were discussed rather than any reference to high cultural tastes. Instilling in their children a strong work ethic was everything. For those interviewees with young teenagers, the pressure – subtle or otherwise – was kept up to the extent that parents spent much time organising their children's activities. As Paula Bailey, and many of the other mothers, explained:

When they have a test or a project or something they write it up on the calendar. I keep a big desk calendar up there so, that way, I can remind them that I am kind of aware what big things are going on at the school and they have things to do and stuff so that I can remind them as far as that goes, and it helps them to remember.[9]

When the interviewees spoke of their children's performance and application, they often did so in a highly gendered fashion. Thus, it was not unusual for daughters to be described as diligent and hard working (and, indeed, their capacity for hard work and striving for perfection sometimes had to be checked) while sons were often described as typically underperforming as young teenage boys do and, therefore, in need of constant pressure. Ken Bailey, for example, talked about how he had 'leaned' on his son over many years. Recounting a typical scenario with his son, he explained:

I tell you if I let my son do his homework by himself, it's a disaster. I let him do it and I say 'bring it to me' and I check it and I go 'You didn't do half of it' and, well, he'll give me some excuse. [He says] 'Well, it's not really due tomorrow.' [I say] 'Well, call your friend and find out if it is due tomorrow.' [He says] 'Ah, I'm busy.' [I say] 'I don't care, do it' and so I've got to lean on my kid or my wife leans on my kid.

To a greater or lesser degree, therefore, parents acknowledged that they kept up the pressure on their children to succeed in school and continually emphasised the values of hard work, discipline, perseverance, productivity and responsibility. Arguably, the interviewees exercised considerable control over their children's lives. That said, the interviewees did not want their children to be motivated by external pressures alone. As they got older, they expected their children to embrace these values for themselves. They wanted and, again, anticipated, that their children would be 'self-starters' as they had been. Again, an important component of this motivation is that their children enjoyed learning and that it was something they embraced rather than experienced as a chore. From this enjoyment and application would come success and from success they would enjoy increased self-confidence and a sense of empowerment.[10] They wanted their children, in the words of Nikos Yacoby, to 'feel good about themselves as people. I think it's really helpful because that's what you really need to succeed.' Self-esteem, therefore, was also highly valued as a key to educational and occupational success. As Jane Bennett explained,

'I want them to feel that educationally they are on a par with anybody, there's no question of being secondary or substandard, that they are really as good as anybody else out there so that opens up a horizon from there in terms of what they can do eventually.' Educational success, therefore, would empower them 'because I think they will do much better at whatever they choose if they have had opportunities and they've done well'.

Indeed, the interviewees with teenage children spoke of how they increasingly 'knew the drill'. On the importance of doing homework before anything else, Bernice Hughes said that her two older daughters 'know what they need to do and I don't have to remind them'. Their children, it seemed, had had these values so successfully inculcated in them that they wanted to excel at school. That said, parents often expressed anxiety about their children as they became adolescents and experienced anti-school peer pressures, to 'hang out' at school rather than apply themselves, to become preoccupied with fashion and music rather than with their studies and be diverted by the attractions of the opposite sex rather than enjoy the endorsement of their friends via academic success. Drugs, of course, greatly concerned them, too. David Neale, for example, spoke of the pressures on his second daughter, Caroline, at school. He said, 'In high school people would rather have her be dumb and pretty, she's attractive or whatever, and I just wanted her to do well in school so she could be happy with herself and go somewhere and do something productive.'

It was vital, therefore, that children be kept 'on track'. Like many other parents, David encouraged and facilitated his children's sporting activities as a healthy leisure pursuit. As he went on to explain, 'I emphasise sport for the girls, more sometimes than I emphasise school, because it's been something that's kept them on track and not distracted them with boys and drugs and all the other things that you have to think about.' It was imperative that they were not diverted from their studies and the pursuit of academic success. As parents, therefore, they felt they had to be ever vigilant.[11]

Overall, the American interviewees placed a very high premium on educational success. Often knowledgeable about child development, they wanted their children to embrace learning from an early age and they were very attuned to their children's progress via standardised tests. It was of paramount importance to them that their children fulfill their potential and they expected schoolteachers to push and challenge their children to make the best of their talents and abilities.[12] Like their parents, the interviewees spoke of how their values shaped their lifestyle practices so that television viewing was kept to a minimum, everyday leisure activities were of an educational kind and, again, they monitored their children's school activities closely. As their children became young adults, they were keen for them to be internally motivated, to work hard and be successful and from success they would enjoy increased self-esteem and self-confidence from which further success would stem. There was considerable anxiety about keeping teenagers on track, however, so that they would not be distracted by popular teenage culture – preoccupied with fashion, music, alcohol, drugs and so on – and the attractions of the opposite sex. Accordingly, they sought to monitor their leisure pursuits, encouraging formally organised sporting activities, for example, which would not distract them from scholarly pursuits. In a myriad of ways, therefore, the interviewees sought to mobilise their cultural resources to ensure their children's educational and occupational advancement.

American occupational horizons

Most of the interviewees' children were still of compulsory school age and making their way through middle or high school (while others had gone on to college and community colleges, and will be considered later). The majority, it seemed, were performing well at school as A grade students although some interviewees acknowledged that their children struggled academically having to work hard to obtain B or C grades. There were some youngsters who had ADD or ADHD for which they were medicated.[13] Medication, it seemed, stabilised concentration levels and kept them focused on their studies. All of the interviewees envisaged that their children would go to college as they had done. It was, as Elisabeth Danson said, 'not an option. Since day one, it's just how the story goes. Elementary school, middle school, high school, college. It's just where you go.' It was no surprise, therefore, that her children did not and, indeed, could not think otherwise. Using the same language, Bernice Hughes stressed that her daughters 'don't have a choice. College isn't an option and they understand that.' Without a shadow of doubt, all of the interviewees saw a college education as an absolute prerequisite for a 'good job' that offered extrinsic and intrinsic rewards. With regard to extrinsic rewards, Ken Bailey suggested, 'I do think that they'll need a college education to basically support the kind of lifestyle that they are accustomed to in America because really college education seems to be a requisite for doing OK in America.'

In this respect, the interviewees were very instrumental in their attachment to educational success as educational credentials were seen as the key to high-level professional and managerial jobs. The interviewees, therefore, were well aware of the increasingly tight fit between education and employment (especially income) and also credential inflation meant that graduate school was increasingly important to attain a good position. Accordingly, they very much wanted their children to achieve high SAT scores to gain entry into the better colleges and Ivy League schools. Those parents who went to Ivy League schools very much hoped their children would follow in their footsteps.[14] In these discussions, the intrinsic rewards of an elite education were stressed. All of the interviewees valued the experience of going to college and living in a dorm away from home for the first time. Those who attended the top schools also spoke of how they wanted their children to be taught by accomplished professors and 'to be exposed [to] and interact' with other 'clever young people'. It was no surprise to learn, therefore, that many of the interviewees' children, especially the physicians' children, were expressing aspirations to go to the top New England universities such as Harvard, Dartmouth and Brown. Gillian Wolkowitz recounted a story about how her daughter, Tina, aspired to get into Harvard although when her school principal suggested she consider Brown, 'She took it as a slight. "Didn't she think I was good enough?" So then I explained to her that Harvard is an international college and all of this but people who go to Brown, they always have the professor, that's one thing.'

Indeed, the interviewees' discussions of their children's emerging college aspirations were very revealing as they spoke of what they thought was required to secure entry into the elite colleges. Mary Moran's thirteen-year-old son, Martin, wanted to go to Harvard like his father. She was thrilled but she was concerned that he was not the kind of candidate they would select. As she explained,

He's quietly aggressive but you have to be a very aggressive individual. You have to be a schemer and he is a schemer and you have to be a good advocate for yourself. So self-effacing individuals from my experience, from people I know that have gone there as undergrads, there is a certain type that goes there. I am sure there are geniuses that got thrown in at the edges but your standard Harvard student is of a certain type.

That certain type, as another interviewee put it, is like an old-fashioned 'renaissance man or woman': namely, a good academic (but not so academic as to be 'a bookworm') who is also good at sports, music and so on. The interviewees and/or their partners who had enjoyed a regular education themselves expressed more modest aspirations for their children. They wanted their children to do four-year degree programmes and to complete them within four years.[15] They hoped their children would do well enough in their SAT scores to get into a college of their choice. Their preference was for their children to attend reputable private liberal arts colleges (which tend to be small) rather than state schools (which are very big). At small liberal arts colleges their children would be pushed and challenged by educators while they might be lost in the crowd and have to struggle alone for a decent education in a big state college.

So far, discussion has focused on the interviewees whose children were still making their way through school and, arguably, their hopes had not been tempered by life events. Some of the older interviewees' children, for example, had not been academically successful and neither had they been internally driven by scholarly interests even though their parents – the interviewees – had encouraged them at school. There were many such examples. Bob Farrell's daughter, for example, struggled academically although she had enjoyed the social side of school. He had threatened to remove her from school and send her to his own school if she did not 'buckle down'. She left school with modest exam grades and went to a small commercial arts college in Boston where she completed an associate degree. Barry Waite, as I noted earlier, had to address these difficulties when both of his sons dropped out of college, neither having either interest in or motivation for further study. Early aspirations had been tempered and he too was relieved and very, very grateful that they were back at a local community college. Other life events intervened to undermine parental hopes and plans. In her senior year at high school, Marion Chaves' daughter lost both of her grandfathers on the same day and she suffered subsequently from depression. Leaving home for college soon after, she was unable to cope and dropped out. She had become entangled with a boyfriend who did not want her to go to college. Despite his resistance, she was thinking of returning to college and her parents desperately wanted her to do so and, when the time came, to get out of the relationship 'with a man who had fed on her depression and loss'.[16]

These examples show that while parents might try to create the conditions in which their children are academically successful, they cannot control their children's lives, especially if they are not intellectually inclined and (consequently) have different interests and pursuits of their own. Again, they can increase the chances of academic success but they cannot guarantee it. The majority of the interviewees did not have particular occupational aspirations for their children. They certainly held mixed views about their children following them into medicine or teaching. Despite its high status, many of the physicians described how medicine was a very time-consuming profession, requiring long and unsocial hours of work, and which was only worth doing if considered rewarding. In this sense, it had to be a vocation. Charles and Nadia Khan were both medics who had experience of the British and American health systems. Their 16-year-old daughter, Sukhdeep, wanted to be a physician too, although Charles said:

She is interested in medicine but I think medicine is a very tough life for a woman in this country. That is my observation and it's not a sexist thing. There is not the social support that you have in the British system . . . In Britain, you can take time off, you can split a job-share now. There is no such thing in this country. Here you do a strict job which people do. [It is] full hours and it's very tough.[17]

In contrast, Sarah Neale, who had never had the opportunity to go to medical school that she desperately craved when she was young, was keen that her eldest daughter, a biology major, should go to medical school rather than into a related health field such as physiotherapy, which she was considering – so that 'she would call the shots'.[18] Another interviewee, Roy Morgan, mentioned medicine alongside other high-status professions like law, as a good job for his only daughter, Tina. That said, his wife, Gillian, was one of the few parents to have very firm occupational aspirations for her daughter. Having been thwarted in her desire to go to law school and pushed into teaching by her mother and grandmother, Gillian said of her daughter, 'I want her to go to law school so badly and no-one encouraged me and my mother did everything to discourage me and made my life miserable.' Unsurprisingly, her daughter wanted to be a lawyer. It was more usual for the teachers, like the medics, to have mixed views about their children following them into the same profession. The Walkers discouraged their eldest daughter, Elaine, from a career in teaching. As Mrs Walker suggested, 'To be honest, I kind of guided her away from just zeroing in on teaching because I know the ins and outs of it. I kind of pointed out, that at least with speech and audiology, there is such a spectrum of things you can do.' It was something that she had not enjoyed, being 'pigeonholed' into teaching at school, and she encouraged her daughter to make the best of a wider range of opportunities, teaching in different settings.

The vast majority of parents, therefore, did not have specific job aspirations for their children. Their major preoccupation was that their children enjoy individual self-fulfillment and happiness in their jobs. The intrinsic satisfactions of a career were deemed crucially important. There were some interesting differences between the upper-middle-class doctors and middle-class teachers and their partners however. The former expressed the view that their children would find their jobs rewarding even if this meant they were not always well paid. The interviewees, in other words, could imagine that they would help their children financially so they could enjoy the high levels of job satisfaction that were very highly valued. Michael Reed said of his young son, 'Actually, I really want him to do something that he is really excited about and he is interested in . . . I don't think I have the same aspirations that my parents had of sort of doing the conventional thing like going to medical school to guarantee yourself a nice job.' Jane Bennett spoke of how her choice of career was influenced by the need to 'provide myself with an independent lifestyle'. For her children, she said,

In my heart of hearts, I would love to think I could bring them to the point in their lives where they could really choose whatever they like and pursue that passionately. That was not an opportunity that I had, so in terms of improving for the next generation, I would be very gratified . . . I would like to take the burden of self-sufficiency [and] remove that from the equation a little bit more than I felt my parents were able to do for me.

The desire, therefore, was for their children to exercise free choice in the pursuit of an individually rewarding career unfettered by financial constraints.[19]

For the more modestly situated teachers and their partners, there was a different emphasis in their hopes for their children. To be sure, they wanted their children to enjoy job satisfaction and to find their paid work intrinsically rewarding. They also expected their children to be financially independent, however. These occupational dispositions, therefore, reflected different economic circumstances, as these interviewees knew they could not support their children financially in their adult lives. As Alan Garrett said, 'I want them to pursue what they want to pursue really', although he added 'I want them to be sort of financially independent sort of thing. I also don't want them to be dependent on us. They can't be dependent on us.' Bob Farrell echoed these sentiments. He had supported his daughter when she went to a small commercial arts college where she completed an associate's degree. She was now a billboard designer and very happy in her job. Given some difficult years, he was 'thrilled' at how things had worked out for her. As he explained,

My only criterion was whatever you want to do as long as you can earn a living at it, that's fine. My objective for her was, you can do anything you want to do as long as you are able to support yourself and take care of yourself, because you have to be an independent person, and don't depend on anybody else. You always have to take care of yourself.

Interestingly, Bob very much stressed the importance of this independence for his daughter because of changes in family life. He said, 'I think society has changed and I don't think it's either appropriate or wise for a women to feel that a man is going to take care of her or for a man to feel a women is going to take care of him either. We need to be self-sufficient.' Unlike his parents, who had pushed him on to college but not his sisters,

Bob was of the opinion that educational success and occupational success were as important to his daughter as to any young man. Gendered occupational horizons had shifted across a generation.[20]

In sum, although some of their children were struggling academically, all of the interviewees expected their children to go to college. Those who had enjoyed an education at some of the top schools wanted their children to follow them to these same institutions. Moreover, the interviewees were cognisant of the fact that academic prowess alone would not secure entry to the top colleges and that their children had to be successful in all aspects of life more generally! Those who had experienced a more modest education expressed less ambitious hopes for their children, cautiously hoping they would secure entry into reputable liberal arts colleges rather than large state schools. Again, in higher education, they wanted their children to be individually challenged rather than lost in the crowd. Turning to the interviewees' occupational aspirations, few had specific jobs in mind for their children. The medics were somewhat ambivalent about medicine as a career especially for their daughters given the time-consuming nature of the job that made it difficult to combine with family responsibilities. The non-medics, however, were still impressed by its high status and financial rewards. A career in teaching was also viewed with some ambivalence.[21] All of the interviewees wanted their children to enjoy self-fulfillment in their chosen careers. Enjoying the intrinsic rewards of their jobs was viewed as the path to happiness and satisfaction. The more affluent physicians and their partners placed a very high premium on individual self-fulfillment and, indeed, envisaged supporting adult children financially in years to come if need be. The less affluent teachers and their partners shared these dreams, although, without such economic resources, they valued financial independence greatly too.

British educational dispositions

Unlike their American counterparts, many of the British mothers, whether they were doctors, teachers or otherwise, did not work or worked part time before their children went to school at age five. Most of them looked after their children when they were young or relied on informal childcare support from extended kin, neighbours and friends.[22] Consequently, there was much less discussion of choice of pre-school for young children and educational preoccupations regarding those choices than with the American interviewees. Among some of the younger British women interviewees, however, more formal childcare arrangements were to be found. The issue of convenience – of having children in close proximity – was emphasised in the choice of childcare, but so too were educational concerns. Bridget Underwood, for example, sent her two daughters to a 'very expensive' nursery close to her practice and the staff, she said, were excellent about her 'never finishing on time'. She had heard of the nursery's reputation through her mother-in-law and her friends and she found the standard to be high. Describing it she said:

It's like a boarding school for girls. They leave school and they go there to train to be nannies. It's like Norlands in London. They live there. They do really proper thorough training to become nannies and they have an attached little day nursery so they learn, at six months this is what a child can do, and at a year, this is what they can do.

The nannies, in other words, were very aware of children's developmental issues and could be expected to stimulate and interest young children in a manner deemed appropriate for their age.

Like their American counterparts, the British parents wanted certain things from their children's early education in primary school. To be sure, they were concerned that their children made friends with other children in the local community and learned to interact and share with them. They were keen that their children went to a school that had a warm and happy environment where the teachers were friendly and approachable (to both children and parents). Mary Hunt, for example, spoke of how her four children went to the local state primary school which was a very average state school but, 'It's a very nice atmosphere, very warm, the teachers are friendly, there's no worry about drugs or whatever, because you read so much about unsafe environments, and these are young children, so they all went to that school.' They wanted their young children, in other words, to be in a secure and protective environment and to be happy and enjoy their time in school. It was in this environment that, again, they wanted their children to be open to and ready for learning. Again, many of the teachers were well versed in child development theories and wanted their young children to be gradually introduced to a formally structured setting where they would enjoy a mix of play and work.[23] As Susan Parry, an informed teacher, said:

I like to walk into a classroom and feel that there is a good rapport between teachers and pupils. I like bright exciting rooms for infants. I like to see lots of things going on, the chance to play as well as to work and you don't always see that in schools.

The British interviewees, in other words, had remarkably similar views to the Americans about the nurturing of children in their early years. They, too, wanted their children to be curious and to enjoy and embrace learning. Early indications of such abilities were seen as signs of being 'bright' and quick'. Sandra Booth, for example, said her eldest daughter was, 'very questioning and very interested in reading and books and she was always writing and sort of being an earlier teacher, I knew what all the good signs were'. Frequent mention, once again, was made of their children's reading abilities indicating the high value placed on reading skills. Once more, comfort was to be drawn from standardised tests at school indicating that children were advanced in their educational development for their age. Describing her eldest daughter, Bridget Underwood said, 'I think she's very bright because Emily's only 7 and she's already – they do assessments at the school – and she already has a reading age of 11. I mean her reading is superb and she loves it.' Of course, other interviewees had children who struggled, like Janet Jones' second daughter who was dyslexic like herself. As she explained, 'Sarah was a problem. I did a lot of work through the primary years . . . Sarah learnt to read quite normally but she couldn't learn to write. Everything was the wrong way round and difficult to control. I didn't want it to be as hard, you see, as it had been for me.' Crucially, Janet did not want her daughter 'to get depressed and give up'. It was crucial, therefore, to bolster her self-confidence and allow her to enjoy some success that would boost self-esteem and lead on to further success.[24]

The primary years of learning, therefore, were considered important for laying the foundations in literacy and numeracy skills that would facilitate their further intellectual development. Like their American counterparts, the British interviewees wanted their children's intellectual curiosity and excitement about the world around them to be encouraged by teachers. Once more, they expected their children to be challenged and pushed to achieve to the best of their abilities rather than be bored and distracted which would lead only to mischievous behaviour. Thus, the interviewees looked to teachers to educate their children with a varied curriculum in an exciting and demanding way. Many of the parents spoke of wonderful teachers they had encountered during their children's education often emphasising that they were 'firm but fair' teachers who were strong on discipline while nurturing of all children. Other parents, of course, came across teachers whom they did not regard so well. Pauline Lomax spoke of how she met some 'staff who have been teaching one way for years' at her children's primary school and who 'refused to take on new things'. Interestingly, Mary Bull moved her son to another school out of dissatisfaction with his teacher. Alarm bells started to ring when her eldest son was 'put into the bottom group, which I didn't feel, knowing his ability, was the right place for him'. When he was asked to write 400 lines for misbehaving, she went to see the teacher. Mary concluded,

He's one you've got to push a bit so he'd been idle with, no doubt, another group and they probably were lads so she's put them in the bottom group and wasn't pushing him. She was just leaving them to it and giving them lines and what have you. I just thought 'No'. You've only got one chance to go through a year.[25]

As I showed in Chapter 3, most of the British doctors and their partners had sent or were intending to send their children to private secondary schools. They were paying, of course, for high-calibre teachers and other resources including various extra-curricular activities embracing sports, music etc. As with their primary-school years, they wanted their children to be confident in themselves and independent in character. This was one of the reasons why many of the doctors and their partners sent their children, especially their daughters, to single-sex private schools. Many of the British doctors wanted to replicate their own single-sex grammar-school education for their children in the hope that they would enjoy educational success in a similar environment.[26] The advantage of single-sex girls' schools was that young daughters could excel in an environment where they would not be put down by boys or distracted from their studies by them. As Julie Dodd said of her daughter,

I had felt that in the girls' school environment, although it was very different to the one that I'd been in, that one was never led to believe that there was anything you couldn't do. There weren't any ceilings put on and there weren't girls' subjects and boys' subjects. Even though they didn't do science in my school, you know, nonetheless there was an aspiration, you know. You weren't led to believe that there were any sort of gender differences there and I just felt that I wanted the same for Melissa.

They wanted their daughters to achieve educationally as much as any young man and believed that strong self-esteem and high aspirations contributed greatly to educational success.

In various ways, therefore, the interviewees demonstrated the value they attached to their children's academic success. They also wanted their children to perform to the best of their abilities. Accordingly, they supported and encouraged their children with homework and other school activities. Again, schoolwork came before leisure in their everyday family routines. They also stressed the values of hard work, discipline and deferred gratification. As Dennis Parker explained:

I would imagine most parents do it but it's a very difficult thing to do and that is to try and get them to realize it's important and that especially during the period of exams, to try and get them to realize that they might be making a sacrifice for the next couple of months but it pays dividends in the long run.

It was, he concluded, 'a question of trying to convince youngsters that you do know best sometimes'. Many of the interviewees talked of the difficult balance to be struck between encouraging and pressuring their teenage children, and how their children's personalities influenced how they guided them.[27] Mary Bull laughed when she explained that she 'nagged' her oldest son, Damian, about schoolwork. She cajoled her younger son in a different way. She said, 'It's sow the seed and let it grow with the younger one. I mean Anthony doesn't realise it but I can definitely sow a seed and get him to think what I think.' The interviewees, therefore, spoke of how they tried to inculcate their children with their values, taking into account, as Robert Ball suggested, that 'you cannot assume that children are sort of a plain board on which you can write. Children have very different personalities.'

The interviewees, therefore, wanted their children to be increasingly self-motivated as they got older rather than externally pressured to do well. As Graham Dowds said, 'All we have ever said to them is you're doing it for yourself. You are not doing it to please us. You are doing it for one person – that is yourself.' They wanted their children to derive personal satisfaction from academic success and the hard work and self-discipline that sustained success. Again, they wanted their children to enjoy their education so that schoolwork was not a chore but readily completed. Some of the interviewees talked about their very successful children. Daughters, it seemed, were often very conscientious and determined to do well. Muriel Crisp said her eldest daughter 'wanted to do well. Alice needs to do well, to compete with other people and doesn't like to be beaten by other people in anything she does. So that's how she is.' Sandra Booth had two very able daughters, one who was very gregarious and outgoing and did well and the other who was quiet and studious who also was successful. As she explained of her second daughter, 'You never had to tell Juliet to do her homework. She did it. Kirsten did it but Kirsten didn't have high standards. Juliet has very, very high standards. You know, she had to get the top grades that she set herself.' Similarly, Hilary Butler talked about how her daughter 'applied herself' in comparison to her son. As she elaborated, 'It mattered to her to do well whereas with Nigel, he did well but it didn't matter with him to do well. As long as he was passing then that was OK whereas Victoria wanted to get the top mark.'[28]

There were other discussions of struggles with teenage children including both young men and young women. Celia Watson laughed when she recalled how her daughter, now in her twenties, 'decided that she didn't like studying and wasn't doing a great deal. She was the most difficult teenager you can imagine!' Muriel Crisp had more recent experience of a similar kind for her 16-year-old daughter was determined to finish school as soon as she could and follow a career in hotel and catering.

She had got to the point where she could not persuade her daughter to stay on: 'It would be a complete waste of time. The last two years have been hell! I'm not going to make her do it any more. I mean, the last year doing all that course work for GCSE was a nightmare, you know.' Interestingly, although her second daughter was not academically inclined, Muriel stressed that she and her husband always did 'things outside school, visiting places and things like that . . . [Like other] parents who aspire for their children to do well. We've done them all. My children have had opportunities to do everything that they've wanted to do.' If they expressed an interest in sport, music or whatever, they pursued these interests and they became shared 'family interests'. Moreover, these types of extra-curricular activities meant, 'I've never had to worry about them hanging around on street corners and things like that. They have always been purposeful and now that they are sort of off on their own, I feel confident in what they're doing.' Like their American counterparts, therefore, the British parents sought to create and control the work and leisure environment of their children, especially their teenage children, to ensure educational success. Again, of course, there were different degrees of success as their children's own interests diverged from their own.[29]

Overall, the British interviewees were very keen, like their American counterparts, that their children be intellectually nurtured and stimulated in their early education. Again, they wanted their children's seemingly natural curiosity and inquisitiveness to be challenged and extended by high-calibre teachers who could give them plenty of individual attention. Some of the interviewees enthused about the great teachers they had encountered and were fully appreciative of the importance of good teachers for their children's continued academic progress. Others recounted negative experiences although, interestingly, they challenged teachers who did not appreciate their children's emerging talents and abilities.[30] Those interviewees who sent their children to private schools attached a lot of importance to the fact that they were single-sex schools. They wanted their daughters, in particular, to learn in an all-female environment that nurtured high self-esteem and career aspirations. As in the USA, the British interviewees spoke of how they tried to inculcate in their teenage children the values of hard work and deferred gratification and their daily lives reflected these concerns as they closely monitored their children's school activities and beyond. Again, they wanted their children to become increasingly self-motivated anticipating that success would boost their self-worth and confidence. Of course, what the interviewees wanted as parents, and their teenage children's emerging interests and talents, were not necessarily the same. It was apparent, once again, that parents might mobilise their cultural capital to facilitate their children's academic success but they could never guarantee it.

British occupational horizons

Many of the British interviewees' children were still making their way through school and the majority of parents anticipated that they would continue with their academic studies, completing A levels at school or college to secure entry into university. Given that Britain has lower participation rates in higher education than the USA, however, it was unsurprising to find some examples of young people who were planning to leave school at 16 or undertake vocational courses at college or who had already done so. Interestingly, the parents of these young people were very keen that they should pursue their education and training and have a career rather than a 'dead-end job'. Mary Bull's 16-year-old son was awaiting his GCSE results when we spoke. He had struggled with dyslexia at school and Mary found out about Modern Apprenticeships (MAs) in accountancy at the local Careers Office. While she appreciated his academic difficulties, Mary wanted her son to pursue a career with training options and opportunities for advancement so that, among other things, he would enjoy a good salary in the years to come. On MAs, she said, 'He would train to be some sort of accountancy clerk but if they get the NVQs, they can, if they wish, take those credits and start doing the Chartered Accountancy examinations.'[31] It could, in other words, lead to a professional occupation. Norman Johns' second daughter, Polly, opted for a vocational course in hotel and catering. As he explained, 'I think, to her surprise, we said, "Fantastic, if that's what you want to do. The only thing I would say to you, that doesn't stop you going to university."' Eventually she went to university, obtained a first-class degree and was headhunted for a managerial job by a large hotel chain.

The majority of the informants, however, expected their children to continue with their academic studies. Like the Americans, they thought it imperative that children obtain education credentials in order to secure a good professional job with extrinsic and intrinsic rewards. Qualifications increased the chances of success and offered more choice.[32] Explaining why education was so important, Heather Foster said:

One of the wealthiest people in my son's school started selling Christmas cards from a van. He's now a multimillionaire, but those people are few and far between, aren't they? Most doctors have a good standard of living. Most people who work on a market stall don't although there are always going to be those people who make it.

While qualifications could not guarantee occupational success, they certainly increased the chances of attaining it. Again, therefore, the interviewees were well aware of how the labour market worked with regard to the link between high-level qualifications and well-remunerated careers. Also, they were very cognisant of the fact that jobs with reasonable pay for the less educated were so few and far between. As Dennis Parker said:

I think education is extremely important and I think more so these days than at any time. I don't think there are many viable alternatives to higher education personally. If I'd have left school at sixteen, there were a range of crafts or skills that I could have trained for which would have given me a fairly decent wage, but I think there are far fewer now. I think there's a big gap in wage or potential wages or earnings between people who leave school early on and those who go on to higher education.

Given these views, the interviewees remained anxious to ensure that their children stayed focused on their education. This was apparent when the British interviewees spoke of their children's transition from school to colleges of further education. Most of the doctors' children continued their studies at their fee-paying schools but Ian Lamb's daughter was one exception. As I discussed in Chapter 3, it seems she convinced her parents that the college of her choice had a good academic record and that she was not risking her chances of academic success. Other parents spoke of how they had directed their children to certain colleges that were 'disciplined' environments allowing young people some independence although not too much freedom. Otherwise, they would be distracted from their studies. Sheila Parker spoke of how her two children went to a sixth form attached to a Catholic school rather than to the local technical college. It had a better academic record, she believed, because it was run on different lines. Sheila said, regarding the technical college: 'It's not run, I don't think, to suit sixteen to eighteen-year-olds. It's run and treats youngsters as adults when clearly most of them are not capable of behaving as adults and so they have large blocks of free time.' In contrast, the Catholic college was not run like 'a college'. She elaborated:

The pupils are expected to fulfill certain criteria like attendance at lectures and they've very little free time. Everything seems to be blocked for them so that they can't disappear and, you know, not turn up. So there's a pressure on them or a greater pressure on them from the college than there would be if they'd gone to the tertiary college.[33]

The high value placed on educational achievement, therefore, influenced how the interviewees directed their children through the system of further education in Britain. A number of the interviewees' children were distracted however. Ian Lamb's second son, Geoff, moved from a single sex to a mixed private school for his A level studies but he obtained poor grades. Ian wondered,

I don't know if it was the fact that his hormones were shooting up and there were females at [C] but he had a mad time for two years and he did badly in his A levels. He was having a ball. Also, I don't think he realized how hard you had to work to do it. He was always coasting by, and they catch people out.

Geoff improved on his grades at a crammer and then went to medical school. For other interviewees, however, a happy outcome was not yet assured. Yvonne Johns persuaded her only son, Karl, to do A levels, since 'I wanted him to stay on. I wanted him to go to university but he didn't want it. I tried hard but I didn't have any success.' Dropping out of college, he found work as a driver but then lost his job and was later arrested and prosecuted for stealing car radios. Returning from a period abroad, Karl secured a job as a care worker in a residential home for the mentally ill. Yvonne was desperate for him to 'settle in it' and even, she hoped, go for social work qualifications later on. She said, 'Karl didn't like being out of work and when he lost the job as a driver that's when he went off the rails really. I hope now he [is] back on them, but I don't know. It's maybe too early to say.' She was grateful that he was in work and, indeed, still hoped he might return to education later in his twenties.[34]

Most of the interviewees with older children, however, recounted stories of their offspring enjoying success in their A levels allowing them to proceed to a university of their choice. Many were, without doubt, highly successful academically. A number of the doctors' daughters went to Oxbridge, including all three of the Jones' daughters. Their second daughter, Sarah, struggled throughout with her schoolwork because of dyslexia, as I noted earlier. Interestingly, however, Janet Jones explained that the top private girls' school they attended encouraged their pupils to sit the entrance exam or go for interview, and their performance dictated what grades they needed to gain entry. It took the pressure off, as top grades might not be necessary. Sarah passed the entrance exam and got into Oxford with two Bs at A level. Still, she continued to struggle. As Janet said,

She took herself to see an educational psychologist when she was at university because one or two of the tutors got angry with her spelling. When she had a whole tutorial on how to spell, she decided to do something. It cost her tremendously. She was frightened she was going to be told there was nothing wrong with her. She was just stupid. She cried and cried and cried. She was very distressed. She realised it would affect her degree. She didn't want that. She found that it really irritates people if your spelling looks ignorant. Her spelling is terrible and it looks ignorant. So, she went to see the educational psychologist through the university. She came out at the top for intelligence and the bottom for spelling, which is horrendous really.

Such difficulties, however, had not stopped Sarah gaining entry to one of the top two universities in Britain.[35]

As in America, a number of the interviewees' young children had expressed a desire to go into high-level occupations. Some of the doctors' children wanted to follow their parents into medicine. Rod Hunt's 12-year-old, Scott, was absolutely certain he wanted to be a doctor and, indeed, he wanted to be a GP in his father's practice. Rod conceded he would be 'delighted if he did'. Indeed, some of the doctors' children did become medics, indicating a high level of occupational inheritance. Just as Edward Myers had followed his father into medicine, so his oldest daughter had followed him into the profession too. Working on the principle that children often do the opposite of what is recommended, he said, 'I have to confess I was a bit Machiavellian. Whenever I talked about what I was doing, I always said how interesting it was. C was mostly neutral and then she talked about it and then I tried to talk her out of it but then she headed that way.' Peter Smith's son, Damian, followed his father into the same medical specialism. Peter admitted that he had encouraged him when he said:

Oh yeah, because there's always been a bit of banter between the two of us. I mean, I don't really know, I still don't know to this day whether Damian decided on surgery because I did surgery or not. He'll be a consultant surgeon in his next job, that will mean he'll have completed the ladder. Certainly, we used to talk quite a bit and, of course, Diane having done nursing, there was the reinforcing of the medical ethos.

Many of these interviewees were especially proud of the fact, therefore, that their children had followed them into medicine. Enjoying their jobs, they hoped their children would enjoy their work too.[36]

Other interviewees were unsuccessful in persuading their children into medicine. Barbara Coombes tried to persuade her two daughters, Sonia and Sallie, into medicine, hoping they would join her practice because 'she enjoyed it so much'. However, they did not 'see a life running round like a scolded cat was very much fun' and, to her bitter disappointment, followed their stepfather into teaching. Like some of the American interviewees, some parents did not want their daughters to go into such a demanding job as medicine, especially if they hoped to have children. Some of the teachers and their partners had ambivalent views about their children following them into education. Few of the young children had expressed such aspirations. Nevertheless, some of the older children became teachers. On his daughter's decision to follow him into teaching, Norman Johns admitted, 'I thought Samantha could do better, I thought, no, better, no, that's not right. No, I don't mean that. I thought she could do better because I felt that there were other jobs that would be more financially [rewarding] and interest wise [would] be better.' Teaching was not considered a desirable occupation because of the low levels of pay and the volume of work involved. Jill Dowds thought that her second daughter, completing her A levels at the time of interview, 'would make a good teacher. I've mentioned it. What you put in, you get out.' Graham Dowds had a different view, however, when he considered his wife's workload. He said, 'Yes, but you take work home very night, marking books every night, all weekend planning work and you get paid a pittance for that. You've got to really want to do it to do that.'[37]

Like the Americans, most the British interviewees did not have specific occupational aspirations for their children. Their more general hope was that their children would pursue a professional career of their choice that was both extrinsically and intrinsically rewarding. They hoped, for example, that their children would secure financially rewarding jobs that would allow them to match or improve upon the quality of life they had enjoyed in their childhood. Like their American counterparts, they wanted their children to enjoy their jobs and, indeed, firmly believed that from enjoyment came success. They wanted their children to be happy and fulfilled in their jobs. Like the Americans, the more affluent British doctors and their partners stressed the intrinsic rewards of the job over financial considerations. As Andrew Underwood said of his two young daughters, 'So long as they do something that they enjoy and that makes them happy, that's more important even if its not a particularly well-paid job. I still think it is more important to enjoy it. I want them to be happy rather than rich.'[38] That said, he acknowledged that they would inherit a lot of money from him, so that 'money wasn't a problem'. The teachers and their partners wanted their children to be happy in their jobs too although they stressed the importance of financial independence. Laughing, Martin Webb said he did not want to 'subsidise' his children in their adult life! Mulling over the idea further, he said philosophically, 'You know, if they think, "No, I'll have a low income and not work hard", then that's up to them I suppose, but as long as they know what they're doing and think and sort of take responsibility for the consequences of that decision, then that's fair enough.' On balance, however, his preference was that they worked hard and went to university so that they had more choices.

Given that the British education system has more branching points than the American system, the interviewees' children were pursuing a variety of routes into employment, through further education, into higher education and beyond. Some of the interviewees' children, for example, were looking to leave school at 16. Even so, the interviewees were keen for them to take up vocational training options so they could advance in their chosen career. Most of the interviewees, however, were keen for their children to continue their future education and wanted their children, now young adults, in an appropriate learning environment where everyday movements were still monitored. Be that as it may, there were a number of interviewees' children who dropped out of college or flunked their studies. Most of the interviewees' children went on into higher education, the privately educated doctors' children often going to the most prestigious educational establishments in Britain although they sometimes still struggled with their studies.[39] Further, a number of the doctors' children had followed them into medicine although, as in the USA, there was some ambivalence about medicine as a suitable career for daughters. Similarly, some of the interviewees' children had followed them into teaching although there were mixed views about teaching as a rewarding job. For the most part, the interviewees did not have specific occupational aspirations for their children. A high premium was placed on individual self-fulfillment, especially among the more affluent medical families, while the more modestly paid teachers and their partners wanted their children to be financially independent too.

Conclusion

This chapter has drawn on the American and British interviewees' accounts of how they were mobilising their cultural resources to increase their children's chances of educational and occupational success. Now all well-educated middle-class parents in professional jobs, they knew how the education system worked and the importance of acquiring credentials in order to secure entry into high-level jobs. Cognisant of child development theories, they took a keen interest in their children's intellectual development, monitoring their progress against standardised tests to ensure their children were performing appropriately, if not better, for their age. They sought to inculcate in their children the values of hard work, discipline and deferred gratification and translated these values into how they conducted their everyday family life as their watched their children's educational activities and carefully controlled their free time too. In this way, they sought to increase their children's chances of doing well at school and going on to higher education. To be sure, the interviewees from well-established middle-class backgrounds who had enjoyed an elite education themselves, approached the business of educating their children with more confidence than those from more modest middle-class backgrounds who had experienced a regular high school education, for example. They wanted their children to follow them to elite colleges of higher education while the educational horizons of other interviewees were not so high. Be that as it may, this empirical material seems to confirm Bourdieu's ideas about how middle-class parents utilise their cultural capital to ensure their children's educational and occupational advancement.[40]

However, what the empirical material also clearly demonstrated is that life is not that simple. Parents may seek to provide all the seemingly right cultural conditions to facilitate their children's educational success; namely, nurturing their children's intellectual abilities, monitoring their academic progress and carefully guarding the boundaries of their leisure activities. Doing all the right things, however, does not necessarily guarantee educational success with implications for occupational success. After all, there were plenty of examples among the interviewees whose offspring were struggling at school, who had obtained poor grades or who were simply not motivated and had dropped out of college. Not all of the interviewees' children, therefore, were academically able or, at the very least, always successful the first time around. Arguably, it was at these turning points, when setbacks were confronted, that the importance of economic resources became fully apparent, allowing children the time and space to retake examinations, pursue other educational options and so forth until they found their niche. In this way, downward mobility into blue-collar or manual employment was avoided as far as possible. Indeed, it appeared that those who enjoyed the most economic resources had the greater power to monitor and control their children's lives, which might explain why the more affluent medics and their families encountered fewer of these difficulties in comparison to the less affluent teachers and their partners. Be that as it may, even medics and their partners experienced disappointments and setbacks in the education of their children. The reproduction of middle-class privilege and power was a complicated affair.[41]

6   Contacts, luck and career success

Attention now turns in this chapter and Chapter 7 to the mobilisation of social resources in the reproduction of advantage. As I outlined in the Introduction, Goldthorpe defined social resources in terms of involvement in social networks that can serve as channels of information and influence in getting a job. He cited the famous research by the American sociologist, Mark Granovetter, on the importance on contacts on careers.[1] Moreover, Goldthorpe argued that social resources are especially important when academic success is not forthcoming. That is to say, parents can call on family and friends to help their less academically able children get good jobs. In the development of an explicit theoretical explanation of middle-class reproduction, however, his initial discussion on the importance of social resources in the reproduction of advantage disappeared from view. In his desire to assert the significance of economic resources and downplay the importance of cultural resources in his critique of Bourdieu, it seemed that Goldthorpe had to ignore social resources as well. Again, I thought this was a shame for precisely the reasons that Goldthorpe initially acknowledged: namely, that networks of a formal and informal kind are often an important source of information and advice in the job search process as Granovetter described. The consequence of this neglect – probably an unintended rather than an intended consequence of Goldthorpe's attack on Bourdieu's ideas – was that he could no longer consider the interconnections between social resources and economic (and cultural) resources.

Goldthorpe's concept of social resources is, of course, remarkably similar to Bourdieu's notion of social capital and the idea that networks of relationships or groups can be exploited in the reproduction of advantage. Bourdieu also notes that those in positions of dominance 'have all sorts of ways of evading scholastic verdicts' and that 'the effects of social capital (a "helping hand", "string pulling", the "old boy network") tend to correct the effect of academic sanctions'.[2] Interestingly, neither

Goldthorpe, nor Bourdieu consider the way in which social resources might be mobilised in the pursuit of educational success as well as career advancement. That it to say, the exploitation of social capital is considered only when other investments have not yielded returns in terms of academic success. The person who has considered the role of social capital in the pursuit of education credentials is the famous American sociologist, James Coleman.[3] Accordingly, this chapter draws on Coleman's ideas about social capital and the creation of human capital. It focuses on the interviewees' reflecting back on their education once more and thinking about how neighbours and friends in their local communities influenced their expectations and behaviour and how it may have contributed to their educational success. Drawing on the insights of Granovetter, it also considers the importance of contacts in the interviewees' careers in medicine and teaching.

The American interviewees were very eloquent on the influence of local interpersonal relationships on their educational expectations. The interviewees from middle-class families spoke of communities populated by other parents preoccupied with educational success whose children were often their children's school friends. The wider social pressures to succeed were reinforced by the strong academic ethos of their schools and of these friends. Overlapping social networks between private schools and Ivy League colleges reinforced norms about going to the best colleges. Peer pressures were also important to the interviewees from modest class backgrounds. School friends were also bright children propelling each other forward towards higher education in a competitive way while also acting as a source of social support. That said, there were others who had to search for group reinforcement and experienced a somewhat lonelier education. Both the medics and educators spoke about the influence of contacts on their careers. Contacts were important in securing laboratory work that facilitated entry into medical school. Being already known to hospital staff meant some medics were considered favourably for prestigious residency programmes. Contacts were important for advice and information in the pursuit of career success and in being recommended for high-level jobs. Educators discussed the value of contacts as a source of information and influence about jobs. They were important in facilitating women's return to teaching after the birth of children as well as in job moves. Mentors also helped interviewees acquire all-important experiences and recommended them for promotion into high-level managerial positions in education.

The British interviewees also spoke at length about the way in which wider community relationships with neighbours, friends and others shaped their educational expectations and more. Again, those from middle-class backgrounds spoke of how it was the norm among their parents' friends to send their children to reputable private schools and the overlap in social networks between these schools and top universities was apparent too. As in the USA, the interviewees from working-class backgrounds highlighted the importance of peer pressure as their bright friends pushed them onwards and upwards. The strong academic ethos of Britain's grammar schools and the strict codes of discipline acted as powerful social pressures to succeed, and teachers were an important source of encouragement.[4] Still, others did not enjoy such group social support until later in life. Contacts were clearly important in forging medical careers in Britain. It helped to have been taught by and know senior staff in securing pre-registration jobs at highly sought-after teaching hospitals in London and Manchester. Contacts who became mentors were important in facilitating promotion to consultant posts in hospital medicine while both close and loose ties were very important in securing positions and eventually partnerships in general practice. Close and loose ties were valuable in securing entry into teaching and especially re-entry for women who had left employment to raise children. Occupational networks circulated information and advice on opportunities, and fellow teachers, either well known or not, were crucial sources of information and support in the pursuit of senior posts in teaching.

Social resources and American education

The American interviewees were very well aware of the influence of social context – the communities in which they grew up and the schools they attended – on their lives and especially their expectations and aspirations. More specifically, they were conscious of how teachers and, perhaps most importantly, their own networks of friends and acquaintances shaped their early lives and beyond. The interviewees, of course, spoke of very different experiences in this respect depending on the community and school relationships in which they were involved. The effects of the school environments varied since some of the interviewees went to private school, some to the best public schools in affluent areas and others to regular and even poor schools in the areas in which they grew up. The small number of informants who went to exclusive private schools emphasised the competitive academic climate in which they were expected to perform. Everyone was expected to excel and to work hard to achieve success and most children did so. Moreover, there was a shared expectation that almost everyone would apply to the best colleges and, indeed, strive to get into an Ivy League school. Jack Poole, for example, went to an exclusive boys' boarding school and he recalled:

I would say about a third of the graduating class went to Ivy League schools. I would say, if anything, the college officers tried to get people to apply to other places. They didn't want people to be disappointed because it was so competitive. At least three quarters of my class applied to Ivy League schools so it was a huge number. Almost everyone applied.

Revealingly, Jack highlighted the social capital of his private school when he spoke of his own progression to an Ivy League college. With good test scores and high recommendations, he explained:

I applied mostly to Ivy League schools so it was a choice amongst those schools and actually it was more just a personal connection of knowing some of the people who had gone to [Y] in the year before me. I was rowing crew at the time and the [Y] coach had actually come down to visit me so I was very impressed by this.[5]

Attending a school that regularly sent its pupils on to the top schools, it was hardly surprising that Jack also knew older students who were already at such colleges. The overlap in the social worlds of young people at his prestigious private school and the Ivy League college facilitated his choice of one college above another. Michael Reed spoke of how the majority of young people from his private school went to some of the best colleges, including Ivy League schools. Well prepared after doing a range of advanced placement courses, Michael explained how he went to a particular Ivy League school:

One reason I went there is that it was a school that I knew and also it had a fairly liberal curriculum without distribution requirements. You could take what you were interested in. They also particularly liked people from my high school. It was just round the corner and they had a policy where you apply early to one college so I applied there and they took me in.

It was a common route for 'every year [that particular Ivy League school] took five to ten people from my school'. Indeed, all of the privately educated interviewees went on to Ivy League schools.[6]

Those interviewees who grew up in the more exclusive white suburbs and who attended the best public schools noted similar effects. Now critical of the social world in which he grew up, George Marshall described his childhood in a Boston suburb as 'a very insular experience and I didn't meet a lot of different kinds of people and I wasn't exposed to a wide variety of ideas'. Echoing these sentiments, his wife Judy, who was socially mobile from a more modest background, described her husband's social world as very different from her own. She explained, 'When he was growing up, his parents are great people and I don't think he felt pressured in that way but all around him was this ethic of the parents watching the test scores and, "What college is your son going to?"' That is to say, their local neighbours and friends were members of the same class who were doctors, engineers, teachers, managers and so forth. Like the interviewees' parents, they were mostly educated people who also wanted their children to do well in school. At home and school, therefore, the interviewees socialised with friends who were like them: namely, the children of educated parents with similar educational and occupational aspirations. This was the social world in which many of the interviewees grew up. It was a Boston suburb in which a number of my interviewees now lived.[7]

Of course, most of my interviewees, including those from middle-class and lower-middle-class backgrounds, did not occupy such exclusive social worlds. They went to regular public schools where they were in the top tracks with other academically able students. Students in the lower tracks were usually bound for the local community colleges or low-level jobs. Taught by the best teachers offering exciting curricula, however, these interviewees were encouraged to excel and to apply to the better colleges. This was the academic climate in which they enjoyed academic success. Tracking within high school, Mary Moran recalled, meant that the teachers 'kind of tailored the curriculum to those groups so you really felt school could be fun because the teacher would go as fast as the class would let them'. These interviewees found themselves in a competitive environment with other A grade students pursuing educational excellence. Consequently, school was a positive experience for these able interviewees. Interestingly, Jane Bennett, of blue-collar origins, very much emphasised the influence of her fellow schoolmates from different social backgrounds on her aspirations and expectations. As she explained:

I would say most of the other students had families who were quite ambitious and they encouraged you to really strive and that sort of brought the entire group and myself along to have high expectations . . . I would say actually my school environment and exposure to people who were, in particular, better off but also had professional work, more highly educated, that's what brought me into a different prospect.[8]

More specifically, Jane spoke of how her classmates affected her choice of college. As she explained, 'Frankly, when I looked at my classmates and where they expected to go, because my experience with better schools was quite limited, seeing what they were looking at encouraged me to look into those institutions and then I selected on this basis.' Many of the educators also spoke of the influence of their peer group in shaping their desire for academic success, including those interviewees from lower-middle-class backgrounds. These interviewees too spoke of the competitive academic environment in which they and their friends worked hard and how they were anxious to do well at school so that they could go to college. Elisabeth Danson, for example, recalled how she was with the 'right' peer group who were all going to college, in comparison to her sister. As she explained:

My sister had a different lifestyle and a different group of friends where she got heavily into drugs and drinking. They were more laid back and a more defiant group and she never went to college and she has her regrets about that. I had my group of friends that was always involved in sports and always going, going, going as a group together and it [was] just where we all went.

The social pressures of the school and their fellow pupils, therefore, propelled many of the interviewees onwards. Peer group pressure generated competition among friends to excel academically yet group solidarity was also a source of cohesion as they supported and reinforced each other as they trod the same path together.[9]

Parental support, a strong academic environment in the school and peer pressure from academically able friends, therefore, propelled the interviewees from lower-middle-class origins on to good colleges. The strong academic culture of schools and the company of other bright children undercut the effects of race too. Despite the racial turmoil over bussing in Boston in the 1960s, Roy Morgan secured a place at the best public school in the city where selection was determined by an entrance examination. He recalled,

It was racially mixed, but it was funny because at the time, one of the things that happened was the pressure around recognizing race, sort of not evaporated, but absolutely minimized once you got to high school. First of all, there was commonality so when you removed girls from the equation, then boys bond around commonalities that transcend competition with girls and transcend race. The thing that everyone had in common there was everyone was bright. They all wanted to do the right thing.

Roy later attended a prestigious liberal arts college in Massachusetts. Others were less fortunate. Jane Kennedy was directed towards a small Catholic college close to home where she enjoyed a reasonable education offered by dedicated nuns. She recalled:

My boyfriend at the time was very intelligent and was from a family who did pay attention to what was going on and I remember him coming with me to look at this college and walking away and saying I can't believe you are here . . . I don't know. Looking back at it, it was a little crazy, a little undershooting. I don't know. It was just the circumstances. It worked out fine in the long run.[10]

A minority of interviewees recalled how they lacked such peer support or at least struggled to find it. Ray Chapman, for example, recalled his school,

Was definitely, and to this day remains, a very ordinary school through which a lot of kids who are headed to the trades will pass. Academic excellence was nowhere near as important to the culture of that school, which was sports activities primarily, so I remember feeling quite different from most of the peers [although] I didn't have the open conflict you certainly hear about from some kids who are in that situation.

He recalled how his mother helped him find friends who would provide him with social capital. Ray said:

My mother, as I went into ninth grade, and knew by then I didn't have an interest in sports, felt quite strongly that part of high school was finding a connection with things other than academic things that you were good at. I think she was quite concerned that I had friends and that I get comfortable in groups and that I would learn all the social skills you need to get by in the world and she thought being involved in the theatre would be a good choice [since] other than the sports things that was the only opportunity in the schools, so she pushed me quite hard to do something that I wasn't actually inclined to do.

He recalled that the drama club proved to be 'a place where I found my home and found people who were like-minded and were interested in literature and the arts and things that I had as an interest'. In these circumstances, school proved to be a positive experience and these interests subsequently shaped his occupational career.[11]

Others emphasised, more critically, that support from their school was conditional upon academic success. Support from teachers was only forthcoming because they were successful. Yuko Yacoby stressed:

I have always been my own director. I have had teachers that were supportive because I was an A student and I always did very well so I was never in a situation where I had to say, oh my god, I've got to do better or anything like that. I never had teachers necessarily that I felt, looking back, steered my direction and my career. I had already decided what I really wanted to do.

Similarly, Susan Rogers recalled how support and encouragement were contingent on being academically successful at school. Encouragement was forthcoming, she said, 'Only if they thought you had any kind of efficiencies. There was no one there saying, you know, everyone can be successful. If you were an effective student that was doing very well things sort of were channelled.' On the college preparation programme in senior grades at high school, an Upward Bound programme directed towards minority and inner-city children, Susan got to meet recruiters from different colleges.[12] After expressing an interest in working with children, as I noted before, she was directed towards a teaching course at college. It was only later that she embarked on a graduate science programme that led to medical school. She recalled, 'Something sort of clicked and suddenly all these people were saying you should do this, you'd be really good at this, maybe you should look into it. There were people there that could sort of direct me, mentor me.'

The American interviewees acknowledged the influence of people who lived around them when they were growing up on their educational success. The influence of the school, namely teachers and school friends, was very important in shaping their expectations and aspirations. The upper-middle-class men educated in exclusive private schools, for example, spoke of how they were directed towards Ivy League schools. Indeed, the social worlds of their elite schools and Ivy League universities overlapped so the transition from one to the other was a smooth and almost predictable one. Others spoke of living in affluent upper-middle-class white communities where they felt a general pressure to do well. Everyone around them was preoccupied with academic success, the status of colleges they would go to and so on. Most of the interviewees, however, did not occupy such exclusive social worlds. They attended regular public schools, although, as academically able students in the top tracks, they were exposed to good teachers who pushed them onward. More importantly, academically able friends acted as a form of peer pressure, propelling them forward in a competitive way while also acting as a source of group solidarity and social support. These pressures were important in pushing some of the lower-middle-class interviewees on to college and, indeed, good colleges. The effect of school, and peer pressure, also undermined the constraining effects of race. There were interviewees from lower-middle-class backgrounds who struggled to find these networks of social support. Encouragement and support at school were conditional upon academic success. Even so, such support was found later in life and still proved influential in shaping the interviewees' career paths.[13]

Social resources, higher education and beyond

While all of the medics went straight from high school to college, some went on directly to medical school while others followed an indirect path. It was common among the science graduates to work in research labs during college or for a period afterwards. This work experience and the people they met were viewed as crucial in the stiff competition to get into medical school. For financial reasons, Anna Gray worked in a hospital laboratory affiliated to the Ivy League school she attended. Successful in her MCAP (medical college admission text) examination, she was sure her work experience helped. As she explained,

The fact that I had done research helped. That's when you realize if you are going to medical school you have to do something kind of out of the ordinary or more, and working for the lab, I actually published three papers and that was very helpful. Also, one of the people that interviewed me I [had] worked with in the lab before I went to medical school.

These worlds, it seemed, overlapped. For others, such research experience was acquired fortuitously. Luck was important although it was a form of luck shaped by social context.[14] Jane Bennett attended one of the prestigious seven sisters' colleges in New England. Mistaken for another graduate who had applied for a laboratory job at the Harvard Medical School, the Harvard Office contacted her and she 'walked into the job through the back door'. Unsuccessful at her first attempt in getting into medical school, good recommendations from her colleagues at the laboratory facilitated success on her second application. Again, Jane thought the experience crucial for getting into a medical school which valued people with more varied backgrounds. As a women in her mid-twenties she fitted the bill in this respect.

On finishing medical school, the physicians completed internships and residency programmes in their specialties. The interviewees described 'the match', a national system that matched medical graduates with specialist training programmes. Despite the supposed formality of the process, it was noticeable how those who went to the best colleges and the most prestigious medical schools usually secured training programmes in the most highly regarded hospitals. A process of accumulating advantage was in evidence. Again, the social worlds overlapped.[15] Jack Poole explained how he secured a prestigious residency through 'the match'. He said, 'Well, [at the hospital], I had actually done direct rotations so it wasn't just my application and interview. It was also that they had seen me work for a while there.' Some physicians enjoyed highly valued fellowships after their training. Informal processes, again, were in evidence as interviewees drew on the support of their professional colleagues. Michael Reed, for example, explained that he was able to draw on advice from his mentor. He said, 'It was a person who was sort of a mentor for me in residency and he was very plugged into the fellowship programmes so he helped me a lot to get the fellowship.' On the importance of social networks, he ventured,

It's very difficult if you have an application from someone you don't know. Even though they look great on paper, they can be a disaster and it's very different when someone calls them up and says 'I've know this person for four years. I think they did a great job as a resident and they'd be a really good fellow for you.'

Knowing people and being known to people, therefore, was a resource or an advantage in these respects.

The physicians held a variety of jobs in Boston in that some worked in the prestigious teaching hospitals, others worked in the city hospital while a few worked in Health Care Centres dotted around the city. Many of the interviewees had moved smoothly from training residencies to attendant physicians at the same institution, having performed satisfactorily and more than that in their training years. They did not have to apply formally for such jobs as their employment status merely changed from one day to the next. Many of the interviewees spoke at length of how the support and encouragement of mentors who, it must be emphasised they had impressed, had been crucial in their careers. Patrick Dutton, for example, spoke of how his mentor, whom he saw as a 'kindred spirit', taught him much and helped his career in various ways. As he explained:

I was attached to [L] Hospital and that was really my career break. There was a lady there who became my true mentor and friend to me and she taught me a lot about clinical medicine but she also taught me how to do research and how to publish papers and gave me something I was interested in and began to stretch me, I began to think about new things and interesting things and things that weren't just written in textbooks.

Patrick also acknowledged that as he sometimes spoke his mind and did not toe the line, she had often smoothed things over. He said, 'She picked up the phone, wrote letters and, you know, said even though he comes across a little bit hardnosed and driven, consider him. In other words, she would smooth things out.' Such contacts, therefore, were crucial in providing the opportunities to acquire the appropriate experiences that then placed some interviewees in good positions for prestigious jobs.[16]

Interestingly, Patrick also spoke of the importance of strong ties on his career in that family connections had facilitated an important job move. His younger brother was a patient at the hospital at which he worked when I interviewed him. As he explained:

Again, fate and fortune, one of the ladies who is on the board of directors is from [M] and knew my family and she came up and introduced herself to my mother. My grandparents and hers had been acquaintances. And it came about that [my mother said] 'Oh, my son is a doctor' and she said 'Oh, would he like to work here?' and she obviously couldn't get me a job but she could introduce me to people. As it turned out, she introduced me to the Chairman of the Department here and as it came about he asked me if I would like to be a fellow here.

After his fellowship, he was appointed to a permanent attendant physician job. Usually, however, the interviewees described the importance of weaker ties in accounts of job moves and promotion.[17] Daniel Lewis, for example, was completing a prestigious one-year fellowship in his specialism when he was offered a job. His current chairman had also trained at the same university and, 'he knew who I had trained with and called them up and said, "Is there anyone you would recommend for a position?"' On their recommendation, the chairman interviewed him. Since he was looking for a well-established person, he appointed Daniel to a junior position. Before he took up the job, however, organisational change created an opening for a senior position and Daniel found that 'it was congratulations, it's yours'. Daniel was, without doubt, a highly able physician and yet his contacts, and some luck, played a crucial role in advancing his career very rapidly indeed.

The American educators had more varied careers than their medical counterparts. Most went straight to college where they completed degrees in education. A number of them joined the staff at schools where they had completed their teaching practice. They were already known to the school and its principal and hired on this basis. Some encountered difficulties finding permanent positions in the 1970s with falling enrolment. Other interviewees came to teaching later and contacts were important in the forging of careers. Unable to go to college because of financial constraints and family circumstances, Bernice Hughes worked in various clerical jobs until her mid-twenties. Married with a stepdaughter, she volunteered to work as a teacher's aid on an education enrichment programme at a private school that her stepdaughter attended on a Saturday. As she went on to explain:

One of the teachers there said 'You know, you are really good at this. Have you ever thought about going into teaching?' I said, 'Not really but . . .' He said, 'You're really good, you should try' and he said 'I am going to give the Principal your name. Maybe you want to come and be a substitute teacher or something.'

Organisational change at work prompted Bernice to call the principal and she became an unqualified substitute teacher and contributed to the after-school programme. Importantly, as a member of staff, she became eligible for grants that paid her college fees and she completed a degree at the same time as she had two of her own three children. She was subsequently employed as a qualified teacher in the city's public school system. The encouragement of a 'loose contact' had been very important in shaping her subsequent teaching career.[18]

Unlike the women physicians, some of the women educators had given up their jobs when they had their children. It was not uncommon, it seemed, for them to become involved in daycare, looking after other children along with their own to earn some money, or in their children's nursery education. Even so, contacts in the teaching world were not lost and they were often contacted for substitute teaching. Although it was still tough finding a job in the 1980s, Patricia Walker recalled how,

One of the Principals needed someone and called me and offered me a job. It was as a substitute. Someone had cancer and was leaving and it was in the middle of the year. She asked me if I'd like to fill in at least until the end of the year and she said she'd call me tomorrow for my answer. I said 'OK'.

She had worked at the same school for over ten years having been made permanent early on. The experience of daycare often kept women in this occupational community.[19] Joanne Rothman explained how she gradually moved back into teaching. She said, 'Well, Sharon had gone to nursery school at a local school programme at our church and I had stopped in there during the summer and they said, "We need another teacher. Would you be interested? It would be three mornings a week."' The experience was very useful when she applied for a position as a substitute teacher. Joanne then went on to explain,

The Principal of the school where my children went which is right round the corner here said to me, 'You know, there's a dandy job opening up at [E] school, 30 hours a week and I think you'd really enjoy it. I'd like to recommend you for that job.' I said 'OK' and I went over and I interviewed with the principal of [E] school and the next thing I knew I was hired.

Social contacts, therefore, were important in facilitating many of the women educators' return to permanent teaching positions. Some of the male educators also spoke of how they re-entered teaching through teaching contacts. Joel Walker initially taught for eight years. In the late 1970s, in the face of tightening budgets and falling enrolments, 'rather than waiting for the axe to fall', he went into private industry selling computers. He lost this job in the early 1980s and endured a spell of unemployment before finding another job in the same field. Faced with the prospect of unemployment again, he decided to return to teaching. Joel secured his present job with the help of a fellow teacher who was also a neighbour.[20] As he explained:

He had heard of a position, a part-time one that may not have turned into a good thing, he didn't know, but he knew we were having some trouble and we had four young kids at that time. He was nice enough to put me in contact with some people there and the Principal of that high school, as it turned out, was leaving [W] because he was going to this town called [H] because he was going to be a Superintendent that way. In the process of him going down there, he knew of a position down there so he was able to help me get a job down there.

Accounts of job moves within the teaching profession that highlighted the importance of contacts were common too. Barry Waite secured his current job when he was called 'by the then Principal of this building who said "I'd like to talk with you, and here I am."' The Principal knew he was looking to move, he was sure, through the 'networks of principals who all knew each other'.

Contacts were also important in the process of promotion. After ten years as a classroom teacher, Bernice Hughes was encouraged by a new Principal to go into school administration. She directed her towards an education administration course, welcoming the opportunity 'because she could then allocate me some jobs that not only benefited me but benefited her because it was less that she had to deal with and that's what I did'. This work experience was all-important in securing a permanent position as an Assistant Principal. Bernice was grateful for her generosity, since 'She wasn't one who was afraid of allocating or who would get upset if she thought somewhere else was getting the glory. She just pushed ahead and said "you should learn it."'

Roy Morgan enjoyed rapid promotion to become a school principal in his twenties. Later, he was turned down for a senior administrative position and that upset him greatly. Political connections in Boston, he felt, counted more than credentials and experience for senior jobs. Disillusioned, he started applying for jobs outside the city and secured a position as principal in another school system. The person he was replacing 'became one of my biggest cheerleaders'. He said,

I actually adore her. I think she is one of the best administrators I have ever seen. She has obviously done an awful lot for my career by really really going to the mat for me. As a matter of fact, what she said was that if they didn't consider me for this position, she was going to offer to stay in this position and have them recruit me for the job she has now.

Roy very much wanted to 'move into her shoes' when she was next promoted.[21]

The American interviewees, therefore, recounted numerous stories of the importance of contacts and luck as they forged careers in medicine and teaching. Work experience in laboratories, for example, although sometimes undertaken for financial reasons by some of the medics of middle-class and lower-middle-class backgrounds, proved to be an important experience enhancing applications to medical school. Contacts were also important here in advising applicants, providing recommendations and having links to medical schools. For those attending the most prestigious medical schools, knowing people and being known to them via work experience was significant in attaining prestigious residencies and fellowships. Weak ties were also important for career progression as mentors provided all-important opportunities to acquire the necessary experiences to facilitate job moves and promotion. There was evidence of a similar occupational community among the American teachers. They were crucial, for example, for allowing the women educators, irrespective of class background, to hear of job opportunities after raising their children.

Involvement in daycare or nurseries during this period out of the labour market was significant here. The help of contacts in job moves within the teaching profession was evident among the male educators and, again, contacts were important in facilitating opportunities to acquire the work experiences crucial for promotion. To be sure, the class background and educational experiences of the interviewees exposed them to different sorts of social networks and different advantages gained from them. That said, the interviewees from modest social backgrounds could tell stories about people who helped them in their careers and facilitated their occupational success.[22]

Social resources and British education

Like their American counterparts, the British interviewees talked freely about being aware of the social pressures to succeed – both educationally and occupationally – from the local communities in which they lived. Again, of course, these social pressures varied according to the milieus in which they grew up. The doctors and their wives from established middle-class families, for example, talked about how they were sent to reputable private schools like the children of their parents' friends and neighbours. Frequent reference was made to how their parents sent them to schools with 'good reputations', academically and otherwise, and it seemed that information about the reputation of such schools was gleaned from their social networks. By implication, their parents lived in a social space occupied by other middle-class people concerned with educational and occupational advancement. Thinking back to his private education, for example, Bruce Brown said, 'I never sort of queried it except I think most of the people we knew went to private school.' Margaret Brown indicated that it was considered 'fashionable' in her parents' social set to send daughters to a particular ladies' college. Be they family, friends or acquaintances, it was just what other people did around them. The daughter of a doctor, Janet Jones recalled how, 'my sister and I were both sent away. A lot of doctors' daughters in [the town I grew up in] went to [C] Ladies College. They just listened to what people said.' In these instances, as I noted before, they were expected to acquire the appropriate 'social graces' and 'marry well'.[23]

Academic and occupational success was all important for the men from such backgrounds, however, and the schools they attended, including the head teachers, other schoolteachers and fellow pupils, shaped their expectations and aspirations. Bruce Brown, for example, described his private school as 'a very medical school' that moulded his own medical aspirations. As he explained,

I was influenced by the school. We weren't pushed in any direction at all but you're surrounded by a fairly medical atmosphere and, you know, most boys were the sons of doctors and a lot of them were going to do medicine and as far as I was concerned, really, I mean, it was the most interesting thing I could think of doing as it didn't really seem to involve at that time too much maths, which pleased me.[24]

Again, the interviewees also spoke of how their private schools actually facilitated entry to the top London medical schools or Oxford and Cambridge. As Stephen Dodd suggested,

I only did medicine because the headmaster after we'd done O levels summoned everybody in [to his office], one by one, and enquired in my case, 'Boy what are you doing to do? I think you should do medicine. I'll arrange for you to go to [prestigious London teaching hospital]', which he did.[25]

Similarly, Andrew Underwood casually mentioned how he achieved a coveted but little-known scholarship to medical school because 'someone who'd been on it the previous year at school told me'. This, then, was the wider social context or 'atmosphere' that shaped the doctors' early lives and how they went to the best medical schools for their training.

To be sure, like the Americans, most of the British interviewees did not occupy such exclusive social worlds. They spoke, nevertheless, about the influence of people around them in shaping their hopes and plans. A number of the interviewees from working-class backgrounds emphasised the effects of school friends and their parents on their primary education and how it contributed to them passing the eleven plus examination thus facilitating entry into grammar school. Reference was made to how they mixed with other children, often from affluent families, whose parents expected them to do well. Sheila Parker described herself as 'working class', as her family 'lived in a council house and there was very little'.[26] Most of the children at her village school passed the eleven plus examination to go to grammar school and she explained this high success rate with reference to the fact that 'it was quite an affluent area'. As Sheila said, 'A large number of my peers had professional parents. A lot of them were teachers, head teachers, people who owned shops, business people.' Hilary Butler, also from a working-class background, was firm in her view that peer pressure contributed to her passing the eleven plus examination. As she explained:

I quite firmly believe that peer pressure came in there because I mixed with people who were quite bright. Perhaps pressure is the wrong word but because my friends were girls and boys who were expected to do well, I think certainly in my last years in primary school, I perhaps made much more effort to do things, you know, do well because there was always a system of tables and so on and obviously it was a challenge and I think I responded to that.

Mixing with other able children whose parents had high educational expectations, therefore, had quite an effect on the interviewees in motivating them to succeed. The tripartite system also shaped the interviewees' and their parents' expectations and aspirations as it seemingly identified academic ability at an early age. The majority of the interviewees, as I have discussed before, went to direct grant or local state grammar schools that were usually single-sex schools. The expectation was that everyone was directed towards educational success and these were highly disciplined schools where young people were expected to behave. Peter Smith explained:

That was the expectation from the moment I went to the school. The first thing I can remember doing, going to this school in a brand new school uniform, being taken to a great big Honours Board and told that you had not come to this school to play any more. You are expected to achieve and this is where we expect your name to be in x years. So you were left in no doubt that you were at a grammar school you know. Masters wore gowns, you know, and it was a very sort of traditional grammar school ethos.

In retrospect, he thought it was very 'elitist'. The top achievers were expected to specialise in the sciences as the harder subjects in which to succeed and young men, as I noted in Chapter 5, were directed into medicine or other professions suitable for their sex.

Other men who went to grammar school before they became teachers or went into other jobs recounted remarkably similar stories. Ken Butler, from a lower-middle-class family, went to a grammar school and then on to university to do a straight science degree before doing teacher training. He recalled that the school was a place where it was assumed that the top sets would go to university or college. It was unquestioned and there was not really a choice about the matter. As Ken explained,

It was an assumption. We all did, all my friends and contemporaries. I don't think there was very much discussion about it. All of the grammar schools, certainly set 1 and part of set 2 either went to university or college. It wasn't a question of whether you went. I can't think of any of my friends who didn't go to teacher training college or university. It wasn't anything that was discussed as to whether you should go.

Interestingly, as he said, all his school friends, it seemed, shared the same expectation and did the same thing, leading Ken to conclude that 'it was just the norm rather than anything else'.[27] John Willis, of working-class origin, experienced the same pressures at his local grammar school. John recalled how,

It was the traditional boys' grammar school. I mean, looking back on it, it was an appalling sort of place [laughs] where there was an assumption that if you were in the top thirty, you'd go to university and the second set you'd go into one of the local training sets and in the third set you were an also-ran. If you were in the top set, you were going for it. I was always in the top set. I always went for it all the time, always.

The school, it seemed, shaped both able middle-class and working-class boys in the same way.

The academic ethos and the strict discipline of the all-girls grammar schools were much commented upon by the women teachers too. Again, school staff made it clear that they had high expectations of those who had been successful with the eleven plus whether they were middle class or working class. Susan Parry, a working-class girl, who went to her local grammar school, said:

It was [E] Grammar School for 'Gals'. I will always remember 'Gals'. It was very strict. Down to the uniform that cost an arm and a leg. You weren't allowed within 200 yards of the headmistress's study. Silence zones everywhere. You knelt in assembly to make sure that your skirts touched the ground. It was a very typical, I think, girls' grammar school. It had a very sort of way about it. You were just expected to do well. They had a lot of famous old girls and, you know, you were following the [E] Grammar School tradition sort of thing.

The expectation was that the more able girls would continue with their studies and this was, indeed, the norm. As Yvonne Johns said, 'Very few left. It was a scandal really if any of them left.'[28] Similarly, Pauline Hill suggested, 'We were all doing it you see. Just one or two loners who decided they were going to be a secretary and have some money and have some fun, and we were boring and we said no we would rather have an education thank you very much.' Again, therefore, it was the norm for almost everyone to proceed in this way. Those who did not were looked down on while those who did felt rather superior.

Some of these working-class women spoke of the encouragement and support they enjoyed from schoolteachers although it was unusual to be directed into medicine. The norm for women was to go to university and then teaching (for the most able) or teacher training college (for the less academically inclined). Julia Dodd, as I have already noted, enjoyed considerable encouragement to do medicine by her headmistress. She also stressed that she was a 'goody goody sister' to her twin brother who went to grammar school although he 'got in with a bad lot' and did badly in his examinations. Hilary Butler, like Julia Dodd, also talked about the important influence of a head teacher. He encouraged her to apply for university as well as the college route into teaching. As she explained,

I suppose he made you believe in yourself in a way because he was very much for getting people to apply for places and he was very much into people going to Oxbridge and doing Open Scholarships. He suggested I did an Open Scholarship for [C]. I did. I didn't actually get a place but, you know, the fact that he believed you could do it, it was very encouraging.

As in the USA, however, there were others who did not recall such encouragement. When Barbara Coombes expressed her desire to be a doctor, her headmistress considered she had 'aspirations beyond her capabilities' while others spoke of their unhappy experiences of grammar school life – resisting the often hierarchical nature of the school and their lowly position within in – leaving at the first opportunity to pursue choices unavailable to their middle-class counterparts.[29]

The school environment, namely people such as head teachers, other teachers, school friends and their parents, had an enormous impact on the interviewees' expectations, aspirations and the paths they followed into higher education and beyond. In Britain, institutional arrangements – in the form of the tripartite system – played an important part in shaping people's futures. Interestingly, there was one teacher, Norman Johns, who failed the eleven plus and went to a secondary modern school before transferring to grammar school to do A levels at 16. His early life is worth dwelling on for the contrast with his grammar school counterparts. As Norman explained about his school:

A lot of people left before the end of the fifth year and there was only a small group that stayed on. I think they wanted people to stay on and to go forward for exams. Yes, they wanted us to go on but bear in mind, only three of us went on. Obviously, the vast majority went into employment at fifteen or went to technical college, because in the 1960s they were still, I suppose, looking to traditional employment placements although there was not that much. That was already in decline so I don't think education served those children well. It might have served me because I decided to take a teaching job.

He, of course, broke away from the common destiny of other working-class young men in the town in which he grew up. Resentment at being 'written off' by the school system and teachers at his secondary school fuelled a strong motivation to succeed and attain more than his supposed lot.[30]

Thus, social pressures beyond the family, therefore, undoubtedly influenced the British interviewees' educational aspirations and expectations. Some interviewees, for example, spoke of how choice of and knowledge about reputable schools were influenced by their parents' social networks as they followed the lead of their friends and acquaintances. Exclusive schools, and also head teachers, ordinary teachers and school friends, were certainly influential in moulding young men's aspirations towards medical careers. For those attending regular state schools, the influence of other able children, usually the offspring of aspiring parents, of course, propelled the interviewees, irrespective of class background, onwards. Again, competition and cohesion among groups of school friends were a significant social pressure. Institutional arrangements in Britain, namely the tripartite system that channelled the able into grammar schools and the less able into secondary modern schools, had a major impact on hopes and plans. Both the men and women interviewees recalled the quite 'elitist' nature of these single-sex grammar schools which left them in no doubt that they had to succeed. Again, the interviewees spoke of how their friends and contemporaries followed the same route so that it was seen as 'scandalous' to deviate from it. This is how sanctions, it seems, operated to limit deviations of this kind. For the interviewees from working-class backgrounds, the encouragement and support of teachers in making applications to universities and teaching training colleges was very important in propelling them on through the education system. It was in this school environment and with the support of such people that they considered higher education as a preferable option to leaving school at 16 in search of routine white-collar or blue-collar jobs.[31]

Social resources, higher education and beyond

On finishing medical school, all of the British medics took up positions as pre-registration junior doctors (as House Officers (HO)) on one-year contracts, and then applied to the General Medical Council (GMC) to become fully registered doctors. Almost all of the doctors spoke of how they obtained jobs at hospitals attached to the medical schools at which they had been taught. Those who attended the prestigious London medical schools invariably secured highly sought after positions at these teaching hospitals. They spoke of the importance of contacts in their early careers. Bruce Brown explained that 'it was only really worth applying for house jobs with consultants that taught you as a student. If you hadn't been taught by them, you wouldn't get the job.' It seemed that being known as former students was an advantage while those outside this 'circuit', without the seemingly right medical training background, were excluded. Indeed, Bruce spoke of how he also secured a prestigious Senior House Officer (SHO) position via his social contacts. As he explained,

I finished my house job and hadn't another one to go to immediately. Then I suddenly heard they hadn't appointed anybody for this job at [B] so I wandered down there, met one of the two consultants in the square and said, 'Oh, I hear you're looking for a SHO.' He said, 'Yes. Do you want the job?' I said 'Yes'. 'Right', he said, 'OK'. I had been taught by him so I knew him so it was all highly informal.

Describing very similar experiences, Stephen Dodd acknowledged that such positions were very helpful for his career for they provided 'training, contacts, progression, stimulation'.[32]

There was only one doctor, Rod Hunt, who worked at a prestigious London teaching hospital after studying at Manchester. A family contact facilitated entry into this seemingly closed medical world in the capital. As Rod explained:

> I decided I'd like to spend a year out of Manchester and I saw an advert for a job in [T] Hospital in London which normally I wouldn't have had a chance for but I saw the consultant's name. He was a Hungarian chap and he was my babysitter when I lived in [N]. I phoned him up and he said 'Come down' and I worked in London for a year at [T] which was very interesting. It was a fluke co-incidence.

Again, he acknowledged that the experience of working in a well-regarded teaching hospital was crucial in securing his next job as a SHO outside London. The atmosphere of working in a teaching hospital – doing things differently, reading journals and 'picking up the patter' – meant he interviewed well. For those who remained in Manchester, however, it was typical to do pre-registration House Officer jobs and then specialist Senior House Officer jobs in the teaching hospitals attached to the medical school. Similar circuits were in operation. Some doctors, of course, did not work in the prestigious teaching hospitals and took junior positions in hospitals in small towns where competition for such jobs was much weaker. Barbara Coombes, for example, elected to work in a non-teaching hospital since she wanted to be a GP rather than a hospital doctor. Local hospitals were desperate to find people and, she said, 'had to depend very much upon overseas doctors to staff them so there was no competition really'. Anyone who was interviewed was seemingly offered a job and social contacts were not necessary.[33]

Those doctors who chose hospital medicine usually undertook further specialist training and study for examinations that facilitated membership of specialist royal colleges (including the Royal College of Obstetricians and Gynaecologists and the Royal College of Surgeons). They moved into Registrar and Senior Registrar positions before becoming consultants and this usually took about seven years. Promotion often entailed geographical mobility and the interviewees lived in localities without contacts. Still, contacts were important in the promotion process. Ian Lamb was invited by a consultant to work for him in London after he impressed him with a paper presented at a conference. Keen to leave an African country because he did not like the political regime, he and his family moved to London. At the end of the six-month contract, the consultant advised him to apply for a registrar's job at a highly regarded outer London hospital. His application, Ian believed, was successful because 'it was recognised that the person I was working for was an extremely good surgeon and extremely good trainer'. Impressing his peers, therefore, had undoubtedly been important and, in turn, his peers had helped Ian. For Julia Dodd, the geographical mobility of her doctor husband and then having children slowed her progress towards a senior position. Nevertheless, working as a part-time clinical assistant, she took the advice of a senior colleague 'who liked her' and who encouraged her to apply for a full-time Senior Registrar's job rather than 'work part time and always be number two'. She was a consultant within two years, which she modestly claimed was because her field 'was a growing specialism and not many people had trained in it'.[34]

After completing the necessary training, other interviewees went into general practice and both close and loose ties were important in securing junior positions and then senior partnerships. Family or family friends played a role for some interviewees. Andrew Underwood joined his parents' practice and his wife Bridget joined soon after, so the family business was effectively passed from one husband and wife team to another. Peter Smith secured his first position in a practice through his wife's contact. As he explained, 'Well, my wife knew another nurse whose husband was already in general practice. There were two of them and they were keen to take on a third party so it was through knowing friends, you know, it was done on that basis.' Others talked about the networks of colleagues and friends built up in their early working years as they worked long hours in hospital, or how they could 'nose around' doing locum GP work in the community. In the context of this tight-knit occupational community, there was much talk and information passed around on available and anticipated vacancies. Lawrence Foster said,

I mean, I think there is a jungle telegraph. It is a fairly close community. Doctors do meet doctors, certainly socially, but also, more often than not, at educational meetings and other things and the jungle telegraph gets around. It's not necessarily all the time. I mean there's lots of advertising goes on in the *British Medical Journal* for doctors and junior partners and for assistants and for trainers and all the other bits so it isn't primary contacts but some of it is done by contact.[35]

A senior partner suggested that 'the networks are working all the time'.

Contacts were also important in shaping the British teachers' careers. After completing their studies at university or teacher training college, the teachers easily found jobs in primary and secondary schools, often securing positions in schools where they had successfully completed their practical teaching practice. Being known to staff in this way had its advantages as in the USA. Some of the men did not pursue a teaching career with enthusiasm and social contacts helped them explore other options. Ken Butler conceded that he opted to do a PGCE merely to stay at university another year. Still ambivalent after a short spell in teaching, he took a job in local government where his father worked. As he explained, 'I think that was actually talking to my father as much as anything else. He was in local government. The opportunities were there for accountancy and so I gave it a go.' He returned to teaching quite soon afterwards, however, and remained there. Similarly, John Wills had wanted to pursue an academic career although an early opportunity to do so fell through at very short notice, as I discussed earlier. A social contact helped him out via some teaching. As he explained,

I needed a job. I needed money and there happened to be a head teacher at a school in the city who attended the University Chaplaincy at [L] of which I was a member and somebody put a word in for me and by sheer chance, it is absolute chance – it's interesting how chance does formulate your future – he needed a teacher on his timetable of English and Religious Studies.[36]

Finding he enjoyed the job, John applied for a PGCE and went into teaching afterwards.

All of the women teachers combined their careers with children and, like their American counterparts, contacts in the teaching world were often crucial in facilitating their return to work. Interestingly, many of the teachers spoke of how their contacts often propelled them back into work much quicker than they had planned. They found themselves being approached to do *ad hoc* supply work at the schools where they had previously taught. As Mary Bull said, 'It wasn't me approaching them, they rang up and said, you know, "Can you do this?"' For these interviewees, supply work then led into permanent part-time and full-time employment in these or other schools. Muriel Crisp did not work for seven years when her three children, close in age, were young. Then, she explained:

Once I started [supply work], it sort of snowballed and from that, doing a little bit at that school, I did a maternity leave for someone part time and then the head teacher of the school where I am now phoned and said would I come and do some work at her school and I said, 'I only do part time', and she said, 'Well just try it for a term full time' and that was eleven years ago!

Similarly, Sheila Parker spent a long time out of the labour market – fourteen years – raising her children before she went back to teaching via supply, part-time employment and then full-time employment. As she explained:

I was called on supply to a nursery school who had an acting Head in at the time who was there to gain experience of a nursery school and she was the Head of an infant school and she phoned me up for supply there and told me that a job was coming up. So I went back in part time and then eventually full time so from supply it was to part time to full time.[37]

Such contacts in the occupational community, therefore, proved for-tuitous in facilitating many of the women's return to teaching while still raising their children. That said, frequent reference was made to how such opportunities began to close down in the 1980s. As Diane Willis explained:

Well, I went back to [A] to some supply work during that period because they asked me. Just a couple of weeks, you know, here and there. Then the head of English rang me up and said there was this really, really, part-time job and he wanted me to go and teach about five periods a week and would I do it and I said 'Yeah, I will', because I thought, you know, I may as well just get my toe back in the water again. I enjoyed those bits of part-time at [A] and ultimately it might have led to a full-time job but at that time, the whole thing closed up and married women couldn't get back in.[38]

Other teachers spoke of how promotion opportunities also dwindled. Norman Johns enjoyed early success becoming the head of the maths department at a secondary school at his mid-twenties. He then found promotion opportunities to a deputy headship dwindled and he failed to secure a position. That he had only a teaching certificate rather than a degree was a disadvantage. Moreover, his previous head teacher had been uninterested in staff development. A new head teacher, in con-trast, funded a Masters course and he had joined the senior management team. He readily suggested, 'I have to say of the new Head, he has been tremendously supportive of me.' Such encouragement had lit a 'spark' and Norman was applying for senior positions afresh.

The support of colleagues was important, unsurprisingly, to those who had attained senior positions. Ken Butler described how he was encour-aged to do leadership courses that facilitated his promotion. He said, 'The Head actually suggested that I should and I suppose, to some extent, I must thank him for pushing me in that direction. And gradually, I thought, yes, I could do that. If he can do that, so can I. That is how it came about.'[39] Just as peers had shaped educational aspirations, so colleagues at work, it seemed, encouraged the interviewees to consider themselves for senior jobs. Information on vacancies from close and loose ties were important too. Yvonne Johns explained how she secured her first headship. As she explained,

I knew the Head there because I'd been acting Head for twelve months at [B] school and you go on courses and meet people and I knew this headmaster and he dropped dead in his office. I was at the funeral of a child at my husband's school that I'd taught and I was with the boss of [E] education authority who was just retiring and he was asking me had I put in for the headship and I said 'Well, I'm thinking about it.' He said, 'It's a nice school. It's a good school', so I put in for it.

Contacts were an important source of information on anticipated job opportunities. On her current position as Head of a primary school, Rosemary Hill said, 'Somebody had told me that another infant school in the borough was coming up because the Head was retiring and the job came up and I thought, oh, I'll just go in for that one and here I am and here I'll stay!' Contacts with fellow teachers, therefore, were significant in the promotion process.

As in the USA, my British interviewees found it easy to talk about the influence of different people, be they close or loose ties, on their careers in medicine and teaching. Some of the (established middle-class) interviewees spoke of how their former teachers were important contacts as they moved from prestigious medical schools to highly sought after house jobs in teaching hospitals, invariably leading on to prestigious consultant positions. These circuits operated in London and Manchester although social contacts were not so important for positions in less prestigious non-teaching hospitals. Mentors were important to the interviewees, irrespective of class background, in providing information and advice on career progression, crucially facilitating opportunities to acquire appropriate work experience needed for promotion within hospitals. Similarly, both close and weak ties were evident in securing junior positions in GP practices where the existence of social networks was readily acknowledged. The influence of social networks in securing advantages was evident among the teachers who also belonged to an occupational community as such. In remarkably similar ways to the USA, social networks were crucial for the women teachers – of middle-class and working-class origins – returning to the labour market after caring for their children full time, although opportunities to return gradually started to dwindle in the 1980s and beyond. Of course, social contacts were very important as sources of information and advice for both women and men teachers of all class origins as they made job moves and sought promotion; mentors encouraged them to consider promotion in the same way that peer pressure operated in their school days.[40]

Conclusion

This chapter has explored the mobilisation of social resources in the reproduction of advantage by drawing on the interviewees' accounts of how people in their local communities contributed to their educational and occupational success. Both the American and British interviewees willingly acknowledged the influence of local interpersonal relationships on their educational expectations. The interviewees of upper-middle-class and middle-class origins spoke of the wider social pressures to succeed because they socialised with other middle-class children of educated parents at school and in their local milieu who were also all preoccupied with academic success. Educational success facilitated entry into the better universities and colleges where they met and forged contacts of their own which helped their careers. While the middle-class interviewees mobilised their social networks to their advantage, social contacts were not their exclusive preserve, however, as Goldthorpe has acknowledged. The interviewees from more modest lower-middle-class or working-class origins also spoke of the importance of local interpersonal relationships in propelling them forward. Peer pressures from other, academically able school friends and encouragement and moral support from teachers in school were a very important social support system that set them on the path to higher education. Educational success, once again, facilitated entry to higher education institutions where these interviewees made contacts of their own which were drawn upon as their careers developed. These empirical findings confirm Coleman's account of the way in which social capital can be mobilised as a resource in the quest for educational success.[41]

This chapter also considered the role of contacts in the interviewees' accounts of their careers in medicine and teaching. To be sure, those from upper-middle-class or middle-class backgrounds had somewhat different connections to those from lower-middle-class or working-class origins. The sample included American interviewees from upper-middle-class backgrounds who were educated at private schools, who then attended Ivy League colleges, went to prestigious medical schools, secured highly sought after residencies and landed plum jobs in reputable teaching hospitals. The contacts made in each of these contexts certainly provided important sources of information and advice. Very similar privileged life histories were evident in Britain too. That said, those interviewees from more modest social backgrounds also spoke of the importance of contacts in their careers as they enjoyed the moral support and encouragement of mentors, for example, in promotion to senior positions in their chosen professions. Thus, the empirical evidence has demonstrated the way in which social resources are mobilised in the reproduction of career advancement and how social networks have a class character. The class character of social networks may well explain how the upper middle class come to occupy the higher positions within a profession while those from more modest social origins are to be found on its lower rungs. At the same time, however, the interviewees' accounts also showed that social resources are not exclusive to the middle class, as those of modest origins spoke of the ways in which social networks facilitated their career advancement too. In this respect, the pervasiveness of social contacts and, indeed, luck, in the forging of careers, confirms Granovetter's classic study of contacts and careers.[42]

7   Friends and networks in school and beyond

In Chapter 6, I drew on Coleman's work on social capital and the way in which parents use their social networks of interpersonal relations in the local community as a resource to help their children in the education system. According to the interviewees, both middle-class and working-class parents mobilised their social resources to their advantage. I also drew on Granovetter's ideas about the importance of social contacts on careers and considered how the interviewees of different class backgrounds mobilised their own social contacts in becoming medics and educators. The interviewees of upper-middle-class and middle-class origins could certainly draw on their parental social networks but so could my informants of more modest social status. Once again, I now consider my interviewees as middle-class parents mobilising their social resources to ensure their children's educational and occupational advancement. Given that most of my interviewees' children were still making their way through the school system in both countries, attention focuses on social capital and educational success. The role of social contacts in the forging of new careers among the interviewees' older children will be considered more briefly. Attention is not limited to the ways in which social resources come into their own only when academic success is not forthcoming. This is in contrast to both Goldthorpe and Bourdieu who viewed them as important only in terms of a strategy of last resort. Rather, I will consider how social resources are mobilised, indeed deeply embedded, in the process of acquiring educational credentials as well.[1]

As I will show, the American interviewees drew on their social networks of family and friends for information and advice on the best schools to which to send their children. It was through their contacts that they learnt of the most academically reputable schools and they discussed their experiences, choices, decisions and actions with them. Their social networks, therefore, were an all-important source of social support in how to act to secure their children's best interests. Knowledge and advice from both tight and loose ties were especially significant in the USA because of variations in the school system and the importance of choosing the right place to live to get the best education.[2] Furthermore, the interviewees were very anxious that their children should socialise with other children of middle-class parents who could act as a local social support in the pursuit of educational success. They wanted their children to experience 'positive' peer pressures to succeed although they also had to deal with negative peer pressures too. All of the interviewees were aware of the social contacts to be made at university or college and how contact with those in power was to be made in the top schools. Not surprisingly, many of the interviewees' children were expecting to go to the better colleges following the lead of others around them. It was clear that the interviewees' children were also drawing on their own emerging social networks of school friends and so forth in shaping college choices. The importance of both tight and loose contacts in the forging of careers was evident among the older children, be they academically successful or not.

Like their American counterparts, the British interviewees drew on their social contacts for information and advice on the most reputable schools to send their children to, invariably following the lead of other people like themselves. As in the USA, work colleagues were especially important for the geographically mobile medics while the less mobile teachers could draw on their local knowledge and contacts with fellow teachers. Again, contacts were a shorthand way of acquiring knowledge from people they could trust about how the system worked and how to work the system. Similarly, the British interviewees were very keen that their children should socialise with children whose parents were concerned with academic success and they directed their children accordingly. They wanted their children's emerging social contacts to act as a source of social support in the pursuit of academic success, peer pressures reinforcing the cultural capital of the home rather than working against it.[3] The importance of social networks for information and influence was notable for the less academically able in terms of helping children stay in the education system as long as possible. Family and friends were also influential in shaping degree and occupational choices and securing all-important work experience in pursuit of particular careers. That said, parents were also aware of how their children's emerging social contacts were an important influence on their children's aspirations and expectations. They also appreciated how they could only offer limited help if their children pursued careers where they had no social contacts to draw on.

Social resources and American education

The American interviewees drew on their social networks of family, friends, neighbours and colleagues from work for information and advice on the best academic schools to which to send their children. They drew on such advice at every stage of their children's education although, unsurprisingly, this advice was most important as children transferred to different schools at various points in their education and choice could be exercised. As I noted in early chapters, a number of the doctors sent their children to expensive private pre-schools – often Montessori schools – from the age of about three until they were ready for kindergarten at six. Invariably, these informants heard of such schools from their circle of friends who, of course, had the economic resources to send their children to these private pre-schools and shared the same cultural capital regarding their aspirations for their children's early education. Jane Bennett spoke of how, 'We had heard of it from a number of people, including some people who had twenty-year-old children who had been to that school a long time ago, and they just were very excited about it.' Similarly, Susan Pearson explained:

My son went to the Montessori school. My daughter went to a co-operative nursery school where one parent came in every day to assist. It was excellent. How do you choose? You talk to your friends and neighbours who know about it. You jockey for position. It's just like trying to get your kids into the Blue Coats or Dulwich. You put their name down on the list and you play the game.

With such information and advice being passed around among contacts, it was no wonder that competition to get into such schools was tough.[4]

Some of the interviewees sent their children to private elementary schools and they drew on their social networks for advice about school choices. It was the way in which they established the academic reputation and status of schools. Those who had grown up in Boston could draw on their childhood knowledge of local schools. They could call also on the recommendation of siblings and old friends and their experiences of educating their children at such schools. The interviewees described how they spoke to their friends and acquaintances about the education of their children. Judy Kennedy and her husband clearly sought the help of friends and neighbours in making the anguished decision to send their sons to private school. As George Marshall said:

I have friends who have gone through the public school system and most people found it very difficult for themselves and their kids. The teachers in the schools were pretty uneven and at that time there was a fair amount of violence in the schools. I had a friend who did it and she ended up spending a huge amount of time getting involved in the schools, to know the schools, to know the teachers, to know which school was good for third grade, to know which school was good for fourth grade, that kind of thing. Among other things, we didn't have the time to do that.

It was by talking to other people about such experiences that they developed a sense of the choices ahead of them. The emphasis was on how they were not alone in confronting the 'big disarray' of the public school system.[5]

Of course, the interviewees who sent their children to public elementary schools also called on the advice of friends and acquaintances in their choice of schools. Indeed, such help was especially important given variations in the quality of education provided under the auspices of the public school system in the USA. Close ties and loose connections were important although loose connections were often most important for the geographically mobile.[6] Daniel Lewis, for example, moved from the West Coast to Boston just before he sent his daughter to kindergarten. As he explained:

The choice of public schools is based upon where you live and the truth of the matter was we looked very carefully as to where we wanted to live as to how the public schools were. In fact, one of the physicians I worked with, her brother was a teacher at a public school in [N] so I talked to him and he was actually wonderful. He said buy whatever house you like because all the public schools are excellent here in [N]. So he was actually very helpful and that being said, we looked for a house we could afford in the neighbourhood we liked but we wanted to be some place where we were pretty sure of the public schools.

For those mobile into Boston, colleagues from work were important information sources too. Charles Khan spoke of how he acquired information, 'By chatting in the coffee room and most people in medicine, and generally for professionals in this country, they move to suburbia to supposedly the better places for the better schools and better security. The urban violence is a fact of life.'

The effect of this advice was that the medics, in particular, were clustered into the most affluent residential communities in Boston and surrounding cities, educating their children among an elite population in schools with high academic reputations that they ascertained from their various contacts.[7] Indeed, many of the interviewees commented on the fact that their neighbours and friends had high aspirations for their children and there was a high level of involvement in schools. Patrick Dutton, for example, explained how his daughter was participating in an experimental school plan in the small affluent town in which they lived and he noted, 'It is quite amazing how so many of our friends' children who had the same ethos and drive in education that we did got into that class.' Similarly, his wife, Susan noted, 'There are a lot of committed parents, particularly in this district. This is a middle-class white professional town. Go up to [W] and it's blue collar and the school system is not so good.

It's totally about parent commitment.' It is interesting to note how parent commitment was regarded as the key to success. There were some, however, who were uncomfortable living among this elite population. Missing the ethnic and cultural diversity of the West Coast, Anna Gray disliked the predominately white, Jewish area in which she lived. There were a few high-achieving Asians but people of colour were hard to find. She described how,

> The parents are all motivated and much more involved in the classroom than either of us . . . There are a lot of primarily women in this area who had major positions who were CEOs of corporations and they have stopped all this to become mommies and they are people who are type A high power. They have got to focus their energy somewhere. They focus it on their kids.[8]

Information and advice from social networks about good schools was also important for those interviewees, primarily the teachers and their families, who could not afford to live in such places. It was a neighbour, for example, who supplied Bernice Hughes with crucial information about a private bussing scheme that allowed her children to be educated in the suburbs rather than the city. Similarly, Don and Elisabeth Danson lived in his family home in South Boston and their children went to the local elementary school. He explained how his wife had talked to lots of people about the school, her sister had sent her children to the school and she had been very happy with their education. Finally, Don mentioned,

> They get a good education as it seems that the kids from [T] do better when they first get to middle school. It seems that way. One of our friends' teachers at one of the other middle schools said if she had it all to do again, she wished she'd sent her kids to [T]. That's always nice to know.

Contacts with fellow teachers, either well known or known only through others, were a crucial source of reassuring information and advice. Indeed, they could provide inside information about schools and their expert knowledge was highly valued because it was personalised and came from friends or friends of friends whom they knew and trusted.[9] Interestingly, Elisabeth also spoke of people she knew who 'chose to send their children to other schools for various reasons in [M] as [they] prefer more white schools'. They, however, valued the ethnic and cultural diversity of their school instead.

Social networks were clearly mobilised when the interviewees were confronted with a choice of schools as their children progressed from elementary to middle school and/or high school. Again, many of the interviewees observed what their family and friends were doing around them and, more often than not, followed their lead; they shaped their expectations as to what they would do and were a guide as to how to act. Jack Poole, himself privately educated, spoke of how most of 'the people I know, they have all sent their children to private high schools'. Not surprisingly, he envisaged doing the same although he and his family lived in one of the most affluent communities with the best high schools in the state. Similarly, his wife, Jane, spoke of how, 'Many people, I think, probably in my position would expect to send their children to private school from beginning to end. The majority of my colleagues, all their children are in private schools.' Interestingly, Jane had enjoyed a good public school education in which she excelled. She appreciated it very much. Nevertheless, she was aware that her husband had been 'educationally and academically challenged' at his private school 'in a very positive way'. She added, 'Now there's no doubt that people meet people of influence in places like private schools and so financially if we are feeling comfortable at that point, it is going to be very tempting to afford them the opportunity that he felt to be very good.' That such schools might facilitate such social networks did not go unrecognised.[10]

The wider, social effects of sending children to particular schools, therefore, were understood and appreciated. Ken Bailey, for example, made some general observations about how the public school system worked in the USA as well as some particular comments about his son's education. At the general level, he was well aware of how the system worked and he knew how to work the system although he neither emphatically endorsed existing institutional arrangements, nor enthusiastically embraced what he had to do to ensure his children's educational success. As Ken explained:

Its my firm belief that the town of [L], it's a self-fulfilling prophecy in that families who are interested in education, who themselves are well educated, who are going to push their kids in school and make sure they do fine, all live in [L] . . . The kids are basically from families of folks who are doing well professionally and value education.

He also noted that such towns attracted immigrants from Korea and China who valued education even more, and they 'leaned' heavily on their children. More specifically, his son had Asian friends who came from highly disciplined households. As he suggested:

These are the kids that my son plays with. They say 'I guess I should do homework.' [He thinks] 'They're all doing homework, maybe my parents aren't so crazy.' If all your friends are watching TV and playing Nintendo, your parents are the crazy ones and they go, 'Well, Jimmy's outside, how come I can't play?'

Instead, my sons goes, 'Cheers. I'm glad I'm not doing as much as he is' so it's all compared to your circumstances, the way I view it.[11]

Drawing on their experiences at work, many of the teachers were conscious of the importance of their children socialising with other children whose parents occupied a similar socio-economic status and who valued education and tried to inculcate these values into their children. Linda Chapman, for example, spoke of how,

You want your kids to be around other kids that are right for them and have the same values because they work very hard. You really want your children to be in a place where other parents value education and they have similar kinds of backgrounds and interests.

Some of the teachers lived in relatively affluent suburbs where they could increase the probability of their children socialising with other such children, while other teachers did not. There were downsides, however, to placing your children in the more affluent environments. Ray Chapman was greatly concerned about the limited economic diversity. He spoke of how,

There are hardly even people that are like the people I grew up with and that makes me nervous for them, I think . . . In fact, one of the things Lesley and I find a challenge and work consciously to do is to have them interact with people from a lower social class than we are because I am a little bit worried about attitudes that are drifting in because of the [N] community about what it means to be working class. I kind of self-identify having working-class roots so a respect for people in the trades or who have craft skills that not necessarily involve college. I don't know whether that lesson will take. I'm more worried about the Mercedes that you get at age sixteen. That's the value gone.[12]

Overall, it became apparent that the American interviewees mobilised their social networks as soon as their children became involved in the school system. By talking to friends and acquaintances, for example, they established the academic reputation of schools to send their children to. Clearly, there was much 'dinner table' talk about good and bad schools, not least in the context of a variable public school system that many of the interviewees felt had declined since their day.[13] Professional colleagues and loose contacts were very important in establishing the academic reputation of schools for the geographically mobile into Boston – usually the medics – while family and long-standing friends as well as fellow teachers were important for those who remained local to Boston and surrounds. Again, the effect of social networks led to a concentration of the affluent medics into the exclusive white communities surrounding Boston and for the less affluent teachers to seek out the best towns outside the city. The interviewees were also anxious to ensure that their children socialised with other children like themselves, namely, the offspring of educated parents who valued educational success. Socialising with other such children kept their children on track rather than being diverted away from credential success. Many of the interviewees, however, were aware and sometimes concerned that their children were rarely exposed to people from different races and classes so they had little sense of America's diversity. Expectations and norms about high levels of consumption concerned them too.

Social resources, higher education and beyond

All of the interviewees expected their children to go to college and, especially in the case of the medics, to go to some of the top schools including Ivy League schools and beyond. First and foremost, they wanted their children to get into the top schools so that they would enjoy a top-level education that would place them well in the job market. Academic success, in this respect, was crucial. That said, the interviewees also remembered the importance of being around other 'high calibre undergraduates, learning from them and socialising with them'.[14] They wanted their children to enjoy such 'exposure' to other bright people who would go into important jobs and become people of importance (i.e. with power). The advantages that might accrue from this resource were appreciated. Don Danson spoke of the importance of friends and contacts met at college or university. As he suggested: 'With a lot of people, you are sort of setting yourself up for life. This doesn't sound quite right but if you make the right contacts it will carry you on through your life.' At the same time, Don acknowledged that the importance of social networks could not be overstated. He pulled back from saying it was the crucial resource in people's lives. As he said:

OK, I went to [S]. Say, I happen to interview and the guy that interviewed me, maybe, he was alumni [S], he might try to give me a little bit better of an advantage because I am an alumni and then the other guy maybe went to another school down the street. In that way it would help but if someone is smart enough or if they get into the right situation they are going to do well no matter what.

Be that as it may, some of the interviewees' children had expressed a desire to go to an Ivy League or other top school even though some of them were incredibly young to do so. That they knew family and friends who went to such institutions made it a familiar rather than a distant aspiration. Gillian Wolkowitz talked about how her daughter, Tina, aged thirteen, was considering places such as Harvard, Brown and Dartmouth. As she explained:

She is also interested in Dartmouth because we have a cousin who graduated from Dartmouth, well, a couple of them but one that she is very close to who is now sailing around the world who really impresses her and has talked oodles about Dartmouth, and we went to his graduation.

Her husband, Roy, also talked about how Tina's career aspirations to go into law were influenced by 'role models'. He said:

My wife's best friend is a very wealthy lawyer who has a couple of back-to-back beach houses on Long Island. That's where we spend our summers so she gets a first-hand look at the lifestyle. She now knows what it takes to go to school and college and to become a lawyer. She has a chance to see what the rewards bring. They have two big houses. They have a boat, a couple of boats actually. They have cars. They had round the clock help and their idea of summer work is they will come out and spend a week and they will have their faxes and telephones and they do all this business. She's there and hears all this and it's very exciting. Arranging to meet clients and judges from the beach. I think she thinks this is what all lawyers do.

These were the people they socialised with who, in turn, influenced their daughter's social world.[15]

The interviewees' social networks and their children's emerging networks had a powerful influence, therefore, in shaping their hopes and plans. They were powerful in applying negative as well as positive social pressures, however. Financial considerations loomed large for David and Sarah Neale as their eldest daughter, Katy, prepared to go to college. They could not afford the fees to send her to the more prestigious colleges so less reputable institutions had to be considered instead. In the end, Katy successfully obtained a full athletics scholarship to a university in the Mid West. Sarah recalled her daughter's friends 'kind of belittled it' because they had not heard of the university and it was not close by on the East Coast. Sarah was 'really proud' of how Katy dealt with the situation and delighted that her daughter was now travelling the country and enjoying a variety of experiences. David Neale also spoke of the social pressures on his daughter and how she desperately wanted to follow her friends to some of the more prestigious colleges on the East Coast. He explained:

It was very hard for her. She was really upset about it. [B] is so affluent or whatever. It doesn't look like it's affluent around here and it is not, but a lot of her friends are going to great schools or very expensive schools and she was really cognisant of that and there is so much pressure to go to the best school.

This example certainly captured the impact of friends and acquaintances in shaping the expectations and pressures to follow certain educational and occupational pathways on the interviewees' children.[16]

Interestingly, whether as a virtue of necessity or otherwise, David adopted a critical perspective on the social pressures to go to the top schools. He acknowledged the advantages of going to elite institutions like Harvard. That said, he also believed that it was possible to do well elsewhere without spending so much money. David said, 'I am the champion of the smaller university. Learn what you can and then challenge those people.' Other interviewees adopted a critical stance to the status of such schools. Ken Bailey, again, was of the view that it is 'the person that makes the career and not the school you went to'. Reputations, after all, were often overrated and should not be accepted unquestioningly. Similarly, many of the interviewees, for example, Nadia Khan, wondered whether such places offered the best education as it was research fellows and not professors who taught people. The professors certainly did not get to know (and, it followed, did not care about) their students. Yet, returning to David Neale, he felt confident about the decision he had to make for his daughter because he could draw on his social networks for reassurance. As he explained:

I'm from the Mid West and I think she has a great opportunity at [K] and she had some good opportunities that are reasonably priced so I think she is better off where she is. I certainly made an executive decision like you are going there but I knew [K]. I knew the school when I worked at [P] because their chemistry department was outstanding and I worked with maybe five or six people who had gone to the University of [K] so I knew it was an outstanding school and good value.[17]

A number of the interviewees' children had gone to or were making their way through university and college courses. None of the teachers' children had attended the most prestigious Ivy League schools although some had gone to other reputable institutions (such as one of the Seven Sisters' women's only colleges) or small private colleges that had a 'decent name'. The interviewees talked about how their children chose their university or college. Of the utmost importance, to be sure, were entry requirements and likely SAT scores. It was, of course, academic credentials that dictated entry to such schools. In addition, the interviewees made reference to the importance they attached to the status or standing of colleges, of particular departments, courses and so on. Again, the issue of status – academic or otherwise – was established by talking to their friends and acquaintances. Their children did the same. Thus, the social world in which they lived and the social networks in which parents and children were connected to others, influenced their choices, decisions and actions. Interestingly, Carole Gedick felt that the fact that her youngest daughter, Hester, had gone to one of the top high schools in the state contributed, alongside her SATS scores, to her success in going to a good college. Other teachers' children were only able to go to local community colleges that did not have such prestige. Status considerations fell by the wayside.[18]

Some of the interviewees' children were finding their feet in the labour market. The influence of social networks in helping them establish themselves more firmly, however, was readily apparent. Immediate and extended family were important. The interviewees' children and their partners often helped each other. When the Rothmans' son, Jack, considered a career in teaching, Joanna Rothman described how,

> Our oldest daughter, her father-in-law is Principal of an elementary school in [S] and she, through him, arranged for Jack to intern at her father's elementary school so he spent three months there and they loved him over there but, by the end of that, he decided he didn't want to be a teacher.

The influence of other in-laws came up too. Martha Lopez spoke of how her son-in-law helped her son, Phillip, obtain his first job on graduating from college. As she explained:

> He came home in the summer and tried to find a job in Boston and, of course, Boston has this tremendous pool of young people coming out of college who want to stay in the area. He was having trouble finding a job. At that time, Silvia and her husband were living in [C] and Matt was working for [M] and he said, 'If you want to, come out here. I'll see if I can set up an interview.' So Matt set up an interview and Phillip packed up the car and left the next morning for [C]. He went to [M] and sat the interview, got the job and stayed with Silvia and Matt until he could find an apartment.

Phillip got an entry-level job in customer services. It was a 'foot in the door' that allowed him to move on to other jobs in the finance sector relatively speedily.[19]

Friends were influential too. After a spell as a scuba-diving instructor, Jack Rothman returned home and worked in a number of temporary jobs that he obtained through a job placement service where his friend worked. He spent a short period of time in retail but decided it was not for him. On a change of jobs, his father William Rothman said, 'He decided that he didn't think he wanted to do retail and the friend at the placement service knew that and when a job came on his desk [that Jack went for], he called Jack. Then Jack switched over and he worked for [F] which is a pretty large corporation.' He had had a series of entry-level jobs in a big electronics company and after three years was in his third position in systems management. William Rothman was intrigued and excited at the way his son's career was developing at the corporation.[20] Jack enjoyed good pay and benefits, notably health insurance, and the possibility of doing an MBA paid for by the organisation. Jack's friend, in this respect, had played a pivotal role in securing entry into the organisation although, of course, subsequent success depended on his own performance in the job. Similarly, Martha Lopez's son drew on his friends. When his sister and her husband moved, he found himself isolated and alone. Martha described how, 'He had been out to [C] to visit some classmates from college and so he packed up his car and moved to [L] and stayed with these guys for a little while, found a job in about two weeks and a place to live and has done very well.' Although his friends had not helped him directly in the job market, they had facilitated his move with help with accommodation that set him on his way.

Social contacts, therefore, were important but it cannot be denied that luck also played a part in these young men's careers. The 'luck' associated with social contacts was evident among looser ties too. Carole Gedicks' younger daughter, Hester, had majored in biology for example, and while she had enjoyed numerous summers working with dolphins, she knew that the pay in such jobs was poor and she had loans to pay back. After a period travelling, Hester returned home to find a job. As her mother said,

She started to look for jobs and she was on her way to a job fair one day and she had to stop at our Internist. She said, 'Do I look great? I'm going for a job.' Carol said, 'You need a job. My secretary has just had a baby six weeks earlier. Would you like to take her place?' Hester said 'I might just be interested. I go to this job fair and then I'll let you know.' So, that's where she has been working, sort of being a medical secretary I guess is what you'd call it. Although it's been fun to practice, I think she knows it's not what she wants to do for the rest of her life but it's kind of interesting and I think she is learning a lot about medical terms and all that. I would bet, give her another year, and she'll have figured out what she wants to do because until you really know what you want to do it's not worth going to graduate school.

Luck, therefore, was a factor in this example. What is also interesting to note in this brief discussion of early careers is that academic credentials were only one of the factors shaping these young people's careers.[21]

Overall, as well as being academically successful, the interviewees wanted their children to go to top colleges where they would be exposed to other bright young people, accomplished professors and so on.[22] Again, this was seen as part of the challenging educational environment that they hoped their children would enjoy. They also acknowledged that these young people might eventually occupy positions of importance, become people of importance, who could be an advantage to their children. The way in which social contacts could be a resource to be mobilised in this way was recognised, therefore, although it was also felt that smartness always won out at the end of the day. It was clear that the interviewees' social networks of family, friends and acquaintances were already shaping college aspirations and job ambitions. So were the interviewees' childrens' emerging networks of friends although the negative side of these social pressures was keenly felt by those not in a position to go to the best colleges. While some interviewees adopted a critical position on matters of reputation and status, they did so, it seemed, from the vantage point of social contacts who could provide inside information on colleges and so forth. Finally, a small number of interviewees' children – effectively young adults – were establishing themselves in the labour market and the importance of family and friends and some luck was obvious in finding entry-level jobs and temporary work in difficult labour market conditions. Academic credentials, it should be noted, were only part of the story.

Social resources and Britain education

Like their American counterparts, the British interviewees drew on their social networks of family, friends, neighbours and colleagues from work for information and advice about the best schools to send their children to. They drew on such advice at every stage of their children's education. Bridget Underwood (mentioned earlier), sent her two daughters to a private nursery school when they were young and she recalled how, 'It's got a really good reputation because it trains nannies so I'd heard of it. My mother-in-law told me it was wonderful and her friends said it was wonderful.' Indeed, it was by talking to people in their social networks that the interviewees established the reputation and status of schools. Frequent reference was made to the 'good reputation' – primarily defined in terms of good academic results – of the schools they had chosen for their children.[23] Some of the choices, as we know, were about private schools while others were about state schools. Heather Foster, for example, spoke of how she considered a number of private schools for her daughter, Stephanie, and eventually settled on a school that many of her friends' children had also attended. As Heather explained, 'I also knew a lot more people that had had their daughters at [M] – for example, my husband's business partners.' It was the norm, it seemed, for many of her and her husband's friends to send their children to private schools and, of course, to be in a financial position to do so. They invariably took the advice of friends and followed their lead in sending their children to the schools they had recommended.

In taking advice from people in their social networks and acting on those recommendations, the interviewees sent their children to schools where they would mix with the children of parents who could also afford to send their children to such schools and they had similar educational aspirations for them too. Their children mixed with the children of parents with similar economic resources and cultural capital. Celia Watson, for example, spoke of how, 'We sent (our son) to [A] prep school which is a local prep school. It's a private prep school. It prepares all the kids for the grammar schools. The people that we knew sent their children there. It had a good reputation.' Interestingly, she went on to say:

In the area, all my friends, everybody knew about the school, it had a very good name. The local school that Robert would have been assigned to was [F] and it had most of the kids from the council estate. Had he not gone to a private school, the local authority primary school was [F]. So being pushy middle-class parents, we decided our children would go to the private school.

Sending her son to private school, therefore, was also about distancing him from poor working-class children living on council estates, seemingly without ambition.[24] Thus, unsurprisingly, these interviewees often mentioned the positive influence of peers on their children's education. Lawrence Foster talked of how his son had done well, noting 'All his peers, they have all done well. They are all ahead.' It was the norm, therefore, for the affluent doctors' children to be mixing with other seemingly 'bright' middle-class children. Their social networks were in the making and their influence on their children assured.

Of course, drawing on the advice of social contacts was equally important to the interviewees whose children went to state primary schools. Again, they sent their children to schools with good reputations that they ascertained from family, friends, neighbours and colleagues from work. For those who had been geographically mobile in pursuit of their careers – which was more the case for doctors and their families rather than for teachers and their families – colleagues at work appeared to be the most significant source of information and advice. As Julia Dodd explained of her two children, 'They both went to the local primary school which is [B] school, which had a good reputation, and I suppose I picked most of the info from the people in the NHS, probably I guess, at that sort of time when we were thinking about those sorts of things.'[25] For those who still lived in areas close to where they grew up, family, neighbours and long-standing friends were an important font of local knowledge about good schools. That said, many of the teachers also knew teachers in the schools their children attended and these wider contacts in their professional communities were important conduits of inside information. Jill Dowds spoke of how she had 'chatted with a teacher' that she knew at her daughter's school and she was able to say with confidence, 'We were well aware at the time that it was a good school because I knew somebody that taught there. I liked the way the Head ran it. I liked the teachers' attitude to the children and it was a very happy school.'

These interviewees valued the academic reputation of their local primary schools although, again, they also attached considerable importance to their young children settling into school and being happy in a friendly school setting. Moreover, an extremely important dimension of their children's early education was that they mixed with other 'nice' children. Muriel Crisp, for example, was very happy that her children went to 'a nice school and they met nice friends in the environment'. The definition of 'nice children' was rarely made explicit although the subtext was that they were well-behaved children who were eager to learn and whose parents had high educational aspirations for them too. Interestingly, Susan and Nick Parry had a bad experience with their son, Luke, who attended a playgroup close to Susan's workplace in an inner city. As she explained:

He'd been going to a playgroup where he picked up rather a lot of foul language and one or two other bizarre things that I wasn't happy about and I realised that the child that he was picking them up from was a child who was going on to the same infants school as he was which was meant to be the best infant school in the area. I decided I wasn't very happy about this.

Initially envisaging her son attending the local school as it had a good reputation, she decided otherwise since this 'other' child was a 'horrendous influence' on her son. Acknowledging the influence of peers, it was apparent that the interviewees were anxious that their children socialise with other nice, usually middle-class children.[26]

The interviewees also called on information and advice from their social contacts as their children transferred to high school. As was noted earlier, many of the doctors and their partners transferred their children to private schools at an earlier age – usually 8 or 9 – so that they had a greater chance of passing the entrance exam at eleven and they could continue on at the same selective fee-paying school. They turned to friends and colleagues for information on how the system worked and, most importantly, how to work the system. Some of the doctors, for example, talked about how they 'heard' that some state primary schools or private prep schools were better than others in securing entry to private high schools and how this information influenced their school choices. Ian Lamb, for example, acted on the advice of colleagues to the advantage of his children.

Friends and networks in school and beyond   161

He felt 'worried and insecure' about the local high school education when he spoke to friends at work. He decided to transfer his two sons from a local state school to a private prep school that would facilitate access to a decent private secondary school. He admitted:

I didn't look at [the secondary schools] very carefully. I just took for granted what a lot of people said. The people I worked with or came into contact with, their children went to that [private prep] school and my wife and my friend's wife were friendly and talked about education and you get sucked into that system.

It is interesting to note how Ian Lamb did not establish whether the local state secondary schools were good or bad which would have taken some time and effort. He trusted the advice of his friends.[27]

It became apparent, therefore, that the interviewees talked to family, friends, neighbours and colleagues from work about educational issues in general and the education of their children in particular. It was also clear that the social circles included, for example, fellow doctors who had been educated at the schools under consideration, colleagues from work who had sent or were sending their children to these schools, and they often knew teachers at these schools too. Looser ties were also significant.[28] One interviewee, for example, casually mentioned that his accountant had been to the same school as his sons. They also drew on these people's expertise. Peter Smith recalled the discussions about the abolition of the grammar schools 'at dinner parties and things' when his children were making their way through the education system. He decided to assess whether his children would pass the examination for the old grammar schools that had become selective fee-paying schools. As he explained:

A colleague of mine, another doctor, was married to this girl whose father was the headmaster of a school, a very good school. Barry, that's Shirley's husband, asked Shirley if her father would assess our two kids. And really, what I wanted to know was whether they had the ability to go in for the examinations for the old grammar schools. So David, that's the headmaster, he assessed them, he said he thought they did have the potential. So, right, that was it. The primary school they went to, we told them what we'd like them to do and Damian went to [M] and Danielle went to [W].

Most of the teachers' children went on to state secondary schools of academic repute. Again, information on academic standing was obtained from people they knew, sometimes well and sometimes not. Their sources of information included siblings who taught at secondary schools or sent their children to these schools and local families they had got to know, often through their children, who sent their older children to the school or knew of its reputation from others.[29] Such local knowledge, it seemed, was not difficult to acquire. As with those doctors who sent their children to private schools, good academic results were of paramount importance although social considerations – the kinds of children their children would mix with – were highly valued too. As Mary Bull said regarding her choice of secondary school for her sons:

The intake actually mattered to us as well. [It] sounds very snobbish doesn't it? . . . I've always felt that my younger one, sort of when he was ten or eleven, he was one of those who could go either way. Put him with the wrong group and he'd follow the wrong way. So I didn't want him having that opportunity of doing that. Let's put him with the right ones and take him that way. I mean I might be doing him a great disservice here.

Pressed on what she meant by the social intake, Mary said, rather embarrassed, 'Middle class. Yes. Sounds snobbish but . . .' The interviewees, it seemed, wanted their children to socialise with other 'well motivated' children who would influence their motivations and reinforce their parents' educational aspirations.

On the whole, the interviewees talked of how their children's social networks reinforced the pursuit of educational success. For some, the 'inevitability' of their children's progress through school, university and into a good job could be explained by the social worlds to which they belonged. Bruce Brown spoke of how his children 'never contemplated anything else', adding:

I suppose they've seen everybody around them, their contemporaries at school, my sister's children – one went to Oxford, one went to Cambridge – they're all professionals so they're surrounded by people doing professional type jobs so that was the sort of thing they had to do.

Those who sent their children to private schools expressed these views with ease but those interviewees who sent children to state high schools – all teachers and their partners – were more aware of and anxious about school friends who might distract their children. They spoke about the anti-academic pressures that their children had encountered, not necessarily among their friends, but among others in the school. Norman Johns recalled that his two daughters, 'Were picked on and bullied because their work ethos was high and the work ethos of the majority of the parents' children in the school was not quite academic achievement.' Similarly, Pauline Lomax and Martin Webb – whose daughter was not at a highly reputable secondary school – were well aware that her peer group would be small and she would have to be very self-motivated to do well. While other children enjoyed some comfort in being in the company of motivated children, they knew it would be tougher for their daughter to succeed.[30]

As in the USA, the British interviewees drew on their formal and informal social contacts for information and advice on the reputation – primarily academic – of schools and they usually followed their lead in sending them to the same institutions. Similarly, the more geographically mobile medics and their families drew on a smaller network for advice, in which their colleagues from work were important, while the less mobile teachers and their families could cast a wider net embracing extended kin, old friends they grew up with as well as fellow teachers from their occupational community.[31] Whether the interviewees sent their children to private or state schools, they were preoccupied with its social mix because they were keen that their children learn and socialise with the children of other educated parents with high educational aspirations like themselves. This issue was important to the interviewees as they were well aware of the influence of other children – how other nice, well-behaved bright children could challenge them and how badly behaved unintelligent children could distract them – on their own children. They preferred to reduce the risks of these bad influences that might undermine academic success. Again, it was evident that the interviewees relied on their social networks for advice and information about choice of secondary schools and it was invaluable information because it was relatively easily acquired. Moreover, it was information and advice that could be trusted given it came from like-minded friends and acquaintances. Such contacts – including close and loose ties – were important in this respect on how to work the system to their advantage. It was not surprising to find, therefore, that almost all of the interviewees' children were attending academically reputable schools and only one family had knowingly put their child at 'risk' (although they wanted to reject the idea it was a risk).

Social resources, higher education and beyond

The interviewees also talked about the many ways in which they used their social networks to help their children into further education, higher education and beyond. Again, talking to people and getting advice was important as their children moved to different institutions – different schools, sixth-form colleges and so on – and as they embarked on new courses – A levels, BTecs and so forth. Drawing on their social circle of friends often appeared to be crucial in helping those whose path through the educational system was less than straightforward. Celia Watson's son, for example, struggled with a range of health and behavioural problems over a number of years but finally achieved his O levels in his late teens. He then completed an accounting technician's course at a local technical college. On this next step, Celia explained:

We had looked at [S] Technical College and discovered this course and we actually knew one of the lecturers on it so we rang him up to ask his advice about it. And they interviewed Robert and he got accepted on it. I just confess he did help him a bit on the course. He passed the first part of the course but not the second. But he could re-sit which he did twice. And he could do it outside college so you could get a job. Then he got a job on his own merit. We didn't do it for him.[32]

Celia, therefore, could draw on her contact, who happened to be a professional in the field of education, and approach him for detailed information and advice about the suitability and appropriateness of the course for her son. It seemed also that this contact provided additional assistance to her son who needed much help to complete the course.

Other examples of the use of social networks were less dramatic but no less important in shaping the interviewees' children's careers. Julia Dodd's daughter, Amy, struggled with A level chemistry and, indeed, she noted, 'Lots of my medical colleagues whose kids have been to that school found that one teacher has been actually quite instrumental in turning quite a lot of kids off things.' Her work colleagues, therefore, had similar experiences and subsequently advised her when her daughter did badly. On finding a suitable place to retake her A level, Julia explained, 'There was just the one crammer place called [A] that some colleagues of mine's kids had been to . . . and so she did chemistry and re-sat in the February and she got a B.'[33] She went on to university the next year. Similarly, Rosemary Hill spoke of an uncertain time for her youngest son after he finally enjoyed some success at exams in his early twenties and the importance of information from a work colleague in shaping his next step. As she explained:

He got two A levels but didn't know what to do with it. I didn't know what he wanted to do and it was actually my Deputy Head – whose husband is a further education lecturer – who showed me in the booklet, you know the sort of guide to courses, and the [N] Institute had a course in Youth and Community Studies which actually could be converted into a degree course by doing an extra year if he wanted. So Mark decided that would be up his street . . . He got his Youth and Community Diploma and went on to do his degree and is now a BA.

Again, that Rosemary's social circle included fellow professionals in the educational field was an important resource that she could mobilise to her son's advantage.

Networks of family and friends were also important for choice of degree courses, universities and subsequent careers (and, again, often for those young people who were unsure of what they wanted to do). Sometimes, the advice came from specific people like wider family. Margaret Brown's son embarked on a university course in engineering. As she explained:

I think one or two of his friends were going to engineering so he thought he'd do engineering. I had an uncle who was an engineer and he thought it was a good thing to go into though he always said that the engineers were not properly recognised and not properly paid in this country. He rather warned James about this. I don't know whether this was why James wasn't one hundred percent sure about this. I don't know but anyway he got a good degree in the end.

Indeed, James later went into business and she recalled the desire to set up his own business came from 'my father. My father was always very business minded.' He was influential in shaping his desire to set up his own business. He wanted to work for himself rather than anybody else and he believed that it was easier to make money working for oneself than somebody else. Extended kin, therefore, were important in shaping James's aspirations, what he valued about a job and so on. The prevalence of such a family culture, among the self-employed and businessmen has been widely noted. The interconnection between the cultural capital of the family and social networks in the form of extended kin was important here.[34]

Other interviewees drew on their friends when seeking to advise and, more importantly, steer their children through university into good jobs. Their intervention was, again, often crucial in setting young people along particular career paths. As teachers, Ken and Hilary Butler had the pleasure of seeing their children enjoy upward social mobility into the top professions of medicine and accountancy. Their daughter, Victoria, was always clear that she wanted to be a doctor and enjoyed straightforward academic success. Their son, however, was unclear as to what he wanted to do and was not entirely successful in the path towards university. Explaining how his son came to do an accountancy degree, Ken Butler said:

I'm fairly certain it was through my interference in that I got a friend of mine who is an accountant to talk to him in some depth one day at the golf club and he persuaded Nigel it was a good basis for all sorts of jobs and so he went to university to do accountancy. Initially he wanted to do geography. I think he got a place at [L] but changed his mind after this conversation.

Unable to pursue a geography degree because his A levels were not good enough, he found a university that 'took him with his General Studies to do accountancy'. Their son was now a successful accountant so the influence of Ken's golfing friend was highly significant. That said, he noted that his son, Nigel, was 'not the slightest bit interested in accountancy. So he says anyway. You know, he still holds it against us.' The source of some sadness and regret, Nigel has never been happy in his job and was still looking for his niche elsewhere.[35]

The interviewees often acknowledged the importance of their social circle of friends more generally. Reflecting on how his son became a medic (and, indeed, specialised in his own area of expertise), Peter Smith stressed that he did not make his son go into medicine but he conceded, 'I think it was almost inevitable. Things like, you see, people that would come here [to their home] would be doctors, there'd be a lot of doctor's talk . . . So really a lot of our acquaintances are professional people. They are lawyers, they are dentists, they are doctors, teachers.' Indeed, he was 'able to have a word' with his medical friends who provided his son with important work experience. The medical talk was reinforced by the fact that Diane Smith was a nurse and her friends were fellow nurses who talked about hospital life. As Diane Smith said, 'Damian was always interested in medicine. From being a little boy, he'd ask questions about it. That's why I felt really he didn't know any other life.' Indeed, Diane went on to speak of the difficulties this posed for their younger daughter, Danielle, who tried to carve out some space from this seemingly exclusive medical world. She explained:

I think for a while, for a number of years, she may have felt that we wanted her to be involved in medicine in some way but we didn't but, of course, it was being talked about. What was hard, if we went out for a meal together, well I would listen in but I didn't want to upset her but I was aware that Peter and Damian would talk on about medicine and I could sense her tensing up.

They were absolutely delighted when she eventually decided on a career in teaching.[36]

The 'medical culture' of this family was obviously very strong because many of their friends and acquaintances occupied this same social world. There were, of course, teaching couples in the research and their children followed in their parents' footsteps although a career in teaching was not as highly valued, as noted in earlier chapters. Interestingly, it seemed as if some teachers were keen to stress that their social lives did not revolve around fellow teachers and, consequently, the influences on their children's university choices, career options and so forth were wide and varied. Sylvia Harrison's highly academically successful eldest daughter, Jackie, for example, was about to embark on a university degree in genetics, influenced by her interest in biology and a good relationship with a young biology teacher at school who gave her advice.[37] Their younger daughter, Angela, still at school, was considering a degree and career in physiotherapy and she had already spoken to a neighbour who had done such a degree as well as physiotherapists employed in a rugby club in which they were heavily involved. As Sylvia said:

We don't mix with teachers as such. We mix with people in general walks of life around the Rugby Club. There are a lot of teachers there and there are also a lot of people who, like us, don't mix with teachers and who are different people so we come across a lot of people. So, I'm not having a direct influence on what they are doing but by the very fact that we mix with all these other people, come across those in other professions, indirectly we are influencing what they're going to do.

Indeed, many of the interviewees emphasised that as their children got older, there were many influences on their children's views and their own friends were increasingly important at university about career choices. Gerald Jones's eldest daughter, for example, decided to become a management trainee with a major oil company after finishing her pure science degree at Oxford. On his influence here he said, 'No, I mean once they get to that stage, they're talking at university with their friends about what they're going to do. And I think one has relatively little input there.' Indeed, many of the interviewees spoke of the difficulties of advising their children about careers. Jill and Graham Dowds' daughter was training to be an accountant. They had tried to persuade Claire to consider the profession 'but she was adamant she wasn't going to do accountancy'. However, after a year of travelling, she returned home and eventually embarked on a career in accountancy. As they explained:

I think it might have been this bloke at university, that sort of starting talking to her about it because he got a job at [A] and he was talking to her about the big accountancy firms and what it entailed, what you get out of it. She came home one day and said 'I've applied to so and so and so now let's see what happens.'

After taking an aptitude test, Claire was offered a job with one of the major international accountancy firms in Manchester. In this instance, their daughter's friend reinforced her parents' wishes and his inside experience working in a top accountancy firm pushed her towards the pursuit of such a career.[38]

Frequent reference was made to the difficulties of helping young people forge specific careers where social contacts were absent. Muriel Crisp spoke of her nervousness in trying to help her second daughter, Bella, pursue a career in hotel and catering. On her lack of knowledge and contacts, she said, 'I mean I am a teacher. My husband's a teacher. Lots of our friends are teachers, you know. I don't know very much about what it's like in the real world at all. I don't know how you get on if you work in a hotel as a receptionist or whatever. I don't know.' Similarly, Ian Lamb spoke of how he and his wife 'knew nothing' of the television world in which their daughter wanted to pursue a career as a presenter. Janet Jones spoke of how her youngest daughter was interested in theatre management when she finished her degree at Oxford. As she said, 'It is a world that we don't have any connection with so she'll have to find out for herself how she gets on.' Lacking social contacts in these worlds, the interviewees very much stressed how they could not turn to family and friends for advice about how their children could forge a career in unknown fields, and they were unsure what work experiences were regarded as crucial for promotion and the very nature of managerial careers in these occupations.[39] They had looked at information from careers services, university handbooks and the like. Nevertheless, they were keenly aware that if they had had such social contacts, they could have used them as a shorthand way of acquiring basic information, supplying inside knowledge on how their children might enjoy successful careers and advising them on this basis. Again, such knowledge and advice was highly valued because they came from like-minded people they could trust. Without it, they were aware that they could not help their children as much as they would have liked.

Overall, the British interviewees drew on their social networks for information as their children carried on into further and then higher education. Advice on vocational courses, and courses leading to further qualifications, for example, were often important in helping the interviewees' children stay in the education system when setbacks were encountered. Similarly, the interviewees called on information and advice from family and friends as they helped their children choose degree courses with, of course, implications for the kinds of jobs they would do afterwards. More generally, the interviewees noted that their social circle of friends often included fellow medics or teachers who were influential in terms of providing important work experience as well as more general advice on career choices. It explained high levels of occupational inheritance. Even if their social circles did not include fellow medics or teachers, they socialised with other professional people who could give them information and advice on a range of professional careers. At the same time, the interviewees were also well aware of how their influence on their children declined as they moved from home to university and, as young adults, their children had their own networks and friends who influenced their emerging hopes and plans. They were cognisant of how they could not help children when they sought to forge careers where they had no contacts, and effectively reiterated the important point that knowledge and advice from their social circle were so important because they could be easily acquired and were to be trusted since it was personalised knowledge offered by people like themselves.[40]

Conclusion

In this last empirical chapter, I have described the processes by which my American and British interviewees, as middle-class parents, mobilised their social resources to increase the probability of their children's educational success. Again, I considered the way in which social capital was used as a resource in numerous choices, decisions and courses of action as the interviewees' children made their way through the school system. It was not merely part of a strategy of last resort as Goldthorpe and Bourdieu emphasised although, without doubt, social resources were very important when setbacks were encountered as exams were failed or only poor grades achieved. It was revealing to see how social contacts were an important source of information and advice about issues such as the academic reputations of schools or how to work the system to their children's advantage. Most importantly, this information could be acquired easily across dinner tables rather than via research that required a lot of time and effort. Moreover, it was information and advice that could be trusted since it came from like-minded friends and acquaintances.[41] It was, therefore, personalised knowledge, drawn from the experiences of their social circle, and not just objective facts and figures that were difficult to evaluate in the making of choices and deciding on courses of action. These empirical findings are more akin to Coleman's broader approach to the study of social capital as a resource in reproducing advantage and, arguably, also apply to Granovetter's general point about the social embeddedness of action to the sphere of education.

It was also interesting to see how the interviewees sought to shape their children's own emerging social networks to enhance the chances of educational success. They were eager to ensure their children socialised with other nice children who were keen to succeed in school and who were, by implication, the children of well-educated people who valued educational and occupational success. Simply put, the interviewees very much appreciated how local interpersonal relationships could influence their children's educational aspirations and occupational horizons. It became apparent that such social networks had a class character in that affluent, established middle-class medics and their families socialised with other medics and people in the top professions while the less affluent lower-middle-class teachers and their partners occupied a less exclusive albeit (semi-)professional social world. All that said, the interviewees became aware that they were but one influence on their children's hopes and plans as they became young adults and moved away from home and socialised with other young people that their parents did not know as they had known their children's school friends. Although they could mobilise their social networks to create the best social environment conducive to educational and occupational advancement, therefore, they did not have the power to determine how their children made the best of the opportunities presented to them. Despite their best efforts, a level of indeterminacy prevailed.[42]

8   Conclusion

I started this book on an autobiographical note talking about my personal experiences of social mobility and that of my sisters and brother. Despite our modest background, my youngest sister Deirdre and myself had the opportunity to go to university and get good professional jobs. Although Barbara did not go on into higher education, she took up the opportunity to train as a nurse in her early twenties and enjoyed mobility into a semi-profession. My brother John did not take up opportunities at school and college. It meant he started work in a lowly position in a factory and experienced redundancy more than once. That said, he has subsequently enjoyed work–life mobility to secure his current managerial position. In our different ways, we have been very fortunate and, yes, even though I am a sociologist, I would say we have been very lucky. I also stressed in the Introduction, however, that such stories of mobility are 'two a penny'. The sociological evidence shows that lots of people in Britain have enjoyed mobility from working-class origins to middle-class destinations, via education or otherwise, since the 1940s.[1] It has not been unusual for social mobility to be of the long-range kind either – including mobility from unskilled manual origins to high-level professional destinations. Comparative research also indicates that social mobility is very common in America too. To go further, the evidence shows that the experience of social mobility, including long-range mobility from modest agricultural backgrounds to high-level non-manual employment, is greater in the USA than in Britain and most other European countries. It is no wonder that the notion that America is a classless society is so popular.

My personal experiences, therefore, are captured in the sociological findings on patterns and trends in absolute mobility since the mid twentieth century in Britain as described by Goldthorpe. I have grown up in an era of major social change in the character of British society. If I focus exclusively on my family and the opportunities my siblings and I have enjoyed, especially in comparison to my parents, Britain does seem a more open society than it was in the past. Most people tend to believe this too. This is why, as I said at the beginning of this book, the empirical findings on relative mobility have not been easy to grasp as I have taught successive generations of students. It is not that the empirical findings on relative rates of mobility, comparing the chances of people of different origins securing middle-class occupations, in America and Britain, are difficult to understand.[2] On the contrary, the explanation of persisting inequalities – of how the expansion of professional and managerial occupations had created more room at the top thereby increasing the chances of people of working-class origin enjoying mobility into such jobs while not reducing the chances of people of middle-class background also doing so – is highly plausible. Goldthorpe's account of unchanging patterns and trends in relative mobility is very sophisticated. I can see also why his empirical findings led him to conclude that government attempts to reduce class inequalities have not been successful. I can also see why, in their comparative research, Erikson and Goldthorpe stressed America is not exceptionally open in comparison to Britain or other older, European nations.

Because the empirical findings have been counter to my own experiences and those of many of my students, my academic curiosity has focused on the stability of class relations in the context of change. To repeat the questions I posed earlier: How is this so? What are the processes by which class inequalities are reproduced over generations and thereby over decades and centuries? How do members of the middle class retain their privileges and power across different nations like America and Britain as well as other parts of the world? How have the middle classes proved successful in resisting legislative attempts, like increased educational opportunities, to create more equality? Does it mean such efforts have proved a complete failure? Should more or less be done? In the Introduction, I outlined the development of Goldthorpe's theoretical explanation of mobility patterns in some detail. I discussed his early ideas, buried in the fine empirical work, on how middle-class parents mobilise their economic, cultural and social resources to ensure their children also enjoy advantaged positions of privilege and power in their adult life. Against the background of debates about meritocracy, I noted how he developed this argument with reference to educational success and the importance of economic resources in the mobility process as parents try to ensure their children get the educational credentials that increasingly secure entry into middle-class occupations. At this juncture, I registered my disappointment with the way Goldthorpe developed his theoretical explanation of class stability, namely, emphasising the importance of the economic and ignoring cultural and social processes in class reproduction.

Finally, I discussed his account of how available resources shape the mobility strategies of middle-class and working-class parents in the seemingly meritocratic competition for educational and occupational success.[3] Again, as I am sure was evident, I found this account of middle-class reproduction and, for that matter, working-class reproduction, to be compelling in a number of respects. The theory certainly works as a micro-sociological explanation of macro-sociological regularities. Judging the theory in its own right, however, it is not so convincing. As I suggested, the characterisation of the working class, seemingly bereft of any resources, and the middle class, abundant in those resources, sounds like the classes of yesterday. His description of the working class certainly did not chime with my experiences of growing up in Britain in the benign economic climate of the post-war period of affluence when income inequalities were reducing, there was full employment and little job insecurity and members of the working class enjoyed affluent lifestyles and consumption patterns never experienced before. This same economic climate, of course, prevailed in the USA. The period was also characterised by a benign political climate as successive governments sought to reduce inequalities including, in Britain, the introduction of a free education system, and the expansion of opportunities for higher education including maintenance grants for children from low-income families. Again, this optimistic political climate existed in America and included federal and state attempts to reduce racial inequalities via the desegregation of schools.[4] Arguably, these favourable conditions allowed some children of working-class or blue-collar origins to exploit opportunities for higher education alongside children of the middle class. In this respect, everyone benefited in this era, which explains why class differentials in education did not decline.

To be sure, the economic boom and political optimism of that era have long gone. It is not hard to imagine that it is probably harder now for working-class children to go into higher education in Britain and America. Nor is it difficult to imagine how children from working-class or blue-collar backgrounds would be daunted by the introduction of tuition fees and the lack of maintenance grants in Britain and the spiralling fees of colleges and the amount of debt to finance higher education required in America. The implication of this argument, as I am well aware, is that Goldthorpe's theory of working-class reproduction might work better today. This leads me to his characterisation of the middle class. Again, it does not chime with my current experiences as I watch my siblings and friends around me, many of them members of the middle class of course, concerned and anxious about how their children will get on at school. It makes me think that Goldthorpe's characterisation of the middle class sounds more like the smaller privileged class of yesteryear and not the much larger, more heterogeneous middle class of today. The changed economic and political climate since the mid 1970s has affected the middle class too. Not all of the middle class enjoy high-level and stable incomes now. Those in the semi-professions do not have high incomes especially if they work in the public sector. Similarly, those in managerial jobs do not have job security especially in the private sector. Similarly, ongoing tax cuts in America and the legacy of twenty years of tax cuts in Britain have undermined the quality of public/state education. The middle and the working classes send their children through a much poorer system than before.[5]

It is in this harsher economic and political climate that middle-class parents seek to mobilise their economic, cultural and social resources to secure their children's occupational and education success. Arguably, the competition is tougher than before – or, at least, people perceive it to be – and the outcome cannot be guaranteed.[6] This monograph has drawn on the stories of a small sample of middle-class parents – medics and teachers – in Britain and America. It is a diverse sample in terms of gender, race and ethnicity. It is also a diverse group in terms of the interviewees' class backgrounds. I spoke to people from long-established upper-middle-class backgrounds, those whose parents had been mobile from working-class or blue-collar origins into the middle class so they were new to their position and those who were upwardly mobile themselves from modest social backgrounds. I had the opportunity, therefore, to talk to people whose parents could mobilise available resources on their behalf and those interviewees whose parents did not have such resources but helped them in other ways to succeed. In these discussions, the interviewees were children so to speak. I also spoke to them about being parents, now all middle-class parents, and how they were helping their children through the education system and, they hoped, into good jobs. Again, I was able to explore how parents with different amounts of available economic, cultural and social resources mobilise them in pursuit of their children's educational and occupational success. In other words, this research has allowed me to explore how the middle class are seeking to remake themselves from generation to generation in both old and familiar and new and novel ways.

The mobilisation of economic resources

Rather than simply summarise the key empirical findings that have emerged out of this comparative study, I want to conclude by reflecting on the theoretical implications of my research too. More specifically,

I want to return to the issue of the mobilisation of economic, cultural and social resources in the reproduction of class advantage. In the Introduction, I outlined Goldthorpe's thesis about the mobilisation of economic resources – including wealth, income and other forms of capital such as business enterprises and professional practices. I noted how Goldthorpe has consistently asserted that economic resources are the most important resources in the reproduction of privilege and power because they are exclusive goods (i.e. not owned by others) that can be easily transmitted from one generation to the next. The ownership of economic resources – and a lack of economic resources – shape mobility strategies in that it influences parents' evaluation of the costs and benefits of different courses of action in pursuit of their children's class stability or advancement. While I found much to commend Goldthorpe's thesis, especially with reference to his account of class differentials in educational attainment, I expressed some misgivings about the narrow focus on economic resources alone and the problems of focusing on family income too. I suggested, for instance, that it might also be important to consider the demands on income in terms of expenditure such as the number of children in a family. I also highlighted the importance of consumption choices – a preference for spending on foreign holidays or a fancy car, for example, rather than private education – on income. Focusing on income alone, I argued, was a narrow and limited way of thinking about the mobilisation of economic resources.[7]

When I spoke to the interviewees about their childhoods, they revealed a lot about how their parents used their financial assets to secure the best education possible for them. The sample included interviewees from established upper-middle-class and middle-class backgrounds who quite clearly used their income and wealth to pay for the best education possible for their children, namely, to pay for a private education directly. Most, however, used their money indirectly in being able to afford to live in affluent communities where they could send their children to good public schools in America. In Britain, economic resources were used directly and indirectly to ensure children secured entry into the best state grammar schools possible. Different institutional arrangements meant that the interviewees' parents employed their economic resources in varied ways to increase the probability of their children's academic success and, crucially, to circumvent different risks that might undermine success.[8] In America, it was crucial to avoid schools involved in desegregation while in Britain, it was imperative to avoid a secondary modern school education. In America, most of the interviewees from advantaged backgrounds enjoyed financial support from their parents through college. Some, however, reported economic difficulties meeting fees and expenses especially when their parents had younger children to support at home. In Britain, the middle-class interviewees' parents did not have to make substantial financial contributions to their children's higher education because they enjoyed the benefits of a free universal education system. The empirical material, therefore, certainly confirmed Goldthorpe's theory of middle-class reproduction although financial constraints were felt in America that were not experienced in Britain.

What, then, of those interviewees from modest lower-middle-class and working-class backgrounds whose parents did not have these economic resources? How did they succeed? The interviewees from such backgrounds were academically able students who enjoyed a good enough education in the top tracks of their large urban public schools in America or in grammar schools in Britain. The successful acquisition of educational credentials allowed them to pursue higher education. Against the backdrop of the period of post-war affluence in the 1950s and 1960s in both countries, their parents, who enjoyed stable and rising incomes, could give them some financial support. At the very least, they did not expect their children to contribute to family income from an early age. Of considerable importance, too, were other sources of economic support beyond the family in the form of federal grants, college scholarships and other forms of financial aid in the USA and state maintenance grants in the UK. That said, financial constraints were often keenly felt in the USA as they restricted the choice of colleges to the less expensive, less prestigious institutions and studies were interrupted when financial matters became most pressing, making the passage through higher education a very tough one for some. Despite these obstacles, however, these interviewees overcame the economic constraints to enjoy educational and occupational success in medicine and teaching. Unfortunately, Goldthorpe's theory of working-class reproduction does not allow for the fact that some members of the working class were able to go into higher education in the benign climate of the 1950s, 1960s and early 1970s.[9]

These are the main findings to arise out of conversations with my interviewees about how their parents helped them through school into good jobs. I also spoke to the interviewees about their roles as parents regarding these same issues. They were, of course, now all middle-class parents, although in selecting medics and teachers to speak to, I was capturing the experiences of a well-remunerated upper middle class and a more modestly paid middle class. Be that as it may, they both encountered different institutional arrangements in the 1980s and 1990s and, arguably, they had to confront a poorer and more variable public or state education system in both countries. Seemingly, the risks to academic success were greater than in their own day and the importance of economic resources to increase the probability of academic success, greater. Accordingly, the most affluent interviewees in both countries simply opted out of the public or state system by paying for a high-quality private education that would facilitate their children's acquisition of educational credentials.[10] With regard to higher education, however, even the affluent physicians and their partners in America were increasingly anxious about the spiralling costs of college fees especially to the more academically reputable institutions that they expected their children to attend. Their decisions and choices were not unfettered by economic considerations. The affluent doctors and their partners in Britain, however, remained untroubled by the introduction of nominal tuition fees and the abolition of maintenance grants. Once again, therefore, the empirical material has confirmed Goldthorpe's theory about middle-class reproduction although my interviewees' narratives suggest that it is not so easily secured in America as in Britain.

At the same time, Goldthorpe's theory of middle-class reproduction does not capture the experiences of a less affluent middle class who do not command the economic resources to pay high private school fees or live in exclusive residential communities. Instead, they have had to confront a variable public or state system where lack of investment, poor facilities etc. do not appear to be conducive to academic success. They are also confronted, as in America, with huge college fees so that financial considerations loom large in the choices and decisions they can make about their children's higher education. Such financial worries about the cost of higher education are increasingly perplexing British middle-class parents too. The difficulties of securing their children's future were expressed more forcefully in the USA than in Britain. Middle-class reproduction, for these parents, therefore, was not easy or straightforward especially when the mobilisation of economic resources could only increase the propensity for academic success, but certainly could not guarantee it.[11] That is to say, there were examples of children who were not academically successful in school and they were found among the medics and teachers alike although less so among the former than the latter. There were instances of further economic investments in search of educational success over a longer time period among the more affluent in order to block downward mobility. Still, not all of the interviewees' children were on course to maintain their parents' social position or had done so, although how far they fell depended on how high they started out. They fell into lower-level professional jobs and not into blue-collar jobs.

Without doubt, the empirical evidence has shown that family economic resources are crucial to the reproduction of middle-class advantage. This simple statement might appear to confirm Goldthorpe's emphasis on the singular importance of economic resources over cultural and social resources in the reproduction of privilege and power. His emphasis implies that economic resources are at the root of all other types of resources. Cultural and social resources are reducible, in other words, to economic resources in the last instance. The empirical findings also show, however, that economic resources are crucial in terms of their conversion into cultural resources. That is to say, their significance lies in the fact that they can be converted into cultural resources in the form of educational credentials. To make this point, of course, is to confirm Bourdieu's view that the importance of economic capital lies in the fact that it can be converted into an institutionalised or objectified form of cultural capital. It is the conversion of economic capital into cultural capital, of course, that is all-important to Bourdieu. Now, Goldthorpe does not deny the importance of this conversion process in that he clearly documents the way in which economic resources are used to buy educational credentials. He places his emphasis, nevertheless, on the importance of economic resources in themselves and not on their conversion to something else (i.e. cultural resources or cultural capital), as Bourdieu prefers. I would contend that economic resources are significant in themselves and in their conversion to other forms of resources. It is for this reason that I remain of the view that economic resources alone cannot explain the reproduction of class positions. The way in which they are so deeply intertwined with cultural and social resources implies that all three types of resources are of equal importance and must be considered simultaneously. At the same time, it should not be forgotten that the mobilisation of economic resources may increase the probability of educational and occupational success but it can never wholly guarantee it.[12]

The mobilisation of cultural resources

In the opening chapter, I discussed how Goldthorpe's early theoretical ideas made reference to cultural resources in the reproduction of advantage. Indeed, Goldthorpe explicitly equated his concept of cultural resources with Bourdieu's notion of cultural capital. As he developed his theory, however, Goldthorpe distanced himself from Bourdieu. He criticised Bourdieu for his overly tight theory of social reproduction in terms of not being able to explain how some working-class children have enjoyed social mobility via the education system. Most importantly, he accused Bourdieu of effectively blaming members of the working class for their lack of educational success by suggesting they suffered from a poverty of aspiration. As I said before, I was disappointed with this development. After all, the way in which Goldthorpe and Bourdieu talk about the mobilisation/exploitation of economic, cultural and social resources/capitals suggests that their theories have much in common bar a few differences in terminology! Rivalry – where differences are emphasised over similarities – does not usually contribute to the accumulation of knowledge about the social world. To be sure, Bourdieu's theory has its shortcoming; the concept of cultural capital is remarkably slippery and how it works exactly is pretty hard to pin down at times. Be that as it may, the importance of cultural values and practices in the reproduction of advantage cannot be ignored or dismissed. It is my view that how cultural values and practices are shaped by class experiences of opportunities and constraints and how they, in turn, shape them, is crucial for any analysis of the reproduction of class inequalities.[13]

I spoke to the interviewees about the ways in which their parents had mobilised their cultural resources in the reproduction of advantage by focusing on their parents' educational dispositions and occupational horizons. This led me to consider Bourdieu's concept of cultural capital and his ideas of how advanced groups use their education, linguistic competencies, dispositions, values and so on to help their children do well in school and beyond. Again, the interviewees from upper-middle-class and middle-class backgrounds, whose parents were highly educated people, mobilised their cultural resources on their children's behalf. To be sure, they expected their children to be academically able like themselves, and that they would be as successful at school as they had been and secure entry into the more prestigious universities and colleges, again, on a par with if not better than their parents. They confidently assumed things would go well unless their children demonstrated otherwise. These interviewees also spoke of how their parents had had high occupational horizons for they expected them to go into high-level professional jobs like themselves. A very important caveat needs to be introduced here, however. Such high occupational aspirations applied much more to the men than to the women interviewees in both countries (although the start of changes in such gendered views could be detected among some of the younger women members of the sample who became medics). Again, therefore, the empirical material confirmed Goldthorpe's ideas about the mobilisation of cultural resources and, of course, Bourdieu's concept of cultural capital.[14]

Goldthorpe, of course, was highly critical of what he saw as Bourdieu's characterization of those in more modest positions suffering from a 'poverty of aspirations'. Was this so? On the contrary, all of the interviewees from more modest social backgrounds spoke of how their parents were very keen that they do well at school. Thwarted in their ambitions when growing up, they were eager that their children should make the best of new opportunities in the 1950s and 1960s. Goldthorpe's criticism of Bourdieu's ideas, therefore, is telling. The trouble with the concept of cultural capital is that it cannot allow for the fact that some members of the working class have been very successful in education and employment. That said, there is considerable merit to Bourdieu's ideas, for he captures the different ways in which those in modest positions engage with the education system. The interviewees from blue-collar or working-class backgrounds spoke of how their parents wanted them to do well but they did not always confidently assume that they would. Rather, they were cautiously hopeful about their children's talents and abilities and then delighted and hugely supportive when they demonstrated their academic prowess. Similarly, in terms of occupational aspirations, their occupational horizons were not as high as their advantaged counterparts and gendered views were again evident. In Britain, most notably, some parents would have been content for their children to leave school early and go into routine white-collar employment that they regarded as a step up from manual employment. Be that as it may, the interviewees' parents did not hold their children back for want of cultural capital and they did facilitate their advancement.[15]

The interviewees also spoke of how they were mobilising their cultural resources to increase their children's chances of educational and occupational success. Now all educated middle-class parents in professional jobs, they knew how the education system worked and the importance of acquiring credentials in order to secure entry into high-level jobs. Their own experiences meant they knew how to work the system too. Cognisant of child development theories, they took a keen interest in their children's intellectual development, monitoring progress against standardised tests to ensure their children were performing appropriately, if not better, for their age. They sought to inculcate in their children the values of hard work, discipline and deferred gratification and translated these values into how they conducted their everyday family life as they watched their children's educational activities and carefully controlled their free time. In this way, they sought to increase the chances of their children doing well at school and going on into higher education. To be sure, the interviewees from well-established middle-class backgrounds who had enjoyed an elite education themselves, approached the business of educating their children with more confidence than those from more modest middle-class backgrounds who had experienced a regular high school education, for example. They wanted their children to follow them to elite colleges of higher education while the educational horizons of other interviewees were not so high.[16] Be that as it may, this empirical material confirms both Goldthorpe's ideas about cultural resources and Bourdieu's ideas about how middle-class parents utilise their cultural capital to ensure their children's educational and occupational advancement.

However, what the empirical material also clearly demonstrated is that life is not so simple! Parents may seek to provide all the seemingly right cultural conditions that facilitate their children's educational success, namely, nurturing their children's intellectual abilities, monitoring their academic progress and carefully guarding the boundaries of their leisure activities. Doing all the right things, however, does not necessarily guarantee educational success with implications for occupational success. After all, there were plenty of examples among the interviewees whose offspring were struggling at school, who had obtained poor grades or who were simply not motivated and had dropped out of college. Not all of the interviewees' children were, therefore, academically able or, at least, not all were successful the first time around. Arguably, it was at these turning points, when setbacks were confronted, that the importance of economic resources became fully apparent, allowing children the time and space to retake examinations, pursue other educational options and so forth until they found their niche. Again, in this way, downward mobility into blue-collar or manual employment was avoided as far as possible. Indeed, it appeared that those who enjoyed the most economic resources had the greater power to monitor and control their children's lives, which might explain why the more affluent medics and their families encountered fewer problems, in comparison to the less affluent teachers and their partners. Be that as it may, even medics and their partners experienced disappointments and setbacks in the education of their children and their inability to ensure that their children maintain or improve upon their position cannot be ignored in any theory of class reproduction.[17]

So, the empirical evidence has shown that cultural resources are crucial to the reproduction of middle-class advantage. Simply put in this way, the findings confirm Bourdieu's theory of class domination. The middle class may have high cultural tastes that they can mobilise to their children's advantage. More important, however, is the way in which parents who have enjoyed educational success know how the system works and how to work the system on their children's behalf. They do so, of course, with a degree of confidence and a sense of entitlement. Those who have not successfully navigated the education system cannot approach and deal with it in the same way. That said, it must be noted that Bourdieu's preoccupation with issues of class domination meant he did not consider issues of class subordination – such as a lack of assurance or a perception of rights – in such detail. Interestingly, Goldthorpe's most recent outline of a theory of social mobility acknowledges the role of cultural resources in the reproduction of advantage once more. Drawing on a positional theory of aspirations, he considers the way in which differential class experiences of (economic) opportunities and constraints shape cultural values and practices. Without doubt, this development is to be welcomed. Arguably, however, Goldthorpe's theory falls into the same trap as Bourdieu's theory in suggesting that members of the working class do not aspire to go into higher education and, thus, lack cultural resources or cultural capital. Any theory of the mobilisation of cultural resources has to embrace the fact that they are inclusive goods that can be owned by members of different classes. This point implies, once again, that the mobilisation of cultural resources may increase the probability of educational and occupational success but they can never wholly guarantee it.[18]

The mobilisation of social resources

Goldthorpe's initial theory of the reproduction of class advantage from one generation to the next discussed the mobilisation of social resources. Drawing on Granovetter's work, he defined social resources in terms of social networks that can serve as channels of information and influence in the pursuit of occupational success. Again, however, social resources were subsequently dropped from his theory as Goldthorpe asserted the importance of economic resources in the mobility process. Indeed, it could be argued that social resources got caught in the crossfire as Goldthorpe placed a renewed emphasis on the economic in his critique of Bourdieu's theory of cultural reproduction. Interestingly, Bourdieu also acknowledges the importance of social capital, defined in terms of social networks, in his theory of social reproduction. It could be argued that his emphasis on the importance of cultural capital in the reproduction process has led Bourdieu to downplay the role of social resources in maintaining class stability too. As I noted, Goldthorpe and Bourdieu consider the mobilisation of social resources only when economic and cultural investments have failed to yield results in terms of academic success. Neither of them discusses the ways in which social resources or social capital are mobilised and exploited during the acquisition of educational credentials themselves. Both, in other words, proffer quite a narrow view of the significance of social resources in the reproduction of advantage. Social resources are tagged on rather than fully integrated into their theories. It is my view that any theory of class reproduction must acknowledge that social, cultural and economic resources are mutually constitutive of each other.[19]

I spoke to the interviewees about how their parents mobilised their social resources, their networks of informal and formal contacts, in the reproduction of advantage, drawing on the work of both Coleman and Granovetter. Both the American and British interviewees willingly acknowledged the influence of local interpersonal relationships on their educational expectations. The interviewees of upper-middle-class and middle-class origins spoke of the wider social pressures to succeed because they socialised with other middle-class children of educated parents at school and in their local milieus all of whom were preoccupied with academic success. Educational success facilitated entry into the better universities and colleges where they met and forged contacts of their own that subsequently helped their careers. To be sure, those from upper-middle-class or middle-class backgrounds had connections to other advantaged people like themselves that they met in various privileged settings. The sample included American interviewees from upper-middle-class backgrounds who were educated at private schools, who then attended Ivy League colleges, went to prestigious medical schools, secured highly sought-after residencies and landed plum jobs in reputable teaching hospitals. The contacts made in each of these contexts certainly provided important sources of information and advice. Very similar privileged life histories were evident in Britain too. The class character of social networks may well explain how the upper middle class come to occupy the most prestigious positions within a profession.[20] Overall, therefore, the privileged parents of my interviewees certainly drew on their social networks, both intentionally and unintentionally, in helping their children do well.

As with cultural capital, social resources were not the exclusive preserve of the privileged middle class, however. The interviewees from more modest lower-middle-class or working-class origins also spoke of the importance of local interpersonal relationships in propelling them forward. Peer pressure from other, academically able school friends and encouragement and moral support from teachers in school were a very important social support system that set them on the path to higher education. Educational success, once again, facilitated entry to higher education institutions where these interviewees made contacts of their own, including contacts with advantaged people, which were drawn upon as their careers developed. Accordingly, the interviewees from more modest social backgrounds also spoke of the importance of contacts in their careers as they enjoyed the moral support and encouragement of mentors, for example, in promotions to senior positions in their chosen professions. Again, there were examples of how they played a crucial role in helping people overcome obstacles in their early lives and allowed them to succeed in later life in America and Britain. At the same time, it was evident that these interviewees' social contacts were not so well placed as the contacts of the upper-middle-class interviewees. It is for this reason, among others, that those from modest backgrounds are more likely to occupy the less prestigious positions in their chosen professions.[21] Thus, these interviewees drew on informal and formal contacts including close ties associated with their family and looser ties beyond, in forging ahead.

I described the processes by which my American and British interviewees mobilised their social resources to increase the probability of their children's educational success. Again, I considered the way in which social capital was used as a resource in numerous choices, decisions and courses of action as the interviewees' children made their way through the school system in a way somewhat broader than that envisaged by either Goldthorpe or Bourdieu and more akin to Coleman's work on the role of social capital in the creation of human capital. That is to say, tapping on informal and formal contacts was not part of a strategy of last resort as Goldthorpe and Bourdieu emphasised, although, without doubt, social resources were very important when setbacks were encountered as exams were failed or only poor grades achieved. Rather, it was revealing to hear how social contacts were an important source of information and advice about issues such as the academic reputations of schools or how to work the system to their children's advantage. Most importantly, this information could be easily acquired across the dinner table rather than via research that required a lot of time and effort. Moreover, it was information and advice that could be trusted since it came from like-minded friends and acquaintances, be they fellow medics or teachers.[22] It was, therefore, personalised knowledge, drawn from the experiences of the interviewees' social circle, and not just objective facts and figures, which were difficult to evaluate in the making of choices and decisions on courses of action. Once more, therefore, these empirical findings confirm that the middle class mobilise their social resources to facilitate their children's educational and occupational success.

Similarly, it was interesting to hear how the interviewees sought to shape their children's own emerging social networks to enhance the chances of educational success. They were eager to ensure their children socialised with other nice children who were keen to succeed in school and who were, by implication, the children of well-educated people who valued educational and occupational success. In the USA, the implication was that children socialised with other white children and maybe Asian children but not African American children from the city. Simply put, the interviewees very much appreciated how local interpersonal relationships could influence their children's educational aspirations and occupational horizons (i.e. their cultural capital). It became apparent that such social networks had a class character in that affluent, established middle-class medics and their families socialised with other medics and people in the top professions while the less affluent lower-middle-class teachers and their partners occupied a less exclusive albeit (semi-)professional social world.[23] That being so, the interviewees were increasingly aware that they were but one influence on their children's hopes and plans as they became increasingly independent young adults and moved away from home and socialised with other young people whom their parents did not know so well. Although they could mobilise their social networks to create the best social environment conducive to educational and occupational advancement, therefore, they did not have the power to determine how their children made the best of the opportunities presented to them. Despite their best efforts, a level of indeterminacy always, it seemed, prevailed.

Thus, the empirical evidence has shown that social resources are highly significant in the reproduction of advantage. They play an integral role in the process by which middle-class parents help their children do well in school and beyond. By implication, therefore, social resources are heavily interconnected with economic and cultural resources. To repeat, social resources – in the form of local interpersonal relationships – were shown to play a crucial part in reinforcing and maintaining the cultural capital to be found inside the family. Community relations reinforced family values and practices by adding additional social pressures to succeed. Further, they were pivotal in the creation of cultural capital in that local relationships often raised children's educational and occupational aspirations above and beyond those of their parents. It is for these reasons that the interviewees in this study attached so much importance to whom their children mixed with and, as well as mobilising their own networks on their children's behalf, sought to nurture their children's emerging social networks too. This discussion goes beyond both Goldthorpe's and Bourdieu's rather narrow discussion of the role of social resources in the reproduction of advantage. In line with Coleman, it suggests that social resources are as important as economic and cultural resources in the pursuit of educational and occupational success. That said, like cultural resources, social resources are inclusive rather than exclusive goods in that people have more or less of them rather than all or none of them. It is for this reason, once more, that I stress that the mobilisation of social resources can increase the probability of success but there are no certainties.[24]

Implications for public policy

Overall, there are two main findings to emerge out of this research. The first finding arises out of the conversations I enjoyed with my sample of medics and teachers of diverse social origins about their own education. It was evident that the interviewees whose parents were in upper-middle-class and middle-class professional jobs mobilised their available resources to increase the propensity of their children's educational success. More importantly, there were interviewees whose parents occupied more modest class positions who had fewer resources to utilise on their children's behalf. Even so, these interviewees enjoyed social mobility from modest social origins to advantaged destinations. Now, the middle-class mobilisation of resources confirms Goldthorpe's theory of class stability without a doubt and, for that matter, Bourdieu's theory of social reproduction too. That some members of the American lower middle class or British working class are mobile, however, poses problems for Goldthorpe's and Bourdieu's theories. They are very tight theories that explain the stability of class relations in Britain and America but they do so without acknowledging the significant levels of absolute mobility, including long-range upward mobility, enjoyed also by many. The theories need to be refined, in other words, to embrace an account of how some members of the working class were able to enjoy educational opportunities that became available in the post-war period of economic prosperity and political optimism. My suspicion is that an elaboration of the theory would require breaking out of the exclusive focus on economic resources on the one hand, and cultural resources on the other, to consider the equally important role that economic, cultural and social resources – and their many and varied combinations – play in the reproduction of privilege and power.[25]

The second major finding arises out of the discussions I had with my interviewees about being parents and helping their children do well in school in order to get good jobs. This is at a time when education credentials are increasingly important as entry requirements into good jobs, especially high-level professional jobs. Again, it was evident that the interviewees, all as middle-class parents, were utilising their available economic, cultural and social resources on their children's behalf. That said, it was also readily apparent that the processes of middle-class reproduction were neither easy nor straightforward, at least for some sections of the middle classes. There were spiralling economic costs to be borne by the interviewees in both countries although those costs were more keenly felt in the USA than in the UK. Thus, while it might be said that middle-class parents readily and, indeed, aggressively participate in the meritocratic competition, the terms on which they do so are not all in their favour. Risks are there to be circumnavigated or not as the case may be. It is for precisely these reasons that middle-class parents have to participate so aggressively to ensure their children do well. The risks to educational and occupational success are many and varied. Arguably, however, one of the most important risks is when children of middle-class parents are not as academically able or inclined as their parents. To be sure, parents do all within their power to ensure their children do not fall into lowly jobs but there is downward mobility within the middle class. Thus, just as working-class upward mobility cannot be ignored, so middle-class downward mobility – disguised within the middle class or within other non-manual occupations – cannot go unacknowledged in any theory of middle-class reproduction.[26] Contrary to Goldthorpe and Bourdieu, the middle classes are not all-dominant and secure in their domination.

These two findings have implications for public policy. Goldthorpe expressed his grave disappointment that the highly favourable economic and political climate that prevailed in the 1950s and 1960s did not lead to more openness in Britain. Legislative and administrative measures proved severely limited because they underestimated the ability of those in powerful positions to utilise their available resources to preserve their privileged positions. Thus, the forces against change are considerable and only highlight the inability of government to effect change. These comments were a remarkably bleak assessment of what had not been achieved in two decades. I would venture a somewhat different conclusion. The benign economic and political climate was crucial in facilitating the upward mobility of members of the working class, via education, into middle-class positions. Without such political initiatives, for example, members of the working class would not have been able to enjoy these new opportunities. A similar argument can be made about the USA. African Americans, for instance, would not have enjoyed new opportunities in the USA either.[27] The evaluation of public policy, in other words, is not a zero sum game where political initiatives are deemed either a success or a failure. The effects of political initiatives were more modest than many had hoped for in the optimistic climate of the post-war period. In the harsher, more pessimistic economic and political climate that has prevailed since, when issues around social inequalities and social justice have not been high on the political agenda, it is possible to appreciate that political pressures and initiatives made some difference. In sum, politics does matter and does make a difference.

Those in positions of privilege and power undoubtedly seek to preserve their position from generation to generation. There is inbuilt resistance to change as Goldthorpe suggests which explains macro-sociological regularities. My micro-sociological project, however, has shown that the reproduction of advantage is not straightforward. The desired outcome is not always assured and there is considerable flux behind the picture of stability. A level of indeterminacy prevails. It was apparent that the difficulties that middle-class parents or, at least, that some middle-class parents encounter have left them unhappy with the present system. Affluent middle-class families just buy themselves out of the system. Opting out in this way was not available to most, however. Thus, in the USA there is much concern about the quality of public schools, the problems of violence and drugs in the school environment, the spiralling costs of tuition fees and the amount of debt children must build up to finance their higher education. Similarly, in the UK, there is much anxiety about the quality of state schools, uneven teaching in the context of a recruitment crisis, the introduction of (nominal) tuition fees and the abolition of maintenance grants. These concerns could be dismissed as middle-class preoccupations. Arguably, however, all parents whose children are currently making their way through school share these concerns and anxieties. Indeed, they are even greater issues for those parents, especially without economic resources, sending their children to poor inner city schools in the USA and the UK. That is to say, there are political alliances to be forged pushing for change that could make important political interventions as in the 1950s and 1960s.[28]

In the 1990s, Anthony Giddens, the British sociologist most closely associated with the Labour Party's Third Way politics, reflected on political responses to issues of equality in Britain. In an ideal world, he suggested, each generation of young people would prove themselves afresh in a meritocratic competition for good jobs. Rather than bring their family advantages with them to the starting block, everyone would start the race equal. There would be winners and losers but the competition would be fair and legitimate.[29] These are radical ideas. Even if initial conditions of equality could be introduced in real life, however, there are problems with meritocratic competitions. They raise questions about whether outcomes would be just. Competitions produce winners and losers and what people win and what people do not win – i.e. what they lose out on – needs to be considered further. Meritocracies can be good in rewarding winners but they can be bad in their harsh treatment of those who lose. It is for this reason that many British academics think America is a very harsh society. American sociologists Claude Fischer and his colleagues considered some of these issues in their powerful critique of the 'bell curve myth'.[30] In an era when income inequalities have widened (as they have in Britain too), it is important to think about whether the gap between winners and losers should be so wide. Should those who win have so much while those who lose have so little? Should people who do not succeed in competition for good jobs be forced to work in bad jobs which pay such poor wages that they barely allow for a minimum standard of living with massive implications for the quality of people's daily lives? I do not think so.

I have begun to consider issues that go beyond the remit of this study. The research has provoked me to dwell on them. It has made me think not just about issues of individual competition but about the system of inequality as a whole. That is to say, thinking about inequalities raises issues of equality of opportunity, equality of condition and equality of result. One further point needs to be made. This book has focused on education. Academics (especially) need to remember that it is not the only game in town.[31] That is to say, we need to keep in mind that people have many talents and not just academic ones or those measured by tests in school. After all, there are plenty of stories of people who were not especially successful in school who are then enormously successful over the course of their working lives. There are, of course, people who are not especially successful in their jobs or careers, however defined, who have talents and abilities in other spheres of their lives. All are worthy of reward and respect. Class and education have a big impact on people's early lives, to be sure, but it does not wholly determine their fate in life. The wider economic and political context in which people live out their lives is a major factor in how things turn out for them. This is why the study of social mobility – be it between generations or across people's working lives – is so fascinating. This is why there is still so much interesting research to be done – talking to different people living out their lives in different places at different times. Everyone has a compelling story to tell.

Appendix A:
The interviewees

Table A.1 *American physicians, partners' occupation and children*

Parents	Occupation	Children
Daniel Lewis Anna Gray	Hospital Physician Health Centre Physician	Amy
Michael Reed Laura Rosen[a]	Hospital Physician Lawyer	Simon
Charles Khan Nadia Khan	Hospital Physician Housewife	Sukhdeep
Ken Bailey Paula Bailey	Hospital Physician Social Worker	Kimberley, Joshua
Patrick Dutton Susan Pearson	Hospital Physician Medical Director	Lauren, Ben
Nikos Yacoby Yuko Yacoby	Health Centre Physician Health Centre Physician	Natalie, Nancy
George Marshall Judy Kennedy	Health Centre Physician Health Centre Physician	Matthew, Jack, Ethan
David Neale Sarah Nies	Hospital Physician Nurse Practitioner	Katy, Caroline, Daniel[b]
Jack Poole Jane Bennett	Hospital Physician Hospital Physician	Bethany, Amanda, Michael
Kerri Clegg Ross Clegg	Hospital Physician Hospital Physician	Thomas, Jacob, Layla
Susan Rogers Stephen Rogers[a]	Hospital Physician Engineer	Christopher, Samuel, David
Mary Moran Colin Moran[a]	Hospital Physician Hospital Physician	Joseph, Martin, Caitlin

[a] These interviewees' partners did not agree to be interviewed although it was possible to gather some information about them from the interviewees.
[b] Some of the interviewees' children were from previous marriages.

Table A.2 *American educators, partners' occupation and children*

Parents	Occupation	Children
Gillian Wolkowitz Roy Morgan	Middle School Educator Middle School Principal	Tina
Bob Farrell Joyce Farrell[a]	High School Educator Retail Clerk	Jennifer
Marion Chaves Christopher Chaves[a]	High School Educator High School Educator	Jessica
Rachel Garrett Alan Garrett	Elementary School Educator Customer Services Supervisor	Chloe, Neil
Linda Chapman Ray Chapman	Elementary School Educator Associate College Professor	Aileen, John
Martha Lopez Al Lopez	Middle School Educator Middle School A. Principal	Silvia, Phillip
Carole Gedicks Paul Gedicks	Elementary School Educator Engineer	Beverley, Hester
Elisabeth Danson Don Danson	Middle School Educator Insurance Broker	Nathan, Ian, Jonathon
Joanna Rothman William Rothman	Elementary School Educator Bank Lending Officer	Lisa, Jack, Sharon
Barry Waite Wendy Waite[a]	High School Educator Computer Systems Manager	Lee, Anthony, Ellen
Patricia Walker Joel Walker	Elementary School Educator High School Educator	Ross, Elaine, Tracey, Sean
Bernice Hughes Robert Hughes[a]	Middle School A. Principal Engineer	Camille, Anita, Melanie, Carla[b]

[a] These interviewees' partners did not agree to be interviewed although it was possible to gather some information about them from the interviewees.
[b] Some of the interviewees' children were from previous marriages.

Table A.3 *British doctors, partners' occupation and children*

Parents	Occupation	Children
Andrew Underwood	General Practitioner	Emily, Alison
Bridget Underwood[a]	General Practitioner	
Lawrence Foster	General Practitioner	Stephanie, Christopher
Heather Foster	Optician	
Stephen Dodd	Hospital Consultant	Amy, Michael
Julia Dodd	Hospital Consultant	
Ronald Watson	General Practitioner	Stuart, Lois
Celia Watson	Medical Secretary	
Peter Smith	General Practitioner	Damian, Danielle
Diane Smith	Nurse[c]	
Bruce Brown	Hospital Consultant	Anne, James
Margaret Brown	Housewife	
Ian Lamb	Hospital Consultant	Ian, Geoff, Molly
Pamela Lamb	Counsellor	
Gerald Jones	General Practitioner	Laura, Sarah, Fiona
Janet Jones	Radiographer	
Edward Myers	Hospital Consultant	Patricia, Catherine, Robert
Sheila Myers	Primary School Teacher	
Roderick Hunt	General Practitioner	Teresa, Scott, Andrew, Stephen
Mary Hunt	Primary School Teacher	
Robert Ball	Hospital Consultant	Lydia, John, David, Daniel
Eleanor Ball	University Lecturer	
Barbara Coombes	General Practitoner	Sonia, Sallie, Laurie, Andrew[b]
Donald Coombes	Secondary School Teacher[c]	

[a] I was successful in interviewing 12 doctors and partners in this case study.

[b] Some of the interviewees' children were from previous marriages.

[c] These interviewees were early retirees on medical grounds.

Table A.4 *British teachers, partners' occupation and children*

Parents	Occupation	Children
Susan Parry Nick Parry	Secondary School Teacher Journalist	Luke, Emma[b]
Pauline Lomax Martin Webb	Primary School Teacher Environmental Officer	Kathryn, Joseph
Mary Bull Alan Bull[a]	Secondary School Teacher Laboratory Scientific Officer	Duncan, Anthony
Diane Willis John Willis	Secondary School Teacher Secondary School Head	Celia, Mark[d]
Sheila Parker Dennis Parker	Primary School Teacher Secondary School Teacher	Melanie, Jonathan
Jill Dowds Graham Dowds	Primary School Teacher Computer Systems Manager	Claire, Rebecca
Sylvia Harrison Roger Harrison[a]	Primary School Teacher Secondary School Teacher	Jackie, Angela
Hilary Butler Ken Butler	Secondary School Teacher Secondary School Head	Nigel, Victoria
Rosemary Hill David Hill	Primary School Head Accountant[c]	Nicholas, Mark
Muriel Crisp Brian Crisp[a]	Primary School Teacher Secondary School Teacher	Alice, Bella, Julian
Yvonne Johns Norman Johns	Primary School Head[c] Secondary School Teacher	Samantha, Polly, Karl[b]
Sandra Booth Malik Booth	Primary School Teacher Businessman	Kirsten, Oliver, Juliet, Alex

[a] These interviewees' partners did not agree to be interviewed although it was possible to gather some information about them from the interviewees.
[b] Some of the interviewees' children were from previous marriages.
[c] These interviewees were early retirees on medical grounds.
[d] Some of the interviewees' children were adopted children.

Appendix B:
Doing comparative research

This appendix is a descriptive account of how I did the research that underpins this book. It focuses on the processes of doing the research by simply discussing the various stages of the project in Britain and America. I have tried to be frank and honest about my experiences in the writing of this narrative rather than offer a sanitised discussion of the methods I employed. Inevitably, however, reflecting back on how I did the research forced me to order my thoughts, think about how I would write up this discussion and so on. I had to find ways of summarising a piece of research that was conducted over quite a lengthy period of time across two countries. This meant that I had to make decisions about topics that I thought interesting and worthy of discussion and issues that I considered less critical and have omitted from this account. It is impossible, in other words, not to 'clean up' narratives of research to some degree and it would be disingenuous to suggest otherwise. Be that as it may, I hope the discussion of my experiences in doing this project will be interesting and beneficial to the readers of this book and researchers on other projects. In the following pages, I describe how I contacted doctors and teachers in Britain and America. Then I go on to consider the experience of doing the interviews – especially the extent to which my *aide memoire* worked – in both countries. I also reflect on the processes of transcribing the interviews, analysing the material and writing it up. Within this remit, I finish with a brief discussion of the politics of researching the middle class.[1]

Contacting doctors and teachers in Britain

As I mentioned in the Introduction, my interest in social mobility developed as I prepared for a series of six lectures on the topic in my first teaching position in the early 1990s. The prospect of giving these lectures was a daunting one and led me to read the sociological literature in (what now seems like) incredible detail. I read the work of the social mobility group – notably, Goldthorpe, Halsey and Heath – at Nuffield to get a sense of the empirical reality of patterns and trends in absolute and relative rates of social mobility since the 1940s. Of course, I was greatly influenced by their interpretation of the survey data they collected and the emphasis on unchanging relative mobility patterns and the implications for the stability of class relations. I also read Savage and his colleagues' book on middle-class formation that was published during this time in which they argued that the middle class in Britain is split into a professional middle class and a managerial and self-employed middle class.[2] The professional middle class is a cohesive and well-established entity because its members enter and then remain in the middle class while the managerial and self-employed middle class is much more insecure and marginal since its members often move in and out of the middle class over their working lives. That said, they found that the children of managers and the self-employed move into the professions in large numbers like the children of professionals thereby ensuring security in the middle class over generations.

This research led me to think about other divisions within the middle class, and especially the division between higher-level and lower-level professionals, managers and administrators (i.e. Class I and Class II of Goldthorpe's class schema). I wondered if (and suspected that) children of higher-level professionals and managers were more likely to enjoy stable and secure positions within the middle class, while the children of lower-level professionals and managers might occupy more insecure and marginal positions in moving in and out of the middle class.[3] It was these initial ideas that led me to design my research on intergenerational social mobility around case studies of doctors and teachers as examples of higher-level and lower-level professions respectively. It was also a way of ensuring that my study also included men and women and, specifically, that women would share the stage with men rather than merely feature as the wives or partners of professional men. That is to say, knowing that the medical profession in Britain has been dominated by men until recently, I expected that I would meet more men than women doctors in the course of my research. Similarly, knowing that teaching in Britain has long been and still is dominated by women, I anticipated that I would come across more women than men teachers while doing the project. Designed in this way, I submitted a research proposal to the University of Manchester and secured funding which gave me leave from teaching to conduct interviews and meet the costs of doing so.

I decided to undertake the research in Manchester for the obvious reason that I was familiar with the city although I had only lived there for a short period of time before I began the research. Travel expenses and so on would be modest. On starting the research, I elected straight away to interview both general practitioners (GPs) working in communities around Manchester and consultants working in the (teaching and non-teaching) hospitals scattered around the city. In this way, I could capture the two main career trajectories to be found in the medical profession in Britain. Initially unsure as to how I would get access to hospital consultants, I started my research by focusing on GPs. I randomly selected medical practices listed in the telephone directory (*Yellow Pages*) for central Manchester (which also includes Salford) and wrote to the GPs concerned. In the letter to them, I explained that I was doing a case study of doctors and their families by way of life history interviews. I indicated that I was especially interested in how they had become doctors and how they were helping their children through the education system into their chosen careers. I had no idea, of course, whether the GPs I wrote to had children or not. I just hoped that those who did not would pass me on to a GP in their practice with children or suggest other GPs I could contact. In this respect, my method of sampling was a hit and miss affair or, at the very least, it did not quite match the descriptions of how to generate a sample in standard methods books.[4]

In the event, I struck lucky in that my letters reached a number of doctors who had children still working their way through the education system who were willing to be interviewed. It was not difficult to find them and they were happy to help. I talked to GPs who worked in some of the affluent suburbs of south Manchester and GPs who worked in some of the most deprived areas of Manchester and Salford. I do not think that I ever appreciated the sense of vocation that influenced those GPs who worked in inner city Manchester and Salford. Their commitment to serving a community of people with considerable needs was humbling.[5] Depending on their preference, I interviewed some of the GPs at their practices and others at home. At the end of each interview, I asked the respondent if their partner would be willing to be interviewed as well. Again, I did not know what their partner's careers were and I certainly did not expect them to be doctors or teachers. I was interested in how they had the jobs they had, of course, and I was also equally keen to hear of how they were helping their children through school. I usually re-contacted my informant a week after the interview and ascertained whether their partner was willing to be interviewed and then made the necessary arrangements to do so. These interviews were invariably conducted at their homes. Some partners did not want to be interviewed. With only one respondent from the family, so to speak, I decided at this stage to omit them from the project.

On the whole, then, I did not encounter many difficulties in finding GPs and their partners with children who were willing to talk to me.

I mentioned earlier that I had delayed what I had expected to be a more difficult task, namely, contacting hospital consultants. The prospect of negotiating access with personnel in the big teaching and non-teaching hospitals scattered around Manchester was somewhat intimidating especially as I wanted to interview only a small number of people. As it happened, I came into contact with hospital consultants while sampling for GPs. Inadvertently, I sent out a few letters to potential respondents listed as doctors in the telephone directory who turned out to be hospital consultants working in a private capacity. I had contacted them at their private practices. When I went to interview them, I was frequently asked how I had got hold of their names and addresses. The issue of National Health Service (NHS) consultants being able to undertake private work is a contentious one in Britain.[6] Not surprisingly, therefore, they were embarrassed about their private work, nervous about how much I would question them on it and quite defensive about the issue. When I explained how I had come across their names and addresses and the issues I was interested in, they were reassured. We talked about their private work to some extent in their account of their work histories. It was not a major topic for me although I was interested to know about the income they drew from this work. They were mostly willing to reveal this information.

Again, at the end of these interviews, I asked my informants if they could speak to their wives or husbands on my behalf about being interviewed for the project. I encountered only a few non-responses here too. Indeed, one of these interviewees' partners was also a hospital consultant and she very kindly put me in contact with other consultants who passed me on to other colleagues in different hospitals. Looking back now, I can see how this couple – both husband and wife – were extremely helpful. It was through this snowballing process that I secured interviews with a small number of hospital consultants.[7] Generating a sample of teachers and their partners was somewhat easier to do although the process was not without its difficulties, of course. I decided it would be good to talk to teachers in both primary and secondary schools about their careers and so on. Again, I used the *Yellow Pages* for central Manchester and after ascertaining the name of the school head teacher with a quick telephone call to the school, I wrote to schools on a random basis around the city. From others, I knew that researchers frequently approach school heads and I expected and experienced some outright rejections. Head teachers have enough on their plate after all and all they need is someone else asking them for some more of their time and effort! It was understandable and I had to accept the situation. That said, there are always people who are interesting and willing to be involved in research and I was fortunate to contact some of them.

In the introductory letter to the head teachers, I asked them if they could find any volunteers among their teaching staff who would be interested in participating in the research. Sometimes, they offered to be interviewed themselves as well as find volunteers and these interviews were frequently conducted at the school too. They were, in other words, very obliging. At the end of the interview, I asked my informants if their partners could be persuaded to participate in the research too. I contacted them a few days later to ascertain if their partners would be willing to help and then established how to contact them. These interviews were usually conducted in their homes. Once again, a number of the interviewees' partners did not want to be interviewed. This proved to be a bigger problem with the teachers than with the doctors and it is related, I suspect, to the gender of the 'main' informant. It was usually men that I was meeting when I conducted the interviews with medics and women who were their partners. It was more often than not women I was meeting when undertaking interviews with teachers and husbands who were their partners. It seemed to me that the women interviewees found it more difficult to persuade their husbands to be interviewed than vice versa. I often wondered if some of the interviewees' husbands were uncomfortable with the thought of being interviewed by a woman alone and, moreover, a woman they had neither spoken to, nor met directly. I think some of the women informants wished their husbands were more helpful.[8]

Consequently, I interviewed a number of women teachers and then found that their partners would not participate in the research. This happened on a number of occasions and I had to decide to include some of the women interviewees in the final sample. As I became more aware of the problem during the course of the research, I asked women interviewees to supply me with some details about their husbands – some basic demographic details, occupation, income and so forth – in these telephone conversations. They often did so and I like to think they did so because they had enjoyed doing the interviews. It was these interviewees – who often referred to their husbands in the course of interviews, of course – whom I included in the final sample. In sum, I have provided quite a long account here of how I generated my sample of doctors and teachers in Britain. On the one hand, I fear my academic colleagues will think this process very unsystematic and haphazard. On the other hand, I am of the view that this is what doing research is really like at the end of the day. Accidents happen although they can have their advantages. Chances present themselves that have to be taken. Some contacts are absolutely vital to a project. This is not to say, however, that the process of generating this sample was disorganised or unmethodical. On the contrary, I thought very hard about the most sensible and orderly way to proceed – with years of reading textbooks on methods, and even writing one, behind me – at each stage of the research process.[9]

Contacting physicians and educators in America

In securing research funds from the University of Manchester for time off from teaching to do a relatively small project, I was also expected to develop it into something bigger and make an application for funding to an external body. This I duly did with my colleague, Mike Savage, who joined the Department of Sociology at Manchester a year after I did. We developed a research proposal to do interviews with professionals and managers in Manchester and Cambridge in the UK and in Durham, North Carolina and Boston, Massachusetts in the USA. I harboured an aspiration to do empirical research in America and Mike was splitting his time between the University of North Carolina at Chapel Hill and the University of Manchester during that period. The application was sent to the Economic and Social Research Council (ESRC), a government-funded body, and the main funder of social science research in Britain. In keeping with the temper of the times, we were both making other research applications as well. I submitted a smaller version of the joint ESRC application to the Leverhulme Trust proposing to extend my study of doctors and teachers to the USA. With a colleague at Salford University, Mike submitted another application to the ESRC on middle-class lifestyle practices. A 'little bird' told us that we had been successful in our application before we heard anything formally from the ESRC. As it turned out, this information was incorrect. The project on which Mike and I had been co-applicants was turned down while it was Mike's other application that was successful. We were both disappointed.[10]

As luck would have it, however, I heard my application to the Leverhulme Trust was successful some weeks later. Given the earlier setback, I was absolutely delighted about the prospect of going to America to do empirical research. I need to explain how I came to do my fieldwork in Boston. When I started as a lecturer at Manchester, I secured funding for a research trip to the USA to do library research for a book I was working on on social class in America and Britain. I called up a former colleague of mine at Liverpool University, Professor Robert Moore, for advice as we had often talked about our mutual research interests, his being in racial inequalities, which frequently led us to talk about the famous early urban sociology conducted in Chicago. Robert suggested I contact his colleague, Professor William Julius Wilson, at the University of Chicago about facilitating a visit to the USA. I did this and Professor Wilson, via Eddie Walker, facilitated my trip as a Visiting Scholar. I know that

Professor Wilson would not mind me saying that our paths crossed only once during my month in Chicago. There was no reason why it should be otherwise. Still, I came to know his team of researchers and administrators well – especially Jim Quane, Bruce Rankin and Eddie Walker – during that time. Jim and I, in particular, got on well and we talked a lot about the research going on at the Center for Urban Inequality.[11] He also showed me around the city, including the notorious Taylor projects. Despite my short stay in Chicago, we stayed in contact and our paths crossed again, for example, when I attended American Sociological Association meetings.

When it came to writing the applications for comparative research, I contacted Jim to ask if Professor Wilson would be willing to sponsor my institutional affiliation once more. I needed such details on my applications. By this time, of course, Professor Wilson had moved from Chicago to the Kennedy School of Government at Harvard University. Professor Wilson was happy to do so and this is how I came to Boston. These were my academic contacts in the city. Of course, I kept my family up to date with all these plans and my mother was very excited on my behalf. She also urged me to write to a cousin in Ireland – one of her sisters' sons – who had worked as a doctor for a while in Boston. She though he might be able to help me start my research. I was a little embarrassed at writing to a cousin – one of the oldest of forty-five cousins whom I had not met in a very long time – but I was pressured into doing so. My cousin John kindly wrote back with five names of physicians attached to two hospitals in Boston that he was happy for me to contact and said I could mention his name.[12] It was with this short list of potential contacts that I went out to Boston in 1998. I was anxious to start my research as quickly as possible and contacted them as soon as possible on arrival. Since I had not stipulated to my cousin that I only wanted to speak to physicians with children – the names of any physicians would be helpful after all – I found that some of these contacts did not have children and I could not, therefore, interview them.

Needless to say, some of these contacts had children and they were willing to be interviewed. The list of contacts gradually increased as they kindly gave me names of other physicians to approach. In this way, my sample of hospital physicians snowballed to include men and women, including women of colour, working in prestigious hospitals attached to Harvard Medical School and the less prestigious City Hospital.[13] Again, at the end of each interview, I asked my informants if they could persuade their partners to participate in the research. I arranged to telephone my informants a few days later and, if their partners were interested, I got details of how to contact them directly. As in Britain, most of the interviews with physicians were conducted at their place of work while the interviews with their wives or husbands were done at home. Somewhat differently to Britain, I came across a number of women physicians working in a variety of hospital settings. Once more, I encountered difficulties in securing interviews with their male partners and my suspicion is that the same reasons for not participating in the research applied as in Britain. I was wise to this situation by now, of course, and collected key information on partners in these follow-up calls. This happened on a number of occasions although I did not have the time to keep interviewing this group of people. I had to include some of these women interviewees in the final sample.

While I was very pleased to be in the field so quickly, monitoring the sample left me a little concerned that I was coming across an elite group of physicians attached to Harvard Medical School and often engaged in research themselves. I talked to my colleagues back at the Kennedy School about these worries and told them about the two types of career open to doctors in Britain. I wondered what the equivalent was in the USA. Here, Jim Quane came to the rescue. Directing the Joblessness and Urban Poverty Research programme across five cities including Boston,[14] he had become very knowledgeable about the city just as he had made it his business to know Chicago inside out. He dug out a directory of medical centres dotted around Boston and suggested I should contact these centres as a way of getting at a different group of medics. After a quick telephone call to establish the name of the medical director of these centres, I sent off letters asking if any of their medical staff would be willing to be interviewed as part of my research. Again, in follow-up telephone calls, I found people to be very obliging, a couple of people offering to be interviewed as well as providing some names of volunteers. Partners sometimes turned out to be physicians too and helped with additional contacts. As in Britain, I came across quite a diverse group of people. These medics were deeply committed to serving poor communities in areas such as Dorchester, Roxbury and so on and they were often passionate about their work with different ethnic and racial groups in Boston. Their sociopolitical values were to the fore and very much shaped their careers in medicine.[15] Overall, it meant I had a good mix.

The first half of my time in Boston – July to September 1998 – was spent interviewing physicians and their partners. The interviews with partners, as I said before, were often conducted at the family home and, unsurprisingly, in some of the most affluent communities in Boston and surrounding towns like Brookline, Newton and, slightly further afield, in Lexington. Ever anxious to be on time for interviews, I would take public transport to these areas, make sure I could find streets and houses and then while away my time in local public libraries if they were close by. Here, I checked out information about the towns and usually found lists of the local public schools. School systems varied in that some had middle or junior high schools while others did not. I wrote to a small number of randomly selected principals of elementary, middle and high schools requesting help along similar lines to my other case studies. Most were very forthcoming and, indeed, one principal gave me the email addresses of volunteers to contact directly. I interviewed a number of teachers working in these school systems and I tried to build up a list of contacts so that interviewees worked in a variety of different schools, to increase the diversity of the sample. Some interviews with partners come off while others did not happen despite my best efforts! Unsurprisingly, these interviewees did not often live in the affluent communities where they taught and, interestingly, they were less likely to have been geographically mobile, having been born relatively close to the areas in which they now resided with their own families.[16]

I was also, of course, acutely aware of the need to talk to teachers in the Boston public school system. One of my contacts from the other suburbs led me to a teacher who worked in Boston – an African American woman – who was very helpful with other contacts. From the city library, I also collected details on the public schools and wrote to a small number of school principals. One of the principals I then contacted on the telephone told me firmly that all such requests to do research had to go through the Boston central school administration located in Park Street. Access would take some time. This news made me very nervous as I did not have a lot of time left in Boston. I feared that I had made a mistake in not thinking about these things at the start of the project. However, when I spoke to other principals, they did not raise the issue and supplied me with a few names instead. I managed to assemble a sufficient list of names of people to interview. The numbers, of course, were always small. While I was doing these interviews, there was this fear in the back of my mind that the administrators at Park Street would find out what I was doing and would banish me appropriately! The school authorities became a great weight on my mind and it left me feeling I was doing something unethical or wrong, even though I was talking to the interviewees about their individual teaching careers rather than the school system for which they worked. I still wonder if I should have talked to them and sought permission after the event.[17]

At the end of my six months in Boston, I had completed all of the interviews with physicians and their partners that I was able to do. Most of the interviews with educators had been completed although I still had some outstanding names to contact. I decided to return to Boston in July and

August of the following year, at my own expense, and complete the outstanding interviews. I contacted the educators I hoped to interview and explained the situation. Cheerfully, they said they would be happy to talk then. I completed these interviews with relative ease during that period of fieldwork. I have to say that I think my American interviewees were as considerate and courteous as they were because it was a novelty factor to be interviewed by an academic over from Britain. More than once, the interviewees commented on how charming they found my accent. If they were charmed by me, I was equally charmed by them. It is easy to be romantic about interviewees – especially over time – and to forget about the ones who were not that friendly. There were some informants who could have been a bit more cooperative but they were few in comparison to the majority who were very kind. I have set out, in some length, how I came to do my research in America. I suspect it is now obvious that it involved drawing on my small network of colleagues and friends for information and advice, chasing potential contacts all the time so I never really stopped generating a sample and enjoying a ton (as they would say in America) of luck. I guess these experiences are not dissimilar to those of others.[18]

The conduct of the interviews in Britain and America

When I started the interviews in Britain, I had an *aide memoire* that took the form of a semi-structured life history. I had a checklist of questions under a series of headings that included background information, educational experiences, work histories, children and their educational and work experiences and a concluding section on reflections. In the opening conversation, I asked my interviewees to tell me a little bit about themselves so I could ascertain some basic demographic details about them and their families. I also collected some basic information on their socioeconomic background, about their parents' occupations etc. To round off this opening discussion, I asked the interviewees to tell me about their standard of living when they were growing so I got a feel for their childhood. The very final question I asked them was if they could say whether they and their families belonged to a social class when they were growing up. For the most part, the opening discussion was relatively easy and pleasant as the interviewees touched on aspects of their childhoods. The discussion on class, however, was the source of much discomfort and awkwardness. My first couple of interviewees just did not want to talk about it at all and they were anxious to dissociate themselves from class labels.[19] In other words, my rapport with the interviewees was seriously undermined by this discussion and early on in the interview too!

Given the unease that was felt on both sides, albeit for different reasons, I decided to drop the question. An explicit discussion of class was not crucial to my research focus on class processes.

The opening discussion, therefore, was brought to a close with a question on the interviewees' standard of living. In Britain, most of the interviewees of middle-class origin talked of how their parents owned their own home, an array of consumer goods, whether they went on holidays and so on. Occasionally, some of the interviewees made an unprompted reference to being middle class. Some of the interviewees were from working-class backgrounds and had enjoyed social mobility into medicine and teaching and, more often than not, they immediately discussed their standard of living in class terms and explicitly described it as working class. The same format of questions was followed in America. To my surprise, virtually all of the American interviewees discussed their families' standard of living explicitly in class terms and, more often than not, described their families' origin as middle class. In one respect, the frequent language of class was very surprising since it is the British rather than the Americans who are supposed to be obsessed with class! In another respect, the interviewees' responses were unsurprising since the tendency to describe their class background as middle class was to be expected. What was also interesting here was the way in which the British were rather uncomfortable about using the term middle class because of its baggage – especially the status connotations – from the past. Such concerns did not seem to deter the American interviewees who used the class category with apparent ease and comfort. The label middle class did not appear to have all this history.[20]

These different discussions were interesting as were the British and American accounts of education. I expected these conversations to be different, however, since I knew the school systems varied across the two countries. The British interviewees' accounts of the tripartite system were familiar since I was a product of that system myself. Still, I learnt an awful lot more listening to my informants reflecting back, for the most part, on their grammar school education in the 1950s and 1960s. The interviewees conveyed the powerful impact of institutional arrangements on their lives, namely, the importance attached to passing the eleven plus, the way in which young people went to separate schools – this separateness being hugely significant – and how all of these things were seen to determine their fate in life. For the most part, the interviewees were the successes of this system and their experiences were mostly happy ones. This is not to say they were uncritical, however. Many of them recalled that it was a quite hateful system and that the snobbery and elitism of their grammar schools were hard to deal with. Similarly, the few interviewees who experienced a secondary school education bristled with resentment when they recalled that their education was secondary in all respects. Some of these discussions, therefore, evoked strong feelings. Now, during this same period, there was a tracking system within American high schools that was effectively dividing students into classes according to their talents and abilities in very similar ways. Such strong feelings were rarely voiced, it seemed, because the process occurred within the school, even though people's life-chances were greatly affected by it.[21]

In the USA, I learnt a huge amount about school desegregation. It really is one thing to know about such important events from books and quite another to hear people speak of their experiences of it and its impact on their lives. I certainly did not appreciate the violent conflict that had occurred over racial desegregation in Boston, for example. The African American interviewees who grew up in Boston during this time described how their parents tried to ensure they got a decent public school education and how they had to find ways of protecting them from the violence in their schools and local communities. Their stories were vivid and compelling. Most of my white interviewees grew up in the suburbs of Boston rather than in the city itself. Consequently, the issue did not feature in the stories of their education although I detected some oblique reference to white flight from south Boston in one example. In this respect, it was possible to see how it was not their history, and how they might view school desegregation as black history.[22] It was also obvious, however, that this was not so. This became apparent as I spoke to the interviewees who grew up elsewhere, where the conflict over the desegregation of public schools was far less violent. Interviewees spoke of how desegregation was introduced relatively smoothly but parents took them out of schools that were being racially integrated because of their fears about the disruption it caused, anxieties about the decline in standards and much more besides. In these respects, the placement of inner-city blacks in white suburban schools is part of white history in America. It still is so.

The conversations about the interviewees' education, therefore, were very insightful and they, along with the discussions about their children's education, were the best parts of the interviews in both countries. Reflecting back, I am not so sure that education was so obviously the central focus of this book at the onset of the research. The issue of education became key over time. Because these conversations could be quite lengthy, the discussions of the interviewees' work histories got squeezed. To be sure, the informants discussed some interesting topics as they outlined their careers in medicine and teaching to me. I felt, however, that I only scratched the surface of how their careers had unfolded over their working lives. What I did get a sense of was the way in which people's lives are not determined by their socio-economic background. I spoke to people who enjoyed early success and then suffered setbacks later on as well as those who confronted barriers earlier on who then made great strides forward in their later career. I would have loved to have delved much more into how some of the interviewees enjoyed considerable success in their chosen careers while others made modest progress. It would have been interesting to explore the effects of class, race and gender on the many and varied career histories I heard about. The issues touch on intergenerational or work-life mobility, however, and I had to concentrate on intragenerational social mobility.[23]

These comments apply equally to the British and American interviews. Something else became apparent when we discussed work histories. By dint of living in Britain, I became aware of how I knew quite a lot about the processes by which people become doctors and teachers. By comparison, I knew much less about the education and training of physicians and educators in the USA. I acquired lots of information, of course, from my interviewees and from various other sources. I was left feeling that I would have liked to have read much more about the history of these two professions in the USA and especially how they embraced some types of people and excluded others. I would also have liked to have known more about how the professions have changed (or not) and the contribution of affirmative action policies on the social background of medical students and undergraduates majoring in education. I felt this when a male interviewee made a passing reference, albeit with some resentment, about the difficulties that white men now confront in getting accepted into medical schools.[24] Some of the women interviewees, including women of colour, also made some remarks about how they went to medical schools that encouraged candidates like themselves. The work history material, therefore, threw up lots of issues that I could not fully take on board in my project. Again, however, all I can say is that I could not embrace all of these things because my interest was on intra-generational mobility and the mobilisation of economic, cultural and social resources in the reproduction of advantage.

Finally, I want to make one point about the discussion of the interviewees' children and how they were making their way through the education system into employment. Before I started this research, I gave a departmental seminar on what I was hoping to do, to colleagues at the University of Swansea, Wales. My paper was well received, although I was pressed about the difficulties of asking people about their children's educational and occupational success. Rightly, some of my audience wondered if parents would gloss over the difficulties their children might have encountered in the interviews I proposed to conduct. How do you talk about children's talents and abilities that may or may not be of the academic kind?[25] It is a challenging issue. Most parents adore their children. In difficult times, they might admit that their children are the source of both their greatest happiness and their greatest sadness but such feelings are expressed in private to intimate others. Could I really expect people to discuss setbacks and disappointments with me? I did not have an answer to the question at the time and I am not sure that I can exactly pinpoint how I confronted the issue when I did the research. I am sure there was much that was not revealed to me. I certainly spoke to parents whose children were successful and they were genuinely so. I am sure I had parents who sung the praises of their children even if they were not as academically successful as they claimed. To be sure, parents do not think less of their children if they are not intellectually able. There are many more important things in life than that!

At the same time, however, some of the interviewees told me stories about their children that were painful to tell. Sometimes relationships had broken down. One interviewee in Britain, for example, spoke of how she had just re-established contact with her only son after a number of fraught years in which he had been indifferent to education, dropped out of college, gotten into trouble with the police and left the country for some time. Similarly, an American couple spoke of how the second of their four children had serious behavioural problems that had disrupted his education and, more generally, their family life. Without explaining all the details, it became apparent that they had facilitated their son's move out of the family home so that they could all enjoy a calmer life. Finally, another interviewee spoke at length about the difficulties that her only child had encountered in life. The issues for the family were still ongoing and maybe because it dominated her life so much, it was difficult not to talk about them when I interviewed her.[26] Indeed, this interviewee contacted me again after the interview. She was upset that she had revealed so much and she felt she had no right to talk about her child's life as if were her own. She regretted, in other words, how much she had divulged and she sought assurances that I would not disclose too much. I promised I would not do so and I sincerely hope that I have drawn on this interview material appropriately. I am sure her worries did not go away; mine did not. I spent a long time fretting about how to handle the issue with care. The problem was one of how to deal with too much revelation and not too little.

Transcription, analysis, writing and politics

Although my main source of empirical material derives from interviews, I could not have analysed the transcripts and written this book without the observations I made in Britain and, especially, America. I say this because doing a comparative project that involved living and working in another country was almost akin to an ethnographic experience. Britain and America are remarkably similar countries in many respects. Even so, there are aspects of everyday life that are different and my first month in the USA was a little uncomfortable. It was incredibly hot, especially in the apartment I was renting that had no air conditioning, and the heat was confounded by a bout of athlete's foot that felt – at the time at least, since I laugh about it now – very painful. I was miserable! Also, I had to learn basic routines like shopping in the supermarket, using the bank and finding my way around Boston's public transportation system. Nothing, it seemed, could be taken for granted and all usually took twice as long as usual. As I gradually figured things out, however, I came to realise that I was learning a lot. Finding my way to and from interviews, getting rides home from interviewees and talking to them outside the formal interview situation, talking to other people, whether they were friends, acquaintances or just people who I asked for help in the street, reading newspapers, magazines and books avidly and so on were sources of great insight.[27] Observations of and participation in American everyday life, therefore, enhanced my understanding of the interviewees and their lives immeasurably. I got a feel for the context of their lives that I would not have enjoyed from interviews alone. Doing comparative research made me very aware of this.

Back in Britain, I set about having my interviews transcribed. Researchers rarely comment on the transcription process, as if it is a straightforward affair. It is not. When I was a Ph.D. student, I transcribed my own interviews in full because I had no money for transcription costs and I (probably) had the time. Now more established, I had the money but not the time. Although this would seem to make for an easier life, it turned out to be extraordinarily difficult to find someone who would transcribe the tapes, I would find someone and then I would lose them to something else and I cannot deny that the quality of some transcriptions was better than others. Eventually, however, I found a brilliant transcriber. She was brilliant in the sense that she included so much in the transcriptions. She was especially good on laughter and hesitations! The quality of her work challenged me to think about all the non-verbal things that go on in interviews. In all honesty, her transcriptions made me much more sensitive to these issues than I would have been, as I tried to remember the tone in which the interviewees answered my questions, when they laughed, when they were despondent about things and so on. In other words, I thought hard and long about the feelings and emotions the interviewees expressed when they spoke and the ones that were left unspoken when they hesitated and did not voice them. Qualitative interviewers are talking about these issues more explicitly now than was customary in the past.[28] Reflection on these issues is to be welcomed especially in relation to how they might bear on the interpretation of empirical material. The transcription process, therefore, bought some methodological and substantive issues into the light.

The process of analysis was not easy either. Although I was fortunate in having a huge amount of empirical material, I was overwhelmed by it. I read and re-read the individual transcriptions numerous times and I just could not see the wood for the trees. I thought it would help if I wrote summaries of the individual interviews, pulling out the key points as I saw them, but it did not. In fact, I wasted a lot of time getting nowhere and it was very painful. Although it seems blindingly obvious now, especially given my theoretical starting point, I eventually figured that I would pull out the ways in which the interviewees spoke about the mobilisation of economic, cultural and social resources. This way of analysing the data was not simple at first either. When I started to identify bits of text with the mobilisation of economic resources, for example, I still found that I was associating huge amounts of the interview material with this particular process. I realised that I needed to discuss both how available economic resources influenced the ways in which parents helped their children and how the lack of economic resources shaped parents' choices and decisions too. The discussion seemed to raise big questions about how the economic touches on all aspects of life and vice versa. As a consequence, it took a huge amount of additional work sifting through the material I had pulled out to effectively narrow down and really focus in on the key points that I wanted to make. This process continued, of course, as I started to write the first drafts of chapters that were often way too long and unwieldy and had to be seriously chopped. It was hard going.[29]

I really struggled with the mobilisation of cultural resources too although I consoled myself by thinking that it was not my fault. Like many others, I have found Bourdieu's concept of cultural capital to be extraordinarily slippery because it seems to embrace so many things: issues of embodiment, matters of deportment, dispositions and values, lifestyle practices etc.[30] Consequently, my early analysis of the mobilisation of cultural resources was very unfocused too as I pulled out huge chunks of text across the interview transcripts that considered a wide variety of issues. Time and again, I went back to Bourdieu and immersed myself in his writings to try and make things easier. When I did so, I felt I understood what Bourdieu was talking about. When I came away, however, I found it difficult to hold on to the issues he discussed. Eventually, I came up with the idea of homing in on educational dispositions and occupational horizons as the way in which the transcriptions allowed me to consider how social positions shape individuals. I worried about whether I had operationalised Bourdieu's notion of cultural capital in an unimaginative and mechanical way. Then again, I suspect interviews are not the best way of capturing how people carry themselves and how they practise themselves. Seeing how they do so in their everyday lives would be much better. In these circumstances, I had to accept that this was the best I could do and I was certainly not unhappy that issues of gender came to bear in the discussion of educational dispositions and occupational horizons. Once again, therefore, I had to read the transcripts over and over again. I came to know my interviewees inside out.

In contrast, the analysis of the mobilisation of social resources was fun. I found it more enjoyable because I had some space to discuss networks and norms in, dare I say, an imaginative way. As I outlined in Chapter 6, both Goldthorpe and Bourdieu talked about the mobilisation/exploitation of social resources/capital although they focused on their importance as a last resort when academic success was not forthcoming. I thought the mobilisation of social resources could be important in the process of credential acquisition too. This led me to draw on Coleman's work on social capital in the creation of human capital, focusing on social capital outside the family in terms of interpersonal relations with other local people in both informal and formal settings. Again, I did not operationalise the concept of social capital in my interview schedule by asking people directly about their social networks. Rather, as I analysed the transcripts, I extracted discussions about the influence of people on the interviewees' lives, and how they reinforced the cultural capital to be found inside the family or as a counter to it. Indeed, I was very interested to note how my interviewees frequently spoke of the influence of other people on them. I was rarely told stories of individual success as they readily acknowledged the impact of other people on their lives. This spontaneous talk led me to appreciate why the concept of social capital has become so popular in sociology of late for it encompasses a basic premise of the discipline: namely, that who we are, how we are, what we do etc. is influenced by the social context – meaning the other people in those social contexts – in which we find ourselves.[31]

The analysis of the interview transcripts, therefore, involved a process of reading and re-reading the material, extracting text according to the topic that was being explored, sifting though those extracts, discarding some and retaining others and gradually constructing an argument or story around them. It was a very time-consuming affair and, indeed, it was surprising how some ideas only came to me late in the day. That the process was so slow at times revealed something important, however. That is to say, economic, cultural and social resources are heavily intertwined and, indeed, mutually constitutive of each other. I have separated them out in the writing of this book but I hope I have highlighted the ways in which they are so interconnected too. In fact, I wish I could have done that more than I have done. This point also highlights the fact that my analysis of the material and then writing of draft chapters were not separate enterprises, although they are often presented as distinct stages of a research project in methods texts. I was still analysing the material as I was writing draft chapters. In fact, I would say that I did my hardest thinking – that is, analysing the material – while I was writing them.[32] This point also leads me to note that I could have organised the material differently and written a different book. I often wondered whether I should bring the chapters on the interviewees as children together and then follow them with the chapters focusing on the interviewees as parents. I was undecided on this issue for some time until I decided there was no right or wrong way of organising the material. I just had to make a decision and stick with it.

This book was written against the backdrop of considerable public debate about higher education in America and Britain. In America, there has been widespread concern about the phenomenal rise in tuition fees to private colleges, state universities and community colleges over the last ten and more years. At the time of writing, these fees are expected to rise further as the US economy struggles and state governments facing substantial deficits cut higher education funding.[33] Many expect that the rise in fees will exclude those from modest backgrounds, African American and Hispanic children for example, more than they already do. In Britain, there has been great controversy about the introduction of tuition fees and the abolition of maintenance grants over the same period of time. Again, at the time of writing, a government White Paper has just signalled an increase in tuition fees.[34] It is widely believed that these fees will exclude those from disadvantaged positions – young white working-class men and women and young people of various ethnic origins – from higher education even more than they do now. I share these concerns, in part, because I doubt whether my parents could have paid the fees to allow my sister or me to go to university. I am not entirely sure, however, as I could well imagine them making considerable sacrifices for us to go to university. They so wanted us to enjoy the opportunity for higher education given that we were able enough to do so. More importantly, this research has shown the importance of economic resources in the reproduction of advantage. They are important in and of themselves and in their conversion to an immaterial form as cultural capital.

In this political climate, I felt somewhat uncomfortable about interviewing some people who were very affluent indeed. They expressed their anxieties and spoke, for example, of how they would have to cut back on some of the finer things in life. They were extremely nice people but I did not feel very sympathetic. I felt they did not know the half of it, so to speak, in terms of the sacrifices that inner city black parents would have to make in order for their children to succeed. That said, the majority of my interviewees were not so wealthy and they had made or were making sacrifices to ensure their children's educational and occupational success. They were ordinary working people doing the best by their kids. I was sympathetic although I was still a little uneasy when I thought about those in disadvantaged positions again. My colleague, Jim Quane, put me right on this towards the end of this project. Whether I was sympathetic or not was beside the point. The point was that I had undertaken a qualitative study looking at the processes of middle-class reproduction that had tapped into people's experiences of, and feelings about, those processes. My interviewees did not think much of the system of rewards even if they played the game. There is no reason to think that those in disadvantaged positions do not share these experiences of and feelings about the distribution system and, indeed, it is likely they are more keenly felt by parents who have less control over their own and their children's lives. These closing thoughts suggest there are class alliances to be forged to come up with something better so that all children, able or otherwise, enjoy a decent life.[35]

Concluding remarks

In this appendix I have tried to write a frank and honest account of how I undertook a comparative project. I hope that I have made the process of doing the research and my experience of it transparent and open. There are probably instances where I have embarrassed myself and I will cringe in the future! I will not pretend that I have excluded some things that may have embarrassed me even more. It would be deceitful to suggest otherwise. Those searching for criticisms of the book may well find them in these pages. I can imagine some critics will not be impressed by my reliance on informal rather than formal ways of generating a sample of people to talk to in Britain and America. Nor, for that matter, will they like the arguably self-indulgent nature of exercises such as this one since I have struggled with this issue too. Be that as it may, I am glad that I have written this appendix. Much of it has focused on the problems I encountered and dilemmas I faced when doing the empirical research for this book and how I overcame them, circumvented them or just plain had to accept them. This is the reality of doing empirical research. Still, I hope I have conveyed a sense of how theoretically informed empirical research is exciting and challenging. I would emphasise this point to relation to comparative research. Living and working in America, and talking to Americans about aspects of their daily lives, was a fantastic research experience. Despite the trials and tribulations that accompanied this research project, I remain passionate about the discipline of sociology and about doing sociological research. I am still sure it is my vocation.

Notes

1. INTRODUCTION

1. I cannot confirm my father's life history exactly since he died, aged 59, in 1990 of a second heart attack (having had his first heart attack in his early fifties). It is, of course, not an untypical way for working-class men to die. He had just returned from a Post Office Union conference since he served as the union's branch secretary for Bournemouth and Poole for many years. He was very active in the Labour Party, the Fabian Society and his local Catholic Church, was a member of Dorset's Health Authority, a Justice of the Peace and many other things besides. He was, in many ways, a typical member of the 'labour aristocracy' that was the bedrock of the trade union movement and the emerging Labour Party in early twentieth-century Britain. See Crossick (1978) and Gray (1976).

2. The 1944 Education Act required all children to be provided with a secondary school place, free of charge, in England and Wales. Prior to the Act, most children attended one school between the ages of 5–14 and only a minority of children went to separate selective secondary schools that charged fees. Under this Act, the tripartite system was introduced. Children took the eleven plus examination and, on the basis of the results which were seen to measure individual abilities and aptitudes, went to a grammar, technical or secondary modern school. In reality, technical schools were not universally provided so children went to either a grammar or secondary modern school. These schools were supposed to be of equal status and to offer equal educational opportunities to all. In reality, grammar schools were held in high esteem while secondary modern schools were poorly regarded in a very hierarchical system. See Chitty (1993), Simon (1991). Middle-class children dominated the former while working-class children dominated the latter. See Halsey, Heath and Ridge (1980). See also the extensive research on British institutional arrangements conducted by American sociologists Kerckhoff *et al.* (1996).

3. I attended my local Catholic secondary school between 1973 and 1978 even though the tripartite system was being gradually phased out in the 1960s and replaced by a comprehensive system where children of all abilities and aptitudes were sent to the same secondary school. However, there was much resistance from local government authorities, dominated by the Conservative Party, to the introduction of comprehensive schools supported by the Labour government of 1966–70. Bournemouth was one such area that resisted

the comprehensive system. The first comprehensive school in Bournemouth resulted from the merger of my old school with the two Catholic grammar schools (St Peter's School for Boys and Boscombe Convent School for Girls). The bishop of Portsmouth, whose diocese included Bournemouth, and not the local education authority initiated the merger. The tripartite system is still found in other parts of the country including parts of Greater Manchester – i.e. Trafford Education Authority – where I undertook the British arm of my comparative project.

4. Initially, under the tripartite system, the more academically able grammar-school children took GCEs – often referred to as O Levels – at 16 while the less able secondary modern school children took CSEs (and a Grade 1 in a CSE was the equivalent of a GCE). Gradually, it was recognised that young people in the top streams at secondary modern schools were intellectually able enough to take GCEs. Five GCEs at Grades A–C were usually required to do A levels (Advanced Level Examinations) after two years of study between 16 and 18, usually in a sixth form attached to a school or a college of further education. For a discussion of changes in educational qualifications under the tripartite system, see Heath, Mills and Roberts (1992), in Crouch and Heath (eds.), 1992.

5. See Goldthorpe (in collaboration with Llewellyn and Payne) (1980; the 2nd edition appeared in 1987). This work and the work on education and class by Halsey and his colleagues (see n. 2) were the main publications to emerge out of the work of the Social Mobility Group at Nuffield College, Oxford.

6. See Glass (1954). The interpretation of their empirical findings on patterns and trends in social mobility in the 1920s and 1930s has been the subject of debate. For contrasting views, see Heath (1981), Payne (1986).

7. Goldthorpe *et al.* 1980.

8. Ibid.

9. See, especially, the pessimistic 'conclusions and prospects' in Goldthorpe *et al.* (1980). Space limitations do not allow me to discuss the huge debate that Goldthorpe's work generated in Britain throughout the 1980s. Two issues are pertinent here. First, there was much unhappiness with the schema that Goldthorpe devised and especially his definition of a seemingly all-embracing middle class that ranged from businessmen to semi-professional and middle-level managers and administrators. For the original statement on this problem, see Penn (1980). The second source of considerable dissatisfaction was the exclusive focus on men, since women were excluded from the national survey undertaken by the Oxford Social Mobility Group. Again, for the original argument on this highly problematic issue, see Crompton (1980). Gordon Marshall and his colleagues (1988) in their national survey of class in Britain (part of an international class project directed by the American sociologist, E. O. Wright) established a national picture of women's mobility patterns in the late 1980s. Marshall *et al.* (1998) established that women had not enjoyed as much absolute mobility into the middle class – especially long-range mobility into the middle class from working-class positions – as men. Rather, many women experienced downward mobility from the middle class to

intermediate-class positions in low-level clerical work. These gendered patterns in absolute rates of mobility, they argued, are the product of the gender segregation of the labour market. In this respect, their findings were different from Goldthorpe's results on absolute mobility rates for men. With regard to relative rates of mobility, however, they found that women of middle-class origins have better chances than women of working-class origins of securing middle-class destinations. This finding confirmed Goldthorpe's analysis of trends in the relative mobility patterns of men. See Marshall *et al.* (1988). On the international class project, see Wright (1996).

10. Seemingly eager to apply his account of patterns and trends in social mobility in Britain to other countries, Goldthorpe, with his colleague Erikson, very much downplays the higher levels of absolute mobility and the higher levels of fluidity into elite positions they found in their reanalysis of Featherman and Hauser's data. See Erikson and Goldthorpe (1993). For the empirical data, see Featherman and Hauser (1978). Featherman and Hauser's study was a replication of the classic study of social mobility in America by Blau and Duncan (1967). Erikson and Goldthorpe's interpretation of American data is at odds with Hout (1988). For Hout's view on Erikson and Goldthorpe's comparative findings, see the exchange in *European Sociological Review* (1994/5).

11. The stability of class relations came to be a key issue in the debate on class between various protagonists, mostly American, in the journal, *International Sociology*, and among British sociologists in the pages of *Sociology*. In relation to the former debate, see, for example, Clark and Lispet (1991), and Hout *et al.* (1993). With regard to the second debate, see Goldthorpe and Marshall (1992) and Pahl (1993). For an overview of the two debates, see Devine (1997).

12. I became aware of this argument, hidden as it was in a very detailed discussion of patterns of intergenerational fluidity in Goldthorpe's book, ch. 4, as part of my teaching preparation for a six-week slot of lectures on social mobility in my first job at the University of Liverpool. It was a very tough initiation into teaching! See Goldthorpe *et al.* (1980), pp. 98–104. I would contend that the other person who appreciated the theoretical argument outlined here in the early 1990s was Ray Pawson, although he seemed overwhelmed with the idea of doing empirical work on social mobility! See Pawson (1993).

13. See Goldthorpe *et al.* (1980), pp. 104–8 although note how the relationship between Goldthorpe's theory and how it is operationalised in his empirical research is unclear. For an elaboration of this point, see Savage (1996). Another neglected aspect of Goldthorpe's findings is his point that, 'It is in fact possible for the closure and buffer-zone theses still to retain some merit if they are reformulated so as to refer to fluidity rather than absolute mobility rates'. See Goldthorpe *et al.* (1980), p. 114. On the two theses, see Parkin (1971), Giddens (1973), and Westergaard and Resler (1975).

14. Erikson and Goldthorpe (1993, p. 397). On the self-maintaining properties of the class structure, see their interesting discussion of Lieberson's point that 'Those who write the rules, write rules that enable them to continue to write the rules.' See Lieberson (1987).

15. See Goldthorpe (1996). Clearly, this article was a continuation of the argument in defence of class analysis with reference to the stability of class relations as outlined by Goldthorpe and Marshall (1992). Arguably, this interest in education, in particular, needs to be placed in the context of the debate on meritocracy and social mobility initiated by Peter Saunders in the mid 1990s. For his initial statement, see Saunders (1995). In his way, Saunders was the first sociologist to critically evaluate Goldthorpe's substantive findings on patterns and trends in social mobility. He argued that Britain is a meritocracy and it is intelligence that explains why middle-class people get middle-class jobs. He was influenced by arguments on intelligence in America and especially the work of Herrnstein and Murray (1994) that was comprehensively challenged by Fischer *et al.* (1996). Saunders' position was also subsequently undermined by empirical research by Breen and Goldthorpe (1999). See also Savage and Egerton (1998). The role of education in the mobility process, for example, was explicitly addressed by Marshall *et al.* (1997). Interestingly, in contrast to Goldthorpe's predictions, Marshall and his colleagues found that the direct influence of class on chances of securing salariat employment has declined over the past twenty years. See Marshall *et al.* (1997, pp. 127–30). For a cautious alternative account of the declining effects of class origins on destinations, see Heath (2000).

16. See Devine (1998). I also commented on Goldthorpe's very selective use of Boudon's work on education. For the key statement of his ideas, see Boudon (1974). One of the major criticisms levelled against the embourgeoisement thesis, that members of the working class saw themselves as middle class in the postwar period of prosperity, is that class is more than income for it embraces, among other things, particular lifestyles and socio-political values. See Devine (1992).

17. See the same article (Devine 1998) for a critique of Rational Action Theory. See also Scott (1996b). For a balanced evaluation of rational choice theory, see Scott (1995) and also Collins (1994).

18. See Goldthorpe (2000, pp. 238–43). His concepts of 'strategies from above' and 'strategies from below' bring to mind Parkin's discussion of social closure and strategies of exclusion and usurpation. See Parkin (1979). The way in which Goldthorpe re-employs a culturalist theory in his theory of social mobility confirms Savage's criticism of Goldthorpe's rational action approach. See Savage (2000, pp. 85, 88).

19. Goldthorpe (2000, pp. 247–50). Interestingly, Goldthorpe explicitly reintroduces a discussion of the mobilisation of cultural and social resources in his outline of a theory of mobility that disappeared from view in earlier publications. There is an insightful discussion, for example, of how social skills may be as important if not more important in service sector jobs such as public relations and promotions work, hotel and catering careers.

20. As part of my undergraduate degree, I would say I was taught to think critically about what I read irrespective of whether the focus of attention is theoretical or empirical. Such thoughts, which often draw on personal experience, can be the starting point of further reading around a topic and the basis of doing

empirical research. Goldthorpe has been dismissive of what he refers to as my earlier 'discursive criticism' of his theory of mobility. See Goldthorpe (2000, pp. 23–4). Engaging with the literature on class and social mobility for over twenty years has led me precisely to do empirical research on the 'adequacy of his theoretical explanation'. I have long thought it a shame that one of the most influential British sociologists of the twentieth century has always been so contemptuous of his critics (see n. 9). The consequence is that he has alienated many British sociologists over the years. Arguably, his theoretical ideas and empirical work have not been as appreciated by younger generations of sociologists as they might have been.

21. I find myself in the strange position of noting, once again, how Goldthorpe's criticisms of other sociological ideas often apply to his own theories! In relation to the embourgeoisement debate, see Devine (1992). See also the thoughtful discussion on the 'question of the working class' in Scott (1996a).

22. See Marsh and Blackburn (1992). They note that without such grants, the expansion of educational opportunities in the 1950s and 1960s might have led to a worsening of class inequalities as children of the middle class exploited those opportunities while working-class children were not in a position to do so. Instead, the benign economic and political climate of that era allowed children of all classes to enjoy unprecedented access to universities, even if class differentials remained unchanged.

23. One of the easiest criticisms that could be levelled against the meritocracy thesis as espoused by Saunders is that there is little empirical evidence of downward social mobility from middle-class to working-class positions. That said, given that low-level manual employment has dropped so substantially in the last forty years, this finding is hardly surprising. Given the substantial growth in high-level and routine white-collar work, it might be worth paying more attention to downward mobility of less academically able middle-class children into lower-level professional occupations, for example social work and other forms of care work for men. See Crompton (1999).

24. My view, which has guided the research undertaken here, is that the divide between high-level professionals and managers and lower-grade professionals and managers, is a significant one within the middle classes (i.e. Goldthorpe's Classes I and II). Certainly, a reading of Anthony Heath's now rather old, but wonderful interpretation of social mobility data, would suggest this. See Heath (1981). The divide between professionals and managers was the focus of the excellent research by Savage et al. (1992). The book has a very interesting discussion of patterns of social mobility of professionals and managers.

25. There are numerous books on the fears associated with downward mobility in the USA. See, for example, Ehrenreich (1989) and Newman (1993). The theme has not been a dominant concern in Britain in part, I suspect, because job insecurity and movement is higher in the USA than in the UK (even though unemployment has been higher in the UK than the US). See, for example, the excellent study by Smith (2001). Perceptions of job insecurity and risk are greater than reality in Britain. See Burchell et al. (1999) and Devine et al. (2000).

26. On US income inequalities, see Levy (1995). On British income inequalities, see Hills (1996). On comparative inequalities more broadly, see Gottschalk and Smeeding (1997).
27. See Mills (1959).
28. On the US education system, see Demaine (2001). On the British education system, see Coffey (2001).
29. Medicine in America was once highly male dominated although it is less so today. On the growing number of women completing medical degrees, see Bianche (1995, vol. I). The same trends are evident in Britain. On the male domination of medicine, see Witz (1991). On the increasing number of women entering medical school, see Crompton and Sanderson (1990). By focusing on occupational groups in this way, I also take up Grusky and Sorensen's suggestion that more research could be conducted on occupations and the mobility trajectories associated with them. See Grusky and Sorensen (1998).
30. On women's dominance in the teaching profession in the USA, see Bianche (1995). See also Mare (1995) and Goldin (1990). On women's domination in the teaching profession in Britain, see Crompton (1992). Crompton provides a wonderful account of how highly educated girls were directed towards teacher training colleges where they completed a degree in education. Cutbacks in teacher training places 'bumped' women into university where they completed a wider range of degrees and entered a wider range of jobs than in the past. Despite all this, teaching remains a female dominated profession as many women do a Postgraduate Certificate in Education (PGCE) after their degree. There is a crisis in the falling number of men going into teaching.
31. On America's diversity, see Harrison and Bennett (1995) and Chiswick and Sullivan (1995, vol. II). On Britain's ethnic population and immigration history, see Coleman and Salt (1996) and Peach (1996).
32. See Erikson and Goldthorpe (1993, ch. 9).
33. To have secured details on the full range of my interviewees' financial assets would have taken up much of the interview so I only have a partial awareness of those assets as they were revealed to me in the course of the interview. That said, I appreciate the important work that is being done on wealth and how the issue needs to be incorporated into class analysis much more than it currently is. See, for example, Wolfe (1995); Oliver and Shapiro (1997); Shapiro and Wolff (2001).
34. All of the American women physicians had returned to their jobs – often training positions – quickly after the birth of their children although all of them had since reduced their hours (although they worked considerable hours). Most spoke of the difficulties of having two parents employed in highly demanding jobs, especially if there were two medics in the family. Most of the American women educators were employed full time although some had left the labour market for a number of years while they were raising their children. The same pattern was discernible among the British women doctors and teachers.

35. During the interviews, my American and British interviewees used the term 'class' in different ways. The American interviewees frequently distinguished between an upper middle class (very established and affluent professionals and managers) middle class (the middle mass of ordinary people like teachers) and lower middle class (blue-collar workers). The British interviewees distinguished between middle class (affluent professionals etc.), lower middle class (low-level white-collar workers) and working class (manual workers). What was most striking was that American interviewees frequently referred to class – their class background, how it affected their education and so forth – unprompted by me. It was a surprise! The findings seem to undermine Kingston's claim that America is a classless society. See Kingston (2000). I have explored the American interviewees' conversations about class further in Devine (2004b).
36. While conducting this empirical research, I learnt to appreciate the violent nature of the conflict over desegregation and bussing in Boston and other parts of America. See Lukas (1985) and Eaton (2001). For a north-eastern city that prided itself on being very progressive, the extent of the violence in comparison to other cities such as Buffalo greatly tarnished Boston's reputation. For a comparative perspective, see Taylor (1998).
37. While I was in the United States in the mid 1990s, there was considerable media discussion about the spiralling costs of going to college that generated much anxiety among my interviewees. I have visited Boston every year since I completed the research and it still seems to be a salient political issue frequently discussed in such newspapers as *The Boston Globe*, *The New York Times* and *The Washington Post*. While I was doing my research in Britain, student maintenance grants were scrapped and tuition fees of £1,000 per annum were introduced and, again, there was a lot of public debate about university and student funding. This book was finished in the same week as a government White Paper on university funding proposed that universities be allowed to increase their fees to £3,000 although only after the next general election. I take up the politics of these issues in Appendix B.
38. The change in gendered educational aspirations and occupational horizons is another theme that emerged through the course of the interviews. Both Goldthorpe and Bourdieu have been criticised for neglecting issues of gender in their research. It must be said, however, that Goldthorpe has acknowledged these important changes. See, for example, Goldthorpe (1996). Towards the end of his life, Bourdieu also started to consider issues of gender. See Bourdieu (2000).
39. Again, on issues of gender, see n. 38.
40. The 'school effect', therefore, was readily apparent. See Halsey *et al.* (1980).
41. In rational action theory, a basic assumption is that people act rationally in collecting and evaluating information in the decision-making process. Of course, the process is described in a very economistic way rather than embedded in social relationships. The way in which people short circuit a process – that requires much time and effort – by drawing on networks of colleagues and friends for information and advice is discussed fully in Chapters 6 and 7.

2. MATERIAL HELP WITH EDUCATION AND TRAINING

1. See Goldthorpe *et al.* (1987: 100). Goldthorpe developed this theory to under-pin his statistical analysis of patterns of intergenerational fluidity drawing on Hauser's (1978) analysis of mobility regimes. There is no evidence in the text, however, that he actually operationalised the different resources to test his theory using his survey data. More on the problems of this type of theory and research can be found in Savage (1996).

2. In my critique of Goldthorpe (Devine, 1998), I was making two points about economic resources that are important to separate. First, I expressed my dis-appointment with Goldthorpe's focus on economic resources alone and his neglect of cultural resources for it restricted his theory unnecessarily. Second, even if economic resources are the exclusive focus of attention, homing in on income alone is also overly narrow and problematic for the reasons I outline in the text.

3. Of course, I am very aware of the difficulties of drawing on childhood mem-ories and conscious of how people tell stories or narratives about themselves. Interview material, in this respect, is partial and I certainly would not claim that I know the whole of these people's early lives but only what they choose to tell me within the remit of the subject matter of this project. Miller (2000) provides a good account of these issues with specific reference to researching life stories and family histories.

4. On school desegregation in Boston, see Eaton (2001) and Lukas (1985). For a more general discussion of the ordeal of racial integration, see Patterson (1997).

5. That is to say, they attended direct-grant grammar schools that charged fees. The local education authority paid these fees for a small number of children who passed the school entrance examination. In effect, therefore, there were two types of grammar school under the old tripartite system. Given the UK's rigidly hierarchical school system, these direct-grant grammar schools enjoyed a higher prestige than state grammar schools. See Chitty (1993) and Simon (1991).

6. Namely, educated in European Enlightenment thought including John Stuart Mill's particular brand of utilitarianism with its focus on self-improvement and self-culture. On Mill's writings, see Skorupski (1998).

7. On risk, see Beck (1992). In a departmental seminar in the Department of Sociology at the University of Salford, the way in which I spoke of risk in a commonsensical way was brought to my attention by my colleagues. It was they who drew parallels with Beck's interest in risk and the increased risks associated with the postmodern era. I would like to thank Brian Longhurst in particular for initiating a good discussion on this issue.

8. On the higher level of educational attainment and lower level of truancy to be found at these schools, see Coleman and Hoffer (1987).

9. A number of the interviewees spoke of how they attended or they sent their children to schools that were part of a network of schools that participated in a programme for the gifted and talented. In David Neale's case, it seemed that he could successfully pass the test to get into such a school even though

he was obtaining only low grades in the public school system. Similarly, some interviewees' children had learning difficulties in the public school system and yet they also turned out to be gifted and talented. It was very confusing.

10. On residential segregation by race, see the excellent study by Massey and Denton (1993). They provide a very interesting account of how northern cities like Boston became increasingly segregated after the great migration and how that residential segregation by race has proved remarkably enduring ever since. On the great migration of African Americans from the South to northern cities, see Lemann (1995).

11. Tracking (like streaming in Britain) reproduced inequalities of class, race and gender within schools although its gradual abolition between 1965 and 1975 has not resulted in the demise of stratification but new forms of inequality arising in different guises. See Lucas (1999). See Hout, Raftery and Bell's (1993) excellent discussion on the importance of community colleges in America's much-lauded system of higher education.

12. To my good fortune, many of the interviewees explained to me how education was funded both nationally and locally in the USA, emphasising the importance of local property taxes on education spending across towns within states and differences across states.

13. That is to say, these interviewees' parents found ways of circumventing their economic constraints and they did so because they attached so much value to educational success and they were prepared to make sacrifices in their standard of living to ensure their children did well in school. Their cultural resources, in other words, were crucial here in overcoming their lack of economic resources.

14. In effect, therefore, those from middle-class backgrounds were sent to the best private and public schools and economic investments usually yielded a return in that they were then academically successful. The interviewees from more modest class backgrounds, however, had to demonstrate their academic prowess in sometimes less favourable educational settings and then they enjoyed better educational provision. On the issue of demonstrating success, see Gambetta (1987) and Goldthorpe (1996).

15. To be sure, I talked to a small number of (invariably male) interviewees who enjoyed a remarkably smooth life as they went from private schools, to Ivy League colleges, to prestigious medical schools, highly regarded internships/residencies and eventually into 'plum' jobs. Middle-class reproduction was achieved with incredible ease. On the link between prep schools and higher education, see the now classic Cookson and Persell (1985).

16. Given the demonisation of poor black women getting pregnant at a young age, it was interesting and thought provoking to hear this story of a teenage pregnancy in a white upper-middle-class family. How Paula Bailey's parents used their wealth to help their daughter and future son-in-law was revealing. They were no more independent than any poor young couple except that they were dependent on Paula's parents rather than on the state. For a critical take on the problem of teenage mothers in America, see Luker (1996).

17. Anna's immigrant father's experience of social mobility had an incredibly powerful effect on the cultural capital of the family. Indeed, her father was

instrumental in ensuring that all five of his children were socially mobile in one way or another and only the youngest son was indulged in his pursuit of a career in the arts. The experience of mobility, therefore, shaped family values and practices in a very powerful way. A description of this processes can be found in Bertaux and Bertaux-Wiame (1996).

18. Mary's account of her childhood powerfully demonstrates the way in which experiences of economic constraint – the Depression in the 1930s in her parents' case – shape cultural values and practices. Her parents' early lives meant they were financially cautious even when economic conditions changed for the better in the 1950s and 1960s. They remained anxious to save rather than eager to spend and, despite feeling its constraints, Mary was a beneficiary of their frugality. Arguably, this generation – suspicious of high levels of consumption – has now disappeared. See Schor (1998).

19. Again, it was readily apparent that while the US has a much-lauded system of higher education (i.e. see Lipset 1996), it is an extremely hierarchical system and money is very important in securing access (namely, being able to meet tuition fees) to schools at the top of the prestige ladder.

20. Given the high proportion of young people who go on to higher education in the USA in comparison to Britain, it is not surprising that there is a much higher dropout rate in the former than the latter. The USA differs from Britain in that students can elect to take longer to complete their degrees – dipping in and out of the system in the face of economic constraints, for example – although there is growing public anxiety about the large number of young men who find it difficult to complete their undergraduate degrees in four years for financial and non-financial reasons. See Mare (1995).

21. Attending medical school is seen as completing an undergraduate medical education consisting of pre-clinical and clinical components. The programme takes four years. It is residency programmes – which can last from three to seven years depending on the specialism – that are viewed as graduate medical education. This is the usual route for the education and training for medical doctors (M.D.s) although there are a small number of combined M.D./P.h.D. programmes around the USA which are, of course, highly prestigious. The American Medical Association provides considerable information on becoming an MD on its web pages and elsewhere.

22. This is another example of how the interviewees from more modest social backgrounds could turn constraints into opportunity. Judy described how she lived a very frugal existence as a medical student in low rent housing while many of her fellow students from more affluent backgrounds enjoyed lavish lifestyles. In effect, she had inherited her parents' frugal nature and, of course, endorsed the value of education and learning over consumption and pleasure.

23. Thus, these interviewees from more modest social origins experienced a much tougher time in getting to, and making it through, college although they won out in the end. They were, of course, incredibly hard working and highly disciplined people. That they had the opportunity to go to college, however, confirms the empirical findings that America is a somewhat more open society than Britain and other European countries even if it is not exceptionally

open. See Erikson and Goldthorpe (1993). The importance that ordinary Americans attach to higher education as a route to social mobility is well captured by Evans (1993).

24. It is interesting to note how it was almost always assumed that money buys the best and you pay for what you get. I asked the interviewees who were privately educated if their parents had been privately educated too. Often, they did not have this information but, for those who did, it seemed that they had been privately educated. It was all part of their family history and tradition. This point confirms Halsey *et al.'s* (1980) statistical finding that parents' private education is a better predictor than social class as to whether a son is privately educated or not.

25. For an excellent account of the importance of education for girls that emphasises a woman's role with the domestic sphere, irrespective of social class, see Deem (1978, 1980). For a longer historical perspective on this issue, see Purvis (1983). On Ladies' Colleges, see Royle (1987).

26. Ronald Watson's parents, therefore, strategically took him out of one primary school and placed him in another to increase his chances of academic success. The interrelationship between economic and cultural resources, therefore, should be readily apparent.

27. She also went on to equate the middle class with cultural capital when she mentioned that she was still in touch with one of her old school friends who was also a 'scholarship kid. She had a single parent but it was always the more intellectual people that took available opportunities.' Arguably, their cultural capital allowed them to take such opportunities. See Roker (1993).

28. Many of the socially mobile interviewees made reference to the fact that their parents came from large families. A large family was equated with economic hardship and pressures to seek employment at the first opportunity and contribute to family income. The decline in family size, especially among working-class families in the first half of the twentieth century (Gittens 1982, 1985) would have contributed to higher standards of living. It is certainly how my interviewees reflected back on their family histories in the telling of narratives of their childhood.

29. Halsey *et al.* (1980) showed that working-class boys were, indeed, far more likely than their middle-class counterparts to finish school at 15 and 16. Working-class boys who stayed on at school between 16 and 18 to do A levels then had as much chance of going to university as middle-class boys. Unfortunately, Halsey *et al.*'s research focused exclusively on young men and we do not have the equivalent empirical findings on young women during this time. It is easy to imagine that similar processes occurred for young women who went to grammar schools too. It could be argued Pauline Lomax's account of her school days indicates why working-class men and women left school as soon as possible. Pauline's account suggests that the snobbery and elitism associated with such schools made working-class children feel inferior and lacking in the appropriate middle-class cultural capital. For an autobiographical account of life at a girls' grammar school, see Evans (1996). That her parents were delighted that she secured a clerical job confirms Goldthorpe's (2000) positional theory of cultural aspirations.

30. Celia Watson suggested that her parents did not attach a lot of importance to her education but they encouraged her sister. She said, 'She definitely had the ability and they knew she had the ability. She was encouraged.' Celia's point suggests that middle-class parents are like working-class parents in some respects in that they also need their children to demonstrate their academic ability. It is once this academic ability has been demonstrated via exam success etc. that parents shape their educational mobility strategies for their children accordingly. This counters Goldthorpe's point (1996) that only working-class parents' educational aspirations are shaped by their children's demonstrated ability. If this point is acknowledged, it is possible to recognise that children within middle-class and working-class families have different talents and abilities that allow some to go far and others not. It would, indeed, be very interesting to do research comparing the social mobility of siblings seemingly exposed to the same parental economic, cultural and social resources.

31. It should be noted that Bridget was an only child. She recalled periods when her parents experienced financial difficulties because her father was made redundant and other times when they were affluent. In her teens, her mother returned to work and, of course, her re-entry into the labour market was facilitated by the fact that she had only one child to look after. Family size, therefore, could impact on levels of economic prosperity and poverty among working-class families (and middle-class families) in this indirect way too. For the classic study of women's employment in Britain that charted, for the first time, women's increasing participation in the labour market, see Martin and Roberts (1980).

32. Institutional arrangements, therefore, captured the hierarchical nature of Britain with its class rigidities and status consciousness at that time. The school people attended was seen to seal their fate in life. See Simon (1991).

33. The majority of the interviewees stayed on at the same grammar school they had attended from 11 to 16 since the grammar schools were the main route through further education into higher education. Again, see Halsey *et al.* (1980).

34. Crucially, therefore, a state maintenance grant gave Barbara Coombes financial independence from her parents so that she was not a burden on them while at medical school. As their youngest daughter, there was less pressure for her to find paid work at 16 to contribute to family income. She was the only child in her family to attend university, indicating the importance of birth order in enjoying these opportunities.

35. Thus, it was Diane Smith's economic resources that were crucial in ensuring that her husband completed his medical career. Her financial independence gave him the space to complete his studies rather than take a lesser job to fulfill his responsibilities as a husband and father. Thus, how economic resources might be mobilised by young couples in the mobility process is worthy of consideration too.

36. This example certainly confirms Goldthorpe's (2000) argument that economic resources are mobilised when children are not always academically successful. Rosemary Hill was not necessarily unsuccessful but her mediocre A level grades closed down the option of going to university. By supporting

her, financially and in other ways, during an additional year of schooling, they kept her options and, therefore, her choices, as open as possible.

37. Here was another example of an accidental pregnancy at an early age and, again, it is interesting to note how families on both sides helped Rosemary and her husband. The early years of their married life were difficult but having children early later became an advantage as Rosemary could forge a career once her children were at school and she was still comparatively young.

38. Norman's good life at university, therefore, had economic consequences. Although he was fortunate to have a student grant for four years, new parental responsibilities meant that he had to finish teacher training college with a teaching certificate rather than stay on an additional year and gain a degree. Lack of a degree had further consequences down the line as it limited his promotion chances within his own school and in applications to other schools.

39. I would not disagree with Pauline's views about class and how her life had turned out. It is often argued that people are aware of class inequalities in British society but class is something that is 'out there' and they find it difficult to apply class processes to their own lives. See, for example, Savage *et al.* (2001). I would contend that people find it increasingly difficult and they are reluctant to categorise themselves as a particular class especially if they have been socially mobile. Even so, class can be a salient identity in people's lives. See Bradley (1999) and Devine (2004a).

40. Sheila Myers enjoyed marital mobility for she met her husband when she was a laboratory technician and he was a newly qualified doctor. The study of marital mobility is a topic that has not been greatly researched. The debate on class and gender in the 1980s led Goldthorpe (1987) to consider marital mobility and to argue that mobility through marriage rather than employment was the main way in which women enjoyed social advancement. While marital mobility is, I am sure, still important, it is hard not to imagine that changes in women's positions over the last thirty or more years – more women acquiring high-level qualifications, more women entering high-level jobs like medicine – have changed these processes somewhat. A male doctor can now marry a fellow female doctor rather than a nurse or laboratory technician! R. Crompton has long been attuned to these issues of assortive mating. See Crompton and Sanderson (1990) and Crompton and Harris (1999).

41. Thus, the existence of the welfare state certainly helped my working-class respondents in the mobility process in a way that was not so readily apparent among my American interviewees from modest social backgrounds. That said, they found ways and means of securing economic resources to see them through college too.

42. The findings confirm that the middle classes have been the major beneficiaries of the welfare state in Britain. See Goodin and LeGrand (1987). That is why there has long been debate on how the middle class is squeezed in the USA. This issue is now taking off in Britain.

43. It is for this reason that is important to avoid stereotypes of a working class completely lacking in economic resources in contrast to a middle class who

have economic resources. Goldthorpe (2000), of course, is not alone in devis-
ing such sharp dichotomies between the middle class and working class. See,
for example, Reay (1998) who also makes a hard distinction between the
middle class and working class in an otherwise interesting study of women,
education and cultural capital.

3. FINANCIAL CHOICES AND SACRIFICES FOR CHILDREN

1. This argument highlights the limitations of equal opportunities. People may
   be free to compete but they are not able to compete equally. The unequal
   competition, therefore, produces unequal outcomes. I consider this issue in
   the closing paragraphs of this book. See Giddens (1994, 1995).
2. See Brown *et al.* (1997).
3. Over the course of this chapter, it will become apparent that many direct
   grant grammar schools, which operated on the boundaries of the private/state
   boundary, effectively opted out of the state system and became wholly private
   schools with the demise of the tripartite system and the rise of comprehensive schools. That said, children who could not afford to pay fees could still
   attend these schools via the assisted places scheme. In effect, it was another
   form of state subsidy to pay for private school fees. Despite some opposition,
   the scheme was abolished by the new Labour government in 1997. For an
   account of the experience of the assisted places scheme, see Roker (1992).
4. Himself privately educated, Michael Reed was very aware of the benefits of
   a private school education in terms of basic resources including a favourable
   physical environment – good buildings, an excellent library, top sporting
   facilities and so on. He was also cognisant of the fact that private schools are
   very good at providing a range of extra curricular activities that all add to
   children's cultural capital. This is but one way in which economic resources
   are converted into cultural capital (Bourdieu 1986).
5. The issue of time and time pressures have been much researched in recent
   years. See, for example, Hochschild (1989, 1997) and Stacey (1996). The
   'time bind' is a issue of much public concern in the USA because they have
   some of the longest working hours in the world and the implications for family
   life have been noted. See, for example, Schor (1992).
6. It was very interesting to hear the different dilemmas that African American
   middle-class interviewees had to confront in comparison to their white counterparts. Their preference to live in diverse neighbourhoods rather than white
   suburbs had consequences for their children's education. That is to say, they
   confronted a much poorer public school system in the communities in which
   they lived in comparison to those living in the suburbs. On the black middle
   class, see Landry (1988, 1991) and Pattillo-McCoy (1999). On residential
   segregation, see Massey and Denton (1993).
7. As I will argue in Chapters 6 and 7, social networks are certainly important
   in supplying information. Arguably, where they are especially important is in
   making sense of that information, helping people to evaluate it. In the USA,
   realtors make extensive use of information on local school systems in selling

property. If anything, it is easy to imagine being overwhelmed by the statistical information that is available on schools and academic success rates which is why the help of colleagues and friends in making sense of information is so crucial. The link between economic resources and social networks is evident here in the way that social networks often include colleagues from work with similar economic resources making similar sorts of decisions about where to live regarding schooling and so forth.

8. Arguably, Rachel and Alan Garrett were downwardly mobile from their parents' position. They lacked the economic resources of more secure members of the middle class in my sample although they had very high levels of cultural capital. Their high levels of cultural capital dictated the economic sacrifices they made.

9. Bernice's children participated in a voluntary school desegregation programme that bussed her children out of their city neighbourhood to an almost wholly white suburban school. Bernice and her husband had high aspirations for their children but unlike the African American medics in my sample they did not have the economic resources to send their daughters to private school. They circumvented this constraint, however, through this programme. See Eaton (2001).

10. Charles and Nadia Khan, therefore, were highly educated middle-class immigrants to America who had made a very successful life for themselves and their daughter. On the diverse experiences of immigrants to America, see Farley (1995a, 1996).

11. The issue of how parents patrol and control their children's activities will be discussed more fully in Chapter 5. See Lareau (1989/2000, 2002).

12. My interviewees often spoke of their worries about violence at school. They talked, for example, of their children's experiences of other children carrying knives. Unsurprisingly, frequent reference was made to tragic events, such as the shootings at Colombine.

13. I would venture to suggest that the interviewees who had been socially mobile into medicine and teaching expressed a higher level of anxiety about spiralling college fees. Jane Bennett came from a 'blue-collar background' while her husband came from an established middle to upper-middle-class background. She was aghast at the kinds of figures being quoted in the media while her husband was somewhat concerned but more laid back about the issue. The impact of social origins and trajectories on values and attitudes was apparent once again.

14. Here, then, was an example of the transfer of wealth across three generations. The most exciting research on wealth and inequality has focused on black/white differences. See, for example, Oliver and Shapiro (1997) and Conley (1999). These studies highlight the limitations of focusing only on income and how wealth is so crucial for understanding the accumulation of advantage and disadvantage across generations. More research of this kind is needed to ascertain the nature of wealth transfers in terms of class and gender inequalities too.

15. Again, it was evident that the interviewees from modest social backgrounds had fewer savings than those from established middle-class or

upper-middle-class backgrounds. After all, they had often taken out loans to finance their own education and now they had to take out further loans for their children's education. Whether this form of consumption is an example of wanting something that is not needed is open to debate. See Schor (1998).

16. That said, the Chapmans' decision to live in an affluent community to ensure their children went to good public schools had been a financial strain. They struggled to pay a high mortgage and property taxes. While they had been successful in securing a good early education for their children, they were increasingly aware of financial constraints with regard to higher education.

17. There was frequent discussion of the advantages of having athletics scholarships by my American interviewees and many of them promoted sport as a leisure activity for a mix of non-instrumental and instrumental reasons.

18. The Rothmans' youngest daughter was still making her way through a community college. They anticipated that she would take five or six years to complete her degree as she was not intellectually strong. As one of the oldest couples in the survey, they had financed their children's education mostly in a more favourable economic and political climate. William Rothman let it be known very quickly in the interview that he had served in the Vietnam War. He was very proud of his veteran status.

19. On the migration patterns of middle-class and working-class Caribbeans to the USA, see Waters (1999).

20. Barry Waite spoke at length about 'fears of falling' in relation to his two sons. See Ehrenreich (1989) and Newman (1988, 1991, 1993). Decisions they had made to drop out of college were discussed and reference made to the impact of their parent's divorce on their teenage years. While there is a huge body of research on changing family forms, including divorce (see, for example, Waite and Gallagher, 2000), it is surprising that so little research has been done on the impact of divorce on family strategies regarding social mobility.

21. There is a wealth of material that shows that college fees have increased way beyond the rate of inflation in the last ten years in the USA. The interviewees' concerns, therefore, are undoubtedly real.

22. Again, therefore, it was apparent that those interviewees who had experienced private education only considered private education for their children. It was a family norm or tradition so to speak and more powerful than the influence of class on decisions to go private or public. After all, most middle-class parents do not educate their children privately since only 8 per cent of parents with children do so. See Halsey *et al.* (1980). Of course, other interviewees did not experience private education but privately educated their children. Barbara Coombes decided to educate her children privately in the face of the collapse of her marriage, her ex-husband's death not long after their divorce and the huge demands of her job as a GP, of course. See n. 3 on changing family circumstances.

23. Note the connection between economic resources and social networks. The decision to send her son to a private school meant that Susan could ensure, as far as possible, that is, that her son mixed with nice boys who did not say F-off (a shorthand term she used rather than me). Interestingly, her son

only spent a short time at the private prep school. Susan and her husband split up when he had an affair and he subsequently remarried and had more children. He refused to contribute to his son's private school fees citing the demands of his new family on his economic resources. Susan and her son moved into rented accommodation in a small town so she could send him to a good (enough) state school. Again, it is noteworthy that while there are some excellent studies of divorce and its implications for parenting (see, for example, Smart and Neale 1999), little attention has been given to the issue of co-parenting, education, the mobilisation of resources and issues of social mobility.

24. Anecdotal evidence and widespread media coverage do suggest that it is in the major cities like London, Manchester and Birmingham in the UK that parents are having to think strategically about where they live in order to ensure their children get into good state schools. Most sociological evidence has been collected in London where, arguably, the problems of a variable state school system are acute. See, for example, Gewirtz *et al.* (1995) and Reay (1998). Reay and Lucey (2003) have touched on the issues with respect to the growing population of asylum seekers and their children in London. For a wider book that addresses middle-class gentrification in London and touches on issues of education, see Butler (1997) and Butler and Robson (2003).

25. Goldthorpe (2000) spoke of the importance of economic resources to pay for additional tuition. Indeed, many of the medics spoke of how people around them were participating in this circuit where their children sat one entrance examination after another for private schools to ensure that they had a choice of school, and to make sure it would be a private school.

26. It was interesting to hear the discussions about private/state education going on within the Jones family. Janet had been wholly privately educated at a prestigious Ladies' College while Gerald was the successful product of a state grammar school (and an ordinary one at that). Janet was extremely fearful about sending her children to the local state primary schools while Gerald was much more laid back although happy with Janet's preferences. I suspect that if one parent has been privately educated, the chances of their children also being privately educated increase. On Peter Smith's logic, see Swift (2003).

27. Again, Stephen had been privately educated while Julia had enjoyed success at a small girls' grammar school. They were aware that their daughter was not as intellectually able as their younger son. There were some strains in the relationship between a highly intellectually able mother and seemingly less able daughter although they appeared to have weathered them quite successfully.

28. Interestingly, Jill and Graham Dowds attended an open day at a private school (once a direct-grant grammar school, now wholly private) and they described the experience as 'ghastly'. They compared this experience with an open day at the local comprehensive school. As they explained,

When we went to [B] grammar school, we were just one of thousands of parents and they can just treat you as they want because there are so many people trying to get in that they are not bothered. When we went up to the comp, the Head had us in his office, explaining how the school worked and got one of the Deputy Heads in to show us round the school.

The Dowds clearly did not like the private school because it felt like a traditional grammar school where they were expected to defer to the head. He expected respect but he did not appear to respect parents. It reminded them of the status consciousness and hierarchy of their own education under the tripartite system. They did not see themselves or their children as the type of people who could fit in easily in this environment and, culturally and politically, they were correct in this judgement. It sounded as if class, status and hierarchy were alive and well at these private schools. For a fine theoretical discussion of status, see Scott (1996a).

29. Roger Harrison's comment that the local comprehensive school was 'perfectly adequate' captures the critique levelled against rational choice theory beautifully. That is to say, people do not spent their time maximising their goals but often seek to achieve them at a satisfactory level especially as they will often be juggling different and competing goals. See Simon (1982). On the problems of rational choice theory, see also Collins (1994), Przeworski (1990) and Scott (1995). On the more general problem of utilitarian models of social action, see Lockwood (1992). It should be noted that Roger was, apparently, a staunch socialist so his wider social and political values and beliefs clearly influenced his actions.

30. In effect, therefore, these middle-class parents had 'exited' the system. On the classic statement of exit and voice, see Hirschman (1962). Moran (1999) also argues that the middle classes have exited the state health system in Britain by paying for private health care. Once upon a time, sociological debate focused on the incorporation of the working class into society (see Devine 1992). Now, it seems, debate over the welfare state in Britain concerns the problem of sustaining the incorporation of the middle class into society.

31. This is an important example of how economic resources could be withheld. It was readily apparent that the interviewees' decisions about education were heavily influenced by their views of their children's talents and abilities. See Gewirtz et al. (1995) on this issue. To be sure, they did not think that intelligence was a genetically unalterable characteristic as demonstrated by their recognition of the effects of schooling on examination success. They also believed that their children have certain levels of innate intelligence especially when they compared and contrasted their sons' and daughters' talents and abilities. They subscribed, in other words, to the popularly held view that intelligence is both inherited to some degree and subject to environmental factors to another degree. They occupied the moderate middle ground in the nature verses nurture debate. See Dawkins (2003).

32. Making a virtue out of necessity, therefore, is not the preserve of the working class although Bourdieu et al. (1999) would argue that members of the working class face the problems of necessity more than the middle class.

33. See n. 31. The Willis's spoke of how they did not know what their adopted son had inherited in terms of intelligence from his parents. The majority of children now go on to further education although there is still a sharp

class divide since it is middle-class children who take an academic route that leads to higher education while working-class children take the vocational route that leads into employment at the lower echelons of the occupational structure. See Banks *et al.* (1992), Brynner and Roberts (1991) and Brynner (2000).

34. Here was another example of middle-class parents helping their children financially so they could keep their options as wide as possible for as long as possible. The similarities with Rosemary Hill discussed in Chapter 2 are obvious.

35. The Hills sent their two sons to private school although it sounded as if they were always ambivalent about that decision. They also found the private school snobbery distasteful and held very similar views to the Dowds as discussed in n. 28. It is probably not surprising, therefore, that their sons held similar views and took the first opportunity to leave at 16 and attend the local college. The Hills' oldest son had dropped out of university although he was then very successful in the civil service and the second son dropped out for a period of time. There seemed to be parallels between this family and the fate of Barry Waite's two sons (see n. 20 above). Mr Hill and Mr Waite were quite alike in their independent critical stance towards a range of issues, including education, and I often wondered whether their sons had adopted similar attitudes at an early age leading them to make the decisions they did. They seemed to have quite distinctive family cultures.

36. Again, note the interconnection between economic and cultural resources in how money paid for travel. On the importance of cultural capital in this respect, see Brown and Scase (1994) and the excellent article by Brown (1995).

37. Thus, changes in the higher education system were forcing some of the British interviewees to consider fees and maintenance costs in a way that the American interviewees were already well familiar with. They were thinking of how they would have to adjust their lifestyles and plans accordingly.

38. Both Bruce and Margaret Brown's fathers were self-employed businessmen and the ethos of independence was very much a part of the family culture. See Scase and Goffee (1989). Note how this financial independence gave James the freedom to flit between numerous careers in his 20s rather than settle down, much to the consternation of his mother and, to some extent, his father. He was, of course, also in the position of taking risks in his attempts to become a millionaire.

39. The notion of branching points was used originally by Boudon (1974) and subsequently adopted by Goldthorpe (1996). It is very useful in examining the junctures at which important decisions have to be made. It should be readily apparent that the different institutional arrangements in America and Britain throw up different branching points and, therefore, choices and decisions.

40. That said, I am aware of the difficulties of suggesting that the importance of economic resources has grown over time when they have been critical to the mobility process for a long time. A qualitative study conducted at a particular moment cannot say very much about changes over time.

41. This example chimes with the popular discourse about a middle class being 'caught in the middle' in America. See Wolfe (1991). This class discourse is absent in Britain.

4. EXPECTATIONS AND HOPES FOR EDUCATIONAL SUCCESS

1. Bourdieu's work has had a huge influence on British sociology. The publication of *Distinction* in (1984) and subsequently of his many books and interviews, mostly by Polity Press, account for his astounding popularity. See, for example, a thoughtful review of his most recent work (Bourdieu *et al.* 1999; Bourdieu 2000) by Warde (2002). Before the 1980s, Bourdieu was better known for his work on education and cultural capital within the sociology of education. For the classic statement of his work, see Bourdieu (1973; 1986). His work, of course, remains highly influential in the sub-discipline of the sociology of education (see Lareau 2000 and Reay 1998). The significance of his work has now extended throughout the discipline as a whole and his discussion of class in terms of different capitals (Bourdieu 1987) has been very influential in the field of class analysis (see Savage 2000; Skeggs 1997). There is now a vast industry on Bourdieu in terms of a huge number of books commenting on his work and it is easy to be overwhelmed by the choices on offer. To my mind, the best short introduction to Bourdieu for students, written in his usual jovial and accessible style, is the book by Jenkins (1991). The more advanced book which I enjoyed reading most and which led me back to re-read Bourdieu is by Swartz (1997). It is an excellent discussion of Bourdieu's work and I would recommend it highly. I also found the work of Bourdieu and Wacquant (1992) useful although I was disappointed with Wacquant's hostility towards Jenkins' critical engagement with Bourdieu. In a seminar in my department, I was asked why I had not used Bourdieu as the theoretical starting point for my research. Quite simply, it was because my interests lay in the topic of social mobility and, by implication, social stability. Unfortunately, Bourdieu has only a little to say about class trajectories. I have, as I hope is obvious in this book, engaged with Bourdieu's work quite substantially. Indeed, I do like Bourdieu's rejection of rational choice models of action. I am of the view that, bar the use of different language, Goldthorpe's and Bourdieu's discussion of the mobilisation of resources/exploitation of capital amounts to much the same thing. To see Goldthorpe and Bourdieu as rivals is unproductive and what is more important is to advance our understanding of the world by taking the best of their ideas forward. While I recognise that the discipline of sociology has its limitations regarding the progressive accumulation of knowledge about the social world, I am cheerful, like Abbott (2001), about what it achieves.

2. On this point, see Lamont and Lareau (1988), Bourdieu and Wacquant (1992) and the discussion in Swartz (1997). See also the work on cultural capital and school success by DiMaggio (1982) and DiMaggio and Mohr (1984).

3. Thus, parents' experiences of education, especially the level of education they had achieved, had a big influence on what they expected of their children. Parents do not wish their children to be less educationally successful than themselves in the same way that they do not wish them to fall into a lower class. Mare (1995) talks about a 'floor' below which they do not like their children to fall.

4. What should also be apparent in this discussion is that aspirations, expectations, hopes, dreams and so on are not shaped by personal experience (or parents' personal experiences) only but the wider economic, social and political climate in which people grow up.

5. Despite Bourdieu's argument that cultural capital is not about high culture, it was interesting to note how some interviewees from long-established upper-middle-class families asserted their families' 'high' cultural tastes. This finding contrasts somewhat with Lamont's (1992) comparative study of the American and French upper middle class. She argued that the former attached importance to their money and downplayed culture while the latter emphasised their culture and downplayed their monetary wealth.

6. It was interesting to note that those interviewees who had a parent who had been socially mobile from a modest class position, and the interviewees' parents who still occupied such a position, proffered an instrumental rather than expressive view of education. While it seemed that education was a means to an end rather than an end in itself, I would not want to overstate this distinction and imply that those from modest social backgrounds do not also value education for its own sake.

7. The way in which Bernice spoke of how she had internalised social pressures to succeed captures the spirit of Bourdieu's ideas about cultural capital (see, in particular, Bourdieu 1986). Note also the links between cultural capital and social networks that will be discussed more fully in Chapters 6 and 7. Swartz (1997: 269) alerted me to the fact that Bourdieu and Coleman had engaged with each other's intellectual enterprises. See Bourdieu and Coleman (1991).

8. The interviewees did not like to portray their parents as 'pushy' parents with all the negative connotations that go with this idea. At the same time, it was apparent that interviewees whose parents had been socially mobile, and who had missed out on opportunities presented to them, were quite aggressive in their desire to see their children get ahead. It might be that mothers, whose opportunities as women were very limited before the 1960s, were especially anxious that their daughters and sons exploit opportunities they had never had or could not exploit themselves.

9. Of course, as highly able young people, these interviewees did not need to be pushed by their parents as they were successful on their own. I was frequently intrigued by my interviewees' remarks about siblings and their different experiences within their family, and different levels of educational and occupational success. I presume, for example, given his comments that George Marshall's sister would have given me a somewhat different account of her parents. Research on social mobility tends to focus on differences between families, of course, with little work on variations between siblings within families.

10. Roy Morgan found it rather difficult to talk about class divisions within the African American community, although he explained the situation to me:

> The South had a very different socio-economic hierarchical breakdown. I hate to put it this way but one of the advantages to the historical segregation that the South was known for was that there was a socio-economic hierarchy in the black community and in the white community that didn't meet. So what happened was, my grandparents were very affluent by black standards in the South in those days and my mother and my uncle were raised fairly affluently. They were able to live a very, very fine, very, very upper-middle-class existence that allowed my mother to go to [H] university, graduate and then go to nursing training in Boston.

Although it seemed that Roy came from a modest social background, since his father was a mechanic who had never enjoyed upward mobility, his mother's social background was middle class. Given the gender segregation of the labour market and discrimination (Bianche 1995), his mother was not able to pursue a more upper-middle-class career in a profession or management. Arguably, she experienced downward marital mobility although her educational background was then crucial in ensuring her children's success. Roy Morgan is an example of how it was the more affluent – either economically or culturally – African Americans who enjoyed the benefits of Affirmative Action policies in the 1960s rather than the materially and culturally deprived, who remained in the inner city. See Wilson (1978).

11. Again, the issue of family size was raised frequently in the discussions on family poverty in the first half of the twentieth century. For changing fertility patterns in the US, see Waite and Gallagher (2000).

12. As discussed in Chapters 2 and 3, white-collar clerical work was seen as a step up from blue-collar factory work. In Marion Chaves' case, it was interesting to hear how she experienced social mobility in her thirties with the support and encouragement of her husband. I suspect that research on work–life mobility would reveal the importance, not so much of parents, but of significant others, e.g. spouses, with both husbands and wives helping each other.

13. The optimistic economic and political climate of the times, therefore, fostered high aspirations for educational advancement. After all, there was a substantial increase in government spending on education in the US and the UK during the long boom between 1945 and 1973.

14. This account of the relationship between fathers and sons makes it easy to see how occupational inheritance was evident in medicine and why it remained almost an exclusively male-dominated profession until the 1960s. See Moran (1999) and Riska (2001). The research discussed in this book shows the value of moving down a level to study occupations as a way of studying class. See Grusky and Sorensen (1998).

15. It appeared, therefore, that it was the sciences rather than the arts (for sons at least) that were most valued within these families.

16. The enduring importance of status was apparent once again. For Weber's classic discussion of status, see Turner (2000).

17. For other women in the sample, therefore, career success came later in life. It was later 'exposure' to educators at graduate school that encouraged Susan

to go to graduate school. The interconnection between cultural capital and social networks is obvious here too.

18. On the formidable impact of gender on women's education and employment, see Goldin (1990) and Bianchi (1995).

19. Elisabeth Danson and her husband, Don, were very interesting. They could be described as southies (see Lukas 1985) as they grew up in the dense Irish communities of south Boston. Elisabeth's family moved out to the suburbs in the 1960s as her father's move into teaching facilitated relocation to a bigger house in the suburbs. Whether there was an element of white flight in this relocation is hard to say for sure, although Elisabeth spoke of her surprise at finding lots of old school friends and neighbours at her new school! She also spoke of how most of her white college friends left Boston to find teaching jobs in the mid-West and how she could not get a permanent teaching job for a long period of time because the Boston school system was only hiring minority teachers then. She expressed no resentment about this issue and, indeed, she and Don appeared to place a very high value on their children being 'exposed' to Boston's diversity. Elisabeth taught at an inner city middle school where most of her pupils were African American and Hispanic. Running special classes for the low achievers, she was cognisant of the difficulties many of her pupils would face in the future and the enormous hurdles they had faced so far.

20. The impact of masculinity on expectations and aspirations was evident here. See Connell (1995, 1987).

21. See n. 18 above. Brothers and sisters experienced different opportunities and constraints within families.

22. The impact of gender sterotypes was crucial in shaping the occupational and class mobility of these interviewees. As with Goldthorpe, Bourdieu neglected issues of gender in much of his early work but was forced to consider the issue more centrally in later life.

23. To these interviewees, it was obvious that their parents valued education precisely because they were paying for it. Note how cultural capital was seen to influence the mobilisation of economic resources. It is not merely the case that economic resources shape cultural capital for, in a circular way, cultural capital shapes the mobilisation of economic resources too. They are, in effect, mutually constitutive of each other.

24. Among the most affluent members of the British sample (although not unlike their American counterparts), there was a tendency to speak of their educational histories and educational success as effortless. They were gentleman who did not talk of the effort required to become successful. This was how they carried themselves. See Scott (1982) on gentlemen.

25. More often than not, it seemed that those parents (usually fathers) who had experienced upwardly mobility via work experience (sometimes combined with study at night school) did not want their children to have to suffer the hardships and make the sacrifices that they had to make in order to be successful. They appreciated that early educational success made life much easier, especially if it facilitated entry into the professions. This might explain why managers as well as professionals want their children to enjoy educational

success and enter the professions, which are, of course, also more secure. See Savage *et al.* (1992). In this respect, they were cognisant of how the system worked and how to work the system.

26. Many of the interviewees were at pains to emphasise the intellect and culture of at least one of their parents, despite the lack of formal qualifications. Indeed, there were some moving accounts of how a parent was only semiliterate but that did not mean they were unintelligent in their lives and work and beyond. In other words, they were well aware that intelligence is not captured in intelligence tests in school! On the intellectual life of the British working class, see the excellent historical study by Rose (2001).

27. The interviewees frequently used the word 'trust' and said how once their parents got them into good schools, they did not need to worry any more because they could trust the school and its teachers. The use of the word reminded me of Putnam's (2000) work on social capital (his definition of social capital focuses on both networks and the norms that arise out of them), and the discussion it has generated on trust. See Gambetta (1990). For an acknowledgement that there might have been a decline in social and political trust in Britain, see Hall (1999). For public concern about the decline in trust and how it is leading to more accountability and surveillance see the concise book from the Reith Lectures, O'Neill (2002).

28. See n. 26 above and the reference to Rose (2001). Interestingly, when Diane Willis spoke of her parents' culture, she also emphasised that they were part of the 'respectable' working class, rather than the 'rough' working class although she was embarrassed to say this since it implied that her family looked down on people. This distinction within the working class has a long history although for a recent discussion of it in relation to gender and class, see Skeggs (1997). Note also the resentment expressed at the lack of opportunities and how her mother did not accept her lot in life. Working-class resentment is often discussed in a derogatory way – dismissed as jealousy – probably because it is a form of resistance or challenge to the prevailing order.

29. The eleven plus examination, therefore, was the key test and public demonstration of academic ability. It represented the external ratification of intellectual talent. See Gambetta (1987).

30. Of crucial significance was the fact that the working-class interviewees did not experience counter-pressures to academic success. On school resistance, see Willis (1977). For an excellent critique of Willis, see Brown (1987). The interviewees' families and friends all supported them in their academic endeavours.

31. The distinction I have drawn between expectations and hopes conveys the different level of confidence to be found among the middle-class and working-class informants.

32. The intimate (although sometimes hierarchical) relationship between fathers and sons, therefore, was influential in occupational inheritance and in the extent to which sons followed in their father's footsteps. Coleman (1988) spoke of the importance of relationships between parents and children when he discussed social capital within families. This point highlights how economic, cultural and social resources are so inextricably bound together that

it is difficult to distinguish their component parts. On intimate relations, see Giddens (1993) and Jamieson (1998).

33. Rod Hunt's parents were middle-class Jewish refugees from Russia who experienced the concentration camps. They were able to get to Britain after the Second World War. They had low levels of economic capital in Rod's early life although his father later enjoyed business success. They had a lot of cultural capital with a taste for high culture with regard to music and the arts. Be that as it may, given their painful life experiences, the security of a scientific career in medicine for their son appealed to them greatly. The desirability of jobs was once a major topic of investigation in the study of class but, unfortunately, it appears to have disappeared off the research agenda. This is a shame, as occupational choices are different today than they were in the past and it would be interesting to know more about careers and jobs that are considered desirable or otherwise among young people. For the old research on this issue, see Goldthorpe and Hope (1974) and Coxon and Jones (1978, 1979).

34. During her teenage years, Bridget had a difficult relationship with her mother. She did not like her mother's snobbery. She talked about the issue with some amusement as if it now troubled her less, although she still disliked snobbery and elitism as was apparent in other parts of the interview. She said:

> My mother was always really anti comprehensive schools. She used to go on and on about comprehensive schools being the pits! So, it was like it was a bit of a nag really . . . She'd gone to a grammar school. Yeah, she was quite snobby. She really went on at me. She really went on about comprehensives so that you felt that nothing you ever achieved or no friends you ever made or nothing you did was going to be any good there anyway because she had such a downer on it, really.

She said her father, a welder, 'wasn't a dominant personality really' and it was her mother who was 'the force' in the family. After grammar school, her mother went into clerical work as opportunities to go into higher education were limited in the 1930s and 1940s. She was desperate for her own daughter to succeed. This may be another example of a sunken middle-class mother propelling her children forward. See Jackson and Marsden (1962).

35. It is important to remember how the older women interviewees who went into medicine were ahead of their time as it was still a very male-dominated occupation. See Crompton (1999).

36. Here was an example of occupational inheritance among women that might explain, in part, why teaching remains such a female-dominated occupation despite attempts to attract more men into the profession. See Coffey (2001).

37. Teaching, therefore, was a good career for middle-class and working-class women up until the late 1960s and early 1970s. See Crompton (1992). Occupational segregation by gender explains why middle-class daughters experienced downward social mobility rather than social stability, as middle-class boys did, and why working-class girls were mobile into the semi-professions (teaching, nursing etc.) while working-class boys enjoyed long-range mobility into the professions and management. On the social mobility patterns of women and men, see Marshall et al. (1988). This situation has now

changed as young women have pulled the qualifications lever, as Crompton and Sanderson (1990) put it, pursuing high-level educational qualifications that have facilitated their entry into the professions and management.
Of course, middle-class women have enjoyed these new opportunities more
than working-class women so that the class divide among women is, arguably,
now more apparent than it was. Class divides women as much as it does men
as Marshall *et al.* found (1988).

38. This is my favourite quote from my British interviewees, as it captures the
ways in which parents' hopes for their children are not static. Mr Willis followed his brother who also was highly successful at school. His father's aspirations, he says, evolved as they enjoyed increasing success at school. The
setback to an academic career was a major one and it is hard not to think he
would have made a great academic.

39. Given his parents' limited knowledge of the education system, the school
culture was important in propelling Norman forward. The culture of the
school was very masculine, of course, as a single-sex boys' grammar school.
Again, see Connell (1995 and 1987). See also Mac an Ghaill (1988, 1994)
on the making of masculinities in British schools in the contemporary era.

40. Thus, the interviewees' educational aspirations were clearly shaped by their
socio-economic backgrounds, and where they started from influenced the
height of these aspirations. This finding confirms Goldthorpe's positional
theory of aspirations. I would argue, however, that it is hard to imagine that
Bourdieu would disagree with these ideas. Over the years, I have come to
wonder whether Goldthorpe's criticism of Bourdieu for characterising the
working class as suffering from a poverty of aspirations is 'over the top'. After
all, Bourdieu's main interests – both theoretical and empirical – are upper-
class/middle-class domination rather than lower-class/working-class subordination. His most recent work on contemporary social suffering (Bourdieu
et al. 1999) is deeply sensitive to those in less advantaged positions, rather
than judgemental. At the same time, I can see how his characterisation of
middle-class power and domination implies a characterisation of working-
class subordination and powerlessness. Numerous writers (see, most recently,
Savage 2000) have stressed the importance of acknowledging the cultural capital of the working class. The dangers of not doing so are evident in Reay's
(1998) work on mothers' involvement in their children's education, where the
contrast between brash, confident middle-class mothers and timid, hesitant
working-class mothers is too sharply drawn.

41. Expectations, aspirations, hopes and dreams are shaped by the economic,
social and political climate and not just by personal family experiences. On
the temper of the times in Britain in the 1950s and 1960s, see Robertson
(1990).

42. The similarities between Goldthorpe and Bourdieu rather than the differences are most obvious here, therefore.

5. FULFILLING POTENTIAL AND SECURING HAPPINESS

1. In this respect, I do not have any difficulty with Bourdieu's theory of social
reproduction and the crucial role of cultural capital in that reproduction,

although I would stress that Bourdieu was more interested in the upper class rather than the middle class in his work in France. Of course, given my focus, I interviewed only people who were successful and, again, I had an inkling that there were other family members – brothers and sisters – who were not as successful, either in education or employment. These discussions have led me to appreciate the important work of Prandy *et al.* (1980) and Prandy (1997) on social stratification, where they ascertained social position by drawing on information on the occupations of family and friends.

2. On the growing importance of intelligence testing in the new American meritocracy, see Lemann (1999). This wonderful book, which weaves personal stories with sociological insight, was brought to my attention by Barbara Reskin when she was a visiting professor in the Department of Sociology at Manchester. Reskin, of course, has long researched issues of inequality and their reproduction and has been highly critical of the idea that America is a meritocracy. See, for example, Reskin (2003). As an aside, Lemann (1991) also wrote a great book on the migration of African Americans from the South to the North in the mid twentieth century using the same style, weaving personal stories with social analysis.

3. It is apparent, therefore, that different institutional arrangements in America and Britain influence educational and occupational aspirations and expectations. The majority of American young people go on to some form of higher education while the split between compulsory schooling, further education and higher education gives people more choices in terms of leaving education or staying on. In this respect, Lipset (1996) is right to point to the different cultural norms and expectations about education in the USA in comparison to a European nation like Britain.

4. In both the USA and the UK, it seemed that Montessori (pre-)schools were highly rated and frequently mentioned. It is a popular form of learning based on a philosophy pioneered by Dr Maria Montessori that emphasises virtues such as curiosity, creativity and imagination. In other words, it captures the preoccupation with the development of individual expression and individuality in a non-competitive environment that the interviewees valued greatly. On the increasing importance of unique individual identities in Western culture, see Strathern (1992).

5. On the key role that Headstart has played in nurturing the linguistic skills of disadvantaged children and also on how easily these can be lost, see the work by Farkas (2001).

6. A number of my American interviewees spoke of how their children suffered from Attention Deficit Disorder (ADD) or ADHD (Attention Deficit Hyperactivity Disorder). I was unfamiliar with these terms and the conditions associated with them as they were not widely used in the UK although they are discussed more widely now. (British parents were more likely to talk about dyslexia.) They talked about how their children had problems with concentration at school that had led them to be labelled as 'learning disabled'. These children were medicated, usually on Ritalin, to harness their energies and ensure success at learning. The condition is associated primarily with young boys. I heard much anecdotal evidence about the growth of ADD and ADHD

in the USA and how as many as 15% of school-aged children are on the drug, the overwhelming majority of them (95%) being young boys. There is a huge debate going on in the US about the over use of Ritalin and how problems of concentration could be contained via a better diet. From the vantage point of being British, it certainly seemed as if there had been a medicalisation of the problem of academic underachievement. Some of the American interviewees put forward this view and noted how it contributed to the greater social control of boys. Their youthful mischievousness was no longer tolerated in modern American society.

7. Yuko had, in fact, been in regular contact with the school to try to ascertain which teacher Natalie would have in her next year of schooling. It was not hard to imagine that the school Principal was well aware of Yuko's concerns and, arguably, was being pressured into ensuring that Natalie be assigned to a good teacher at the next grade. On the relationship between teachers and middle-class parents and how they interact with each other, see the excellent study by Lareau (1989/2000).

8. There was a very notable preoccupation amongst the interviewees with limiting and controlling children's television viewing. Again, it was interesting to see how the interviewees' dispositions and values translated into everyday lifestyle practices. As Lareau (1989/2000) emphasised, it is not enough to demonstrate that families have cultural capital. It is imperative to show how – i.e. the process by which – it is mobilised as a resource in the reproduction of advantage.

9. Lareau's (1989/2000) study has been very influential in Britain (see Reay 1998) for many good reasons. (I have found her personal essay on doing the research for her book that appears in an appendix – the research being her Ph.D. – very helpful for my own Ph.D. students.) Drawing on the work of Bourdieu, she focused on parental involvement in primary schools. Inevitably, she had less time to consider the amount of time parents spend with their children after school and at weekends on homework. Many of the interviewees in America and Britain spoke of how their parents sent them off to do their homework and there was no actual involvement in homework, while they were now heavily involved in projects and other types of work which often involved research with their children. At the same time, as teachers, some of the interviewees spoke of the difficulties of getting disadvantaged children to do homework. They had no time if they went to jobs after school or had to take on responsibilities at home when their parents (or parent) were out at work. The teachers working in inner-city schools were very revealing about these processes and how they might contribute to inequalities. See also Fine (1991) on the relationship of parents to teachers and schools. Note also the discourse on female achievement and male underachievement that was found among my American and British interviewees. See Weiner *et al.* (1997).

10. Note the all-important logic re enjoyment, application, success, self-confidence and empowerment to which so many of the American interviewees subscribed in a more explicit manner than was found in the UK. This line of thinking is part of the individualism that is so strong in the USA in

comparison to European societies like Britain and France. For a comparison between the US and France, see Lamont (1992, 2000).

11. See Lareau (2002) on the increasing control of children's leisure activities. Indeed, a number of the interviewees complained of how society did not let children just 'hang' (as in, hang out as a group on neighbourhood street corners) and how they were 'scheduled to death' with summer camps and what have you. Sports, as ever, was deemed the ultimate healthy (physically or otherwise) leisure pursuit.

12. Thus, the interviewees were crucially aware of the importance of good teachers for their children. In both America and Britain, good (namely, clever) teachers were seen as vital in challenging children to fulfill their utmost potential. The language used was identical.

13. See n. 6 above. All the more confusing to me, at times, was that these children were still expected to be educationally successful and go to college.

14. Again, see Mare (1995). Note the importance of social resources here on continued academic success in higher education. A fuller discussion of these issues is to be found in Chapters 6 and 7.

15. A number of the interviewees spoke of how young people were taking longer to complete their degrees and young men, in particular, were the main culprits. See Mare (1995). The discourse on male underachievement was evident here too.

16. I have thought long and hard as to whether I could explain why some of the interviewees' children were successful and others less so. I suspect I would need to conduct much more detailed interviews to be able to ascertain what was happening within individual families. There were issues to do with divorce, depression, loss and so on that I was only partially aware of but that I am sure contributed to the processes of mobility and stability.

17. Charles and Nadia Khan, as immigrants from the Asian continent, held quite traditional views in comparison to the American-born interviewees. Nadia, for example, had trained as a doctor in her home country but had never practised in America. She was the only woman who was not engaged in paid employment outside the home even though she had only one child. That said, they had some interesting, and what might be considered non-traditional, critical views about American capitalism and its consequences for family life and how (little) value was placed on children.

18. Sarah Neale was an interesting case as she was an example of a woman from a lower-middle-class (working-class) background who had been thwarted in her attempts to go to medical school. There were family pressures to go to work early on and then her own family circumstances constrained her later. Three opportunities to go to medical school had to be passed up much to her regret and pain. Given my decision to focus on physicians and educators, it was obvious that I would be talking only to those who enjoyed social mobility. Given the macro-sociological empirical material (Erikson and Goldthorpe 1993), I would certainly not deny that stability rather than mobility is the common experience among members of the working class in America and Britain.

19. See Strathern (1992). On parental mobility projects in the 1960s and children's reflections of their occupational success in the 1990s, see Sennett (1998).

20. Thus, Bob was cognisant of women's changing position in society over his lifetime and his attitude towards his daughter's education and employment were different to his father's although, like him, he greatly valued economic independence. He was well aware, too, of changing family forms in American society. See Stacey (1991, 1996).

21. On the changing status (and collective downward mobility) of teaching as a profession in the US, see Bullough (1997).

22. American women with young children are much more likely to work full time than their Britain counterparts, who are more likely to work part time. In the USA, the provision of childcare is much more formally organised than it is in Britain. For a rather old but useful comparative study, see Dex and Shaw (1986). On the considerable informality of British childcare arrangements, see McRae (1991).

23. As in the USA, the parents (especially mothers) were cognisant of child development theories and the key ways to stimulate their children's intellectual curiosity and so on. This is hardly surprising given the abundance of popular books on child development to be found in bookstores in both countries.

24. Again, note the concern with self-confidence and how this was seen as a key to all kinds of personal success. In contrast, low self-esteem was seen to contribute to failure.

25. As a fellow teacher, of course, she was confident in challenging the teacher in question and, subsequently, the school Head about her son's education. See Reay (1998). Note the interconnection with social networks here too, namely, Mary's concern that he was with the 'bottom group' of boys who were not academically successful and mostly larking around. See Chapter 7.

26. The issue of single-sex schools was quite particular to the British interviewees, for in sending their children to private schools, most of the interviewees were sending their children to single-sex schools. There is an old debate in Britain as to whether young women's academic success at single-sex schools results from the fact that the schools are single sex or that the girls are usually middle-class girls. It is difficult, in other words, to disentangle the effects of class and gender in this instance. See Kelly (1982). Arguably, it is not a case of one or the other factor being important but both factors playing a role – and being entangled with each other – in examination success.

27. Since doing the empirical research for this book, it has often struck me that sociological theorising on social reproduction assumes that parents can dictate their children's lives in a relatively uncomplicated way. There is, of course, now a growing literature on the relationship between parents and children and a recognition that children have their own 'voice', so to speak. Time and again, my interviewees stressed that they could not impose their views on their children; delicate negotiations were always taking place and,

quite simply, parents did not always get what they wanted. It may be that these comments reflect the changing nature of relationships with children in the contemporary world. On children, see Prout (2003).

28. On male underachievement yet again, see Coffey (2001).

29. Muriel Crisp's quote is interesting because of the way in which she talks about her children's activities being 'purposeful'. It was as if leisure could not be enjoyed for leisure's sake. There is now a lot of time-budget data that suggest that the decline in time spent on housework has been accompanied by a rise of time spent on child-centred leisure. See the excellent work by Gershuny (2000) and an earlier study by Smith (1987).

30. See Lareau (1989/2000) and Reay (1998).

31. Note the importance attached to having a career with prospects rather than a dead-end job.

32. To be sure, the interviewees were well aware of changes in the economic sphere such as the decline of manufacturing jobs, the rise of poorly paid service work, the increasing premium on educational qualifications to secure entry into professional and, increasingly, managerial jobs which paid well. The 'tightening bond' between education and employment (Marshall *et al.* 1997) was well appreciated and they could draw on personal experiences over their working lives, as did Dennis Parker, when they spoke of these issues.

33. On Catholic education, see Coleman and Hoffer (1987).

34. Yvonne and her son, Karl, had had a very poor relationship when he was a teenager. She desperately wanted him to do well and found it very frustrating that he was so indifferent to education. Her frustration was pronounced, she argued, because he was far more intelligent than she was, while she had experienced educational and occupational success as a result of a lot of hard work and determination. It seemed as if social work (like teaching) was an occupation in which underachieving men could find some shelter.

35. Private schools, therefore, provided the facilities where students could enjoy additional preparation to get into the elite colleges at Oxford and Cambridge. Both Oxford and Cambridge take a disproportionate number of students with private school education (namely, just over 50% in both cases, when the proportion of children who attend private schools stands at just 8%). It is not difficult to imagine that additional tuition plays a small part in this process.

36. Indeed, many of the interviewees spoke of how they talked to their children about how they enjoyed aspects of their jobs and, again, it is not difficult to imagine that children would, as a result, also hope to find jobs with intrinsic rewards. Their experiences of high-level professional jobs, therefore, were influential on their children's emerging occupational aspirations and expectations.

37. On the decline in status of the teaching profession in Britain, see Whitty (1997).

38. Andrew Underwood's wealth, therefore, would give his children considerable freedom in their choice of jobs and, if necessary, relieve the burden of financial independence from them if they did a low-paid job that they enjoyed.

39. As in the USA, therefore, it appeared that the middle-class doctors' children were more likely to enter the high-level professions and management than

were the lower-middle-class teachers' children. In the higher echelons of the middle class, they appeared to exhibit a greater degree of intergenerational stability. See Heath (1981) on social closure at the top.

40. In effect, I confirm Bourdieu's ideas about the role of cultural capital in social reproduction with reference to the way in which the interviewees' educational histories shaped their children's education.

41. Thus, just as the mobilisation of economic resources can increase the probability of success but can never guarantee it, so the exploitation of cultural capital can raise the chances of advancement but it can never be assured. The macro-level empirical findings and the theories that have been developed to explain those findings emphasise social stability and social reproduction. My micro-sociological study has thrown up a much higher level of flux and indeterminacy than I expected. Indeed, some of my interviewees' children could be said to have experienced downward social mobility although they remain in non-manual employment and, of course, they may return to higher-level positions later in life. The macro-level theory fits the macro-level findings but not the micro-level empirical material. The theory seems to be too tight, with its emphasis on stability, and unable to explain the flux and change going on beneath the surface. This conclusion reminds me of Crompton and Sanderson's (1990) excellent study on gender segregation in the labour market in Britain. On the surface, it seems that gender segregation in the labour market remains unchanged. Beneath that surface, however, they found considerable change taking place.

6. CONTACTS, LUCK AND CAREER SUCCESS

1. Social resources have been slipped back (like cultural resources) into the more recent theory of social mobility. See Goldthorpe (2000). What is noteworthy is that he argues that social resources are especially important when academic success is not forthcoming. Parents seemingly only call on their family and friends to help their less academically able children get good jobs. He does not, in other words, consider the way in which social resources might be mobilised in the pursuit of educational success as well. It is quite a restricted view, in other words, of the role of social resources in the reproduction of advantage. The focus of attention is on how social resources might facilitate occupational success. It is in this regard that he draws on the work of Granovetter (1973/95). Further reference to Granovetter's work and how it stimulated a massive amount of research on social networks in a variety of substantive areas will be considered more fully below.

2. Yet again, therefore, the similarities rather than the differences between Goldthorpe and Bourdieu are readily apparent in their discussions of social resources or social capital. Bourdieu operates with a narrow view of the role of social capital in social reproduction too. Somewhat surprisingly, given his long interest in education, he talks about the exploitation of social capital only when investments have not yielded the appropriate returns in terms of academic success. How social capital might be exploited during the process of credential acquisition is not considered. Moreover, Bourdieu focuses much

more attention on the conversion of economic capital into cultural capital and vice versa, while the way in which social networks convert into other forms of capital is discussed quite superficially. In both similar and different ways, therefore, I have often been left feeling that social resources/social capital have been tagged on (or not) by Goldthorpe and Bourdieu in the theories of class reproduction and social stability.

3. Given the central focus on education, it was obvious that I should turn to the work of Coleman given his interests in social capital. See, especially, Coleman (1988) and, for his broader sociological thinking, Coleman (1990). Coleman's interests lay in how social capital contributes to the creation of human capital: namely, the skills and capabilities that influence people's life chances. He defines social capital in terms of social networks although he also explores 'how interpersonal relationships generate feelings of trust, establish expectations and enforce norms. He suggests that social capital is a resource that can be mobilised to advantage in that parents can use it to help their children be successful in school. Coleman distinguishes between social capital in the family and social capital outside the family. Social capital in the family includes parent–child relationships and the amount of time and effort devoted to educational concerns. (This definition of social capital sounds so remarkably akin to cultural capital that, I suppose, it goes to show how difficult it is to distinguish the different types of resources! In Chapter 5, of course, I touched on the relationship between parents and children within families to a limited extent.) Social capital outside the family includes wider community relationships and the ways in which the community, including organisations like the local church within it, influences young people's expectations and monitors and guides their everyday behaviour by rewarding educational success and punishing failure. Social capital is, in effect, a form of social support to parents. It reinforces the cultural values and practices of the family inside the home. It also acts as a social sanction if they try to stray from their parents' path. Given that I have discussed social capital within the family under the remit of cultural capital, this chapter focuses on social capital outside the home in the local community. As an aside, the concept of social capital has enjoyed incredible popularity in political science through the work of Putnam (2000) who drew on Bourdieu and Coleman's earlier ideas. See Fine (2001) for a detailed discussion of how differently these three scholars have used the term.

4. When I analysed my interview transcripts for social resources, I noticed how frequently the interviewees spoke of other people who had been very significant in their lives. That they could speak warmly of people who had helped them in school or in work made for some very pleasant conversations. To be sure, there were some unpleasant stories too. They involved people who had thwarted the interviewees' careers, undermined their confidence and self-esteem at work or whatever. Either way, it was rare to hear stories of individual success for the interviewees were often humble in acknowledging the help of others and their good fortune at different times of their lives. The interviewees may have constructed narratives of their lives on my behalf with a neat linear dimension to them but, within those narratives, they invariably emphasised contingency, indeterminacy and so on.

5. Although, to be sure, my interviewees could not be said to come from the upper class, those from established upper-middle-class families reminded me of Domhoff's classic early work when they spoke of their easy passage through an elite of educational establishments! See Domhoff (1970).

6. On the overlapping social worlds of elite private schools and Ivy League schools, see Cookson and Persell (1985).

7. It was a predominantly white suburb too. Thus, time and again, it seemed as if the search for a good public education was crucial for the persistence of racial segregation in Boston in particular and, I suspect, the USA in general. See Massey and Denton (1993).

8. As a bright student, therefore, Jane Bennett found she was amongst mostly middle-class students also deemed to be bright. This bridge to another social world and mixing with those beyond her blue-collar environment had a major impact on her aspirations. In this respect, Jane benefited from the inequities of the tracking system although, of course, it also meant that most public high school students did not do so.

9. Again, it was interesting to hear of the different experiences of Elisabeth's sister and our conversation led me to wonder if she had chosen her particular peer group because she was less academically able and/or less academically inclined. It is not hard to imagine a circular relationship at work here.

10. Jane's quote is important as it counters the preoccupations of the interviewees about the importance of getting their children into good colleges. In the end, after all, she did well in getting to medical school and she had quite a benign view of how things had worked out for her. At the same time, it is important to acknowledge that Jane was very academically successful so it worked out fine for her. For the less successful, going to a small Catholic college might not have led to such a favourable outcome.

11. It was interesting to hear how Ray Chapman talked about how he did not have the 'open conflict that you certainly hear about from some kids who are in that situation'. He did not encounter, therefore, the kind of anti-school culture or feel the pressure to subscribe to a culture among young boys so vividly described in the classic study by Willis (1977). Whether the 'macho front' of Willis's respondents was an extreme case and much resistance is less vocal and more subtle remains open to debate. See Brown (1987). For the US, see Fine (1991).

12. On the persistence of inequalities of race, class and gender in education, see Ogbu (1988). On debates on race and education initiated by the meritocracy debate, see Jencks and Philips (1998).

13. Thus, social resources were resources that could be used to advantage as Coleman (1988) described. Focusing on the interviewees reflecting back on their childhood, however, meant the emphasis was on how they were for-tuitous in finding themselves amongst a group of people who shared their hopes and plans. In this respect, the conversation was less on how resources were mobilised (by parents), although Chapter 7 will show how they, as par-ents, consciously exploited their social networks on their children's behalf.

14. It is important to pause here and talk about the issue of luck. Jencks et al. (1972), in their now infamous study, found that socio-economic status (SES)

was a weak predictor of income and their highly sophisticated analysis of the effects of lots of variables on the attainment process showed that, in the end, luck (or competence) influenced economic success. This study was the source of much criticism and prompted Jencks and his colleagues to do more research on the topic. See Jencks *et al.* (1979). Their new research led them to acknowledge the powerful influence of SES, and education as a reflection of family background, on both occupation and income. In the preface to his book, Granovetter stated that he was interested in this idea of luck (prompted by these debates) and how to explore it sociologically. He did this, of course, by way of analysis of social networks. Despite being 30 years old, and not especially sophisticated in terms of statistical analysis of the data, it remains a fascinating book to read. So does the second edition (Granovetter 1995) that includes his famous article on the social embeddedness of economic action. For the original publication, see Granovetter (1985). See also Granovetter's review of the huge research his book initiated on social networks. I have always thought it a shame that a lot of technical work has gotten in the way of the sociological substance in the analysis of social networks. To be sure, much time has to be spent on describing networks but it is then important to think about what they might explain – such as the reproduction of advantage.

15. The 'match', as I say in the text, is supposed to be a highly formal process and in many respects it is. At the same time, it is not difficult to imagine how someone like Jack Poole does well out of these processes. Whatever the level of formality, it seems that it helps to know people so that they can 'put a name to a face' so to speak, which reminds me of Putnam's (2000) discussion of the importance of face-to-face interaction for the production of social capital. On the issue of formal and informal processes and how they have disadvantaged women and African Americans, see Reskin (1998).

16. In this instance, Patrick Dutton was out on a limb and so was his mentor and the situation was turned from one of disadvantage to one of advantage.

17. Granovetter (1973; 1995) made an important distinction between strong ties (family and friends in work) and weak ties (friends of friends, acquaintances of friends and so on). Somewhat counter-intuitively, he argued that weak ties were most important in the job search process because they introduced people to information and advice about opportunities extending beyond the immediate network.

18. What was also important here, which was especially notable to a British academic studying America, was that Bernice became eligible for grants to pay for college fees. In many respects, the culture of lifelong learning and financial support for it appears to be much stronger in the USA than the UK. On these cultural differences, see Lipset (1996).

19. There was, therefore, a considerable overlap in the lives of the women interviewees in terms of being mothers, often involved in daycare, and their lives as teachers in the labour market. While teaching was often seen as a suitable career for women, this discussion led me to think about how it might have *become* a suitable career for women as a result of employer practices.

20. A number of the American teachers spoke of how they circumvented the prospect of being made redundant – taking a reallocation elsewhere, for

example – or were made redundant as a result of falling school rolls. Their employment histories, therefore, were much more insecure and precarious than those of their British counterparts. The higher levels of job insecurity are the product of the way in which education is financed, with a mix of federal and state money, derived from property and other taxes in the USA. For a very detailed analysis of the funding of education and the implications that flow from it, see Kozol (1991).

21. Roy made a brief reference to the continued dominance of a white Catholic Irish elite in Boston but he was not keen to discuss the issue further.

22. Talking to the interviewees about their careers and how they had unfolded, therefore, really showed the declining impact of socio-economic background over time. SES and education have a powerful impact on the early years to be sure, but competence in the job, getting on with other people and so forth are crucial later on. That is not to say, however, that such background influences ever disappear entirely. See Jencks *et al.* (1979).

23. Janet Jones came from an established middle-class family and she was not embarrassed to say she was middle class like other interviewees (see Devine, 2004a). She talked about class explicitly throughout the interview, including her educational experiences. As she explained:

I grew up in [S]. It was not a very middle-class area which was why we were schooled out of the area . . . Central [S] was a very poor working-class area. It would have been difficult for us because they [other schoolchildren] would have been patients. A lot of the children would know our father. Anyway, I don't think the academic aspirations of the local schools were the aspirations my parents had.

It was important, therefore, to create a (physical and social) distance from working-class children especially if they 'polluted' middle-class children with their lower educational aspirations and expectations. On the idea of class pollution, see Walkerdine *et al.* (2001).

24. Just as some of my American interviewees reminded me of Domhoff's work, so these interviewees brought Scott's great study of the upper classes to mind. See Scott (1982). Scott was a lonely scholar in his research on the upper classes and, from this interest, he is one of the few British sociologists to have taken an interest in social networks although this situation is gradually changing. See Scott (2000).

25. Again, the links between the private schools and Oxford and Cambridge were obvious. It is not hard to see how private school pupils dominate Oxbridge.

26. Sheila Parker had a very strong class identity although, living in a rural area, she found herself mixing with the children of middle-class parents. Bridges into a middle-class world to be found here, therefore, suggest issues of place are important in shaping opportunities for and constraints on social mobility. For a discussion of space/place in class analysis, see Savage (1996).

27. It was fascinating to notice how many of the interviewees made reference to what was the 'norm'. It is a word, of course, that sociologists do not like to use very much given its association with Parsons and functionalism! On Parsons, see Holmwood (1996).

28. Note how the single-sex schools reinforced separate masculinities and femininities. Note also how the scandal of leaving school operated as a form of social sanction discouraging other girls from pursuing this option, as Coleman (1988) described.

29. It may be that the interviewees who recounted their happy experiences of grammar-school life had sufficient cultural capital – from whatever source – to survive and, indeed, thrive in such schools while those without enough cultural capital were overwhelmed by the middle-class culture of school and resisted it strongly.

30. The school effect, therefore, was obvious to Norman who had crossed the boundaries from a secondary modern school to a grammar school. On the school effect, see also Smith and Tomlinson (1989). Acknowledging the cultural effect of the school highlights both Goldthorpe's and Bourdieu's overly exclusive focus on the family. The family, as in parents, do not have total control over their children, not least because their children have many and varied experiences outside the family from an early age. Note, too, in Norman's case, his resistance to being written off and how it shaped his (internal) motivation to succeed.

31. The powerful cultural environment of schools attended was the topic of much discussion among the British interviewees. The way in which the schools seemed to encapsulate the hierarchical and gendered nature of British society is obvious too. I certainly asked my American interviewees to talk about the schools they had attended as well. They frequently spoke of how they were huge urban public schools and they talked about the emphasis on academic studies or sports or whatever. Even so, institutional arrangements did not seem to have such a profound impact on their lives, their aspirations.

32. Bruce Brown, one of the oldest interviewees, in his late fifties, appeared to have secured each of his jobs through social contacts. Like his education, it seemed his career had been achieved without effort and with considerable ease. This is how he talked of securing his current position:

> Well, fairly straightforward really. I wanted a job as a consultant [E-name of specialism]. Jobs for consultant [E] were a bit thin on the ground but [W] hospital was just starting. It was a teaching hospital and I used to meet this chap who was the professor of medicine there then, in the pub quite often, and so we would chat about this and that. It was well known that if you wanted to know what was happening in those days you needed to go to the Red Lion at half past five and you'd invariably find the professor of medicine and one or two other moderately powerful people . . . So I chatted to the professor of medicine and said that I thought I might apply and he said 'Good'. So I came down here and chatted to people and they seemed quite pleasant so I banged in an application and got it.

He went on to acknowledge that competition for the job was quite limited as there are fewer eligible candidates for higher-level jobs. He had the distinctive experience that got him the job over the other nine applicants. Again, it is not hard to see how medicine was such a male dominated profession until recently, and, yet, it is not difficult to imagine that it has changed to some extent now. See Pringle (1998) and Crompton (1999).

33. On the position of ethnic minority GPs, see the work of Robinson (1988, 1990). It seemed they were the less preferred option and at the back of the queue. See Reskin and Roos (1990).

34. It is important to note here that I am not arguing the common cliché that 'It's not what you know, it's who you know' that gets you good jobs. To be sure, Ian Lamb had impressed his superiors and because they were impressed they had sponsored him in job applications. The cliché, therefore, is crude and simplistic in capturing the way in which contacts work to a person's advantage. Note here, too, Julia Dodd was helped by a colleague and by the fact that she was working in a growing medical specialism. She was cognisant of the wider structural context in which her rapid promotion had taken place. See Sorensen (1986). This example shows how numerous factors may be influential at the same time in shaping career mobility.

35. This discussion brought to mind the old sociological material on occupational communities. This literature focused on working-class occupational communities. See the classic study by Dennis *et al.* (1956). Studies of middle-class occupational communities do not immediately spring to mind. It is interesting to note how the notion of community has been replaced by a discussion of networks. The concept of community has troubled sociologists in the last thirty years because it conjures up something that is tightly bounded. Arguably, the concept of networks refers to social relationships which are much more diffuse but no less important. On community, see Crow and McClean (1990). On networks, see Petersen and Kern (1996). On social solidarities more generally, see Crow (2002).

36. It is hard to deny that John was lucky although his luck was shaped by the social world in which he lived. I do not think that sociologists should feel uncomfortable with the idea that serendipitous events take place in most people's lives.

37. Again, note the overlap in the world of the women as mothers and teachers. It reminds me of Hakim's argument that women's employment in the labour market mirrors many of their activities outside it. See Hakim (1996).

38. A number of the British teachers spoke of setbacks in their careers as the wider economic climate changed in the 1970s, the political climate changed and tax cuts reduced the opportunities for supply work and restricted promotion prospects. Rapid advancement for some quickly became stagnation as times changed.

39. Ken's changing aspirations were interesting. He readily confessed that he only stayed on at university to do a PGCE to avoid getting a job and remain a student. In his early years of teaching, his aspiration was to become a top professional in the sense of teaching his specialist subjects to A level students. He had no managerial aspirations at all. His views changed when he realised he could be as a good a head as the next person. This story was not unlike those told about evolving educational aspirations and expectations.

40. In the workplace, therefore, social networks were an important influence on shaping motivations and aspirations to succeed and, crucially, providing the experience to secure promotion and continued advancement.

41. My empirical material, therefore, has confirmed Coleman's account of the effect of social capital on educational success. The one issue that I have touched on, although I wish I had explored it some more as it was referred to, was the effect of religion on people's early lives. I suspect, however, that its impact might be greater in the USA than in the UK. On religion in the USA, see Wuthrow (1988, 1998) and Hunter and Rice (1991). On religion in Britain, see Davie (1994) and Bruce (1995).

42. Social resources, therefore, are not the exclusive preserve of the middle class although they have a class character. I suspect their class character, among other things, may help to explain why the upper middle class tend to occupy higher positions within professions while the middle and lower middle class are positioned in lower jobs within them.

7. FRIENDS AND NETWORKS IN SCHOOL AND BEYOND

1. It is in this chapter, therefore, that I am really able to explore the ways in which social resources are mobilised in the pursuit of educational success. Just as the labour market is embedded in social relations, so the education system is embedded in social relations. On embeddedness, see Granovetter (1985).

2. It is here, too, that I can explore more fully how parents strategically mobilise their social resources to their children's advantage. I still have concerns about the concept of strategy. In my critique of Goldthorpe's adoption of rational choice theory, I expressed my reservations about his discussion of parental strategies. Among other things, I made reference to the debate on strategies initially by Crow (1989) and endorsed the call for an approach which acknowledges that people are not always economistic rational decision-makers and actions are frequently the outcome of negotiations, compromises and so on. Arguably, this is especially true of family life. See also Wallace (1993) and McCrone (1994). My discomfort undoubtedly derives from my distaste for rational action theory. It seems to me that rational choice theory is a particular way of looking at the world with its own language that you either buy into or not. To be sure, it has many virtues and it is not hard to enter into the logic and way of thinking behind rational action theory. Lots of clever people like its abstractions including, of course, Coleman (1990) although note the cutting critique by Tilly (1998). At the same time, I do not see the point in adopting an economistic view of the social world, in terms of means, ends and so on. It is like stripping away the social from social life and reducing the study of actor and actions to economic modelling. Bourdieu, of course, was highly critical of a *homo economicus* view of action like the rational choice theory embodied by one of the other major French theorists in this era, namely, Boudon. See Boudon (1979, 1980). At the same time, Bourdieu uses the concept of strategy, although not in terms of rational action theory but in terms of getting away from a notion of action as governed by rules and norms. In this respect, his notion of strategy embraces a notion of agency engaged in everyday practices and it needs to be understood in terms of his attempt to overcome the structure/agency problem. See Swartz (1997),

pp. 98–100. On the structure/agency problem, see Giddens (1979). Thus, it is very hard to get away from a discussion of strategy so I would emphasise that my interviewees certainly had goals and sought the means to achieve them but decisions and actions should be understood in a cultural and social context as well as an economic one.

3. The key argument of this chapter is that social networks are important for information and, most crucially, for advice. Rational choice theory attaches a lot of importance to people obtaining knowledge and then how they use this to make rational decisions. See Collins (1994) and Scott (1995). Arguably, it is not difficult to acquire information on, for example, the good schools in an area, especially in the USA where realtors happily supply such information when purchasing a property. The difficulty comes in making sense of the mountain of information available and then making decisions on which way to act. Other people are crucial in giving advice on information they supply or that has been supplied from elsewhere. Advice from tight and loose networks is so important because it is personalised in that it comes from people who are known and trusted and who, from their own experiences, are assumed to think and act the same way about, say, school choices. It is for this reason that advice from other people is so valued over and above the dry statistics than can be obtained from realtors, public libraries etc. On the crucial issue of trust, see Gambetta (1990).

4. Indeed, many of the interviewees spoke of the tough competition to get into highly reputable pre-schools and beyond. Parents could not just pay and get their children into the school of their choice. Such schools were heavily over-subscribed and there were waiting lists to secure entry. This was why it was important to learn about the best pre-schools to which to send their children as early as possible so that their names could be added to a waiting list as early as possible too.

5. Thus, as well as their own educational experiences, the interviewees drew on their colleagues' and friends' experiences of the education system and it was extremely helpful if they could draw on the advice of contacts with children who had gone through or who were making their way through the public or private school system. In this instance, George Marshall and his wife Judy were astute in getting a sense of how things had changed over time and they were especially aware of time pressures as two parents in demanding medical careers. That said, Judy had just reduced her hours as she felt she was under tremendous pressure working full time and caring for three young sons. She wanted to enjoy more time with them. Of course, she could pursue this option as she and her husband had two high salaries between them so their economic resources were being mobilised indirectly in this way to secure their children's education success. On acute time pressures in the USA, see Hochschild (1989, 1997).

6. Granovetter (1973, 1995) made the distinction between strong ties and weak ties in his classic study of contacts and careers. Somewhat counter-intuitively, he argued that weak ties were more important than strong ones because they supplied information and advice about jobs that people might not know about through their close circle of family and friends. Subsequent research in various

fields of sociology and economics has confirmed this key finding. See, for example, Granovetter's (1995) review of research generated by his book. It is a little surprising that he does not discuss the issue of social networks and geographical mobility (which often accompanies social mobility, of course) since it is widely known that spatial mobility affects contacts with strong and weak ties. See, for example, Fischer (1982). On the geography of population shifts in the USA, see Frey (1995).

7. Again, see Douglas and Massey (1993) for a powerful exposé of the persistence of residential segregation by race in the USA.

8. Coming from the West Coast, Anna Gray was very scathing of the East Coast and its lack of ethnic and racial diversity. Indeed, it was noticeable how some of the interviewees acknowledged the limited economic diversity of the affluent communities in which they lived although they suggested they were ethnically diverse to some extent. That is to say, they pointed to the fact that their children mixed with Asian children from Korea, China and so on. No mention was made of their children mixing with African Americans, however. They could talk about ethnic diversity but not racial segregation. On ethnicity in the USA, see the wonderful study by Waters (1990).

9. Here, therefore, is a clear case of the argument I make under n. 3 about the importance of personalised knowledge that can be trusted. Also note how information and advice from an insider – a schoolteacher – were especially highly valued. It brings to mind Bourdieu's (1973, 1986) discussion of cultural capital in terms of knowing the system and how to work the system, illustrating the mutually constitutive nature of cultural capital and social networks.

10. As I am sure is not uncommon, husbands and wives can have very different experiences of education and both of these experiences influence how parents confront choices and make decisions about their children's education. Thus, Jane was cognisant of the advantages of her husband's private education, over her own – i.e. meeting people of influence – even though she had been very successful in the public school system. Indeed, Jack's education could be described as an elite education, and how they both talked about social networks within this elite environment brought Domhoff's (1970) classic work on the upper classes in America to mind. Paying for a private education, therefore, not only increased the chance of academic success but also enhanced the probability of social success. The interconnections between economic resources and social networks are obvious here.

11. Like many of the interviewees, Ken did not endorse the educational regime in the USA. He was well aware that his children did well out of the system and there were other children who did not do well out of it. He was, like the other informants, highly sympathetic to the plight of African American children in inner cities and wondered how they could ever escape their predicament. Most thought that the hurdles were too great. Only the most determined, self-disciplined young person could jump them and the majority of ordinary decent black children could not. Arguably, however, being distant from the reality of America's uneven education system meant Ken and others were somewhat laid back about current institutional arrangements. Seeing

they were doing OK, it was not their most pressing concern. On attitudes to inequalities, including racial inequalities, see Kluegal and Smith (1986), Kluegal *et al.* (eds.) (1995) and Hochschild (1995).

12. On different moral universes and value systems, see Lamont (1992, 2000).

13. In this respect, it seemed that parents had to be especially strategic in the context of a declining and variable public school system. Whether they would have been any less strategic in a stable and even public school system remains an open question.

14. Both Goldthorpe and Bourdieu, of course, saw power as crucial to the reproduction of advantage. On how power is the crux of the stability of class relations in the USA, see Zwieg (2000).

15. It was amazing to hear such tales of children and young people with such big ambitions at an early age. They reminded me of the dark side of parental ambitions so well described by Lareau (1989/2000).

16. See n. 8 above on the alleged snobbery and status consciousness of the East Coast. Indeed, I was warned by Erik Olin Wright at a conference in Australia, a conversation I am sure he has long forgotten, that the East Coast and Boston are quite distinct within the USA. Massachusetts and surrounding states – like New Hampshire and Connecticut – are certainly hothouses in terms of their concentration of prestigious private schools and Ivy League colleges! Given the vast size of the continent in comparison to a small country like Britain, I am sure Wright's comments are true. They came to mind often when I was doing the research and reminded me of Edith Wharton's (1905, 1920) novels on upper-class society in New York that I read many years ago.

17. Again, see ns. 8 and 16 above on local preoccupations with status and prestige. David Neale was critical of the system, seeing himself as an outsider from the Mid-West looking in on the preoccupations of the East Coast. It would, indeed, be very interesting to do a comparative study within the USA on these issues. David was aware of the dark side of social pressures on his daughter too. See n. 15.

18. That is to say, the interviewees felt that the reputation of their children's high schools was not inconsequential in how far they were successful in getting into a college of their choice.

19. Most of the interviewees' older children, therefore, were still finding their feet in the labour market in a post-industrial economy. On the increased risks of the United States' new economy, see the excellent study by Smith (2001). Note how there was a very strong belief in children 'getting a foot in the door' so that they could prove themselves in the workplace. On the importance of the meritocratic ideal of being able to prove oneself and thereby improve on one's social position, see also Newman (1999).

20. On generational changes in risks and opportunities, see Smith (2001). Social networks – often extended family, it seemed – were considered crucial during early entry into (sometimes temporary) jobs in the labour market. Academic credentials were only one part of the game!

21. Social contacts, therefore, were often perceived as lucky chances that had to be exploited. See Jencks *et al.* (1972, 1979) once again and see n. 22, chapter 6.

22. Using a language not often used in Britain, many of the American interviewees spoke of the importance of 'exposing' their children to the world, other people and so on.

23. Thus, both academic preoccupations and issues of status and reputation concerned the interviewees, rather than just one or the other. The interconnections between the three main resources discussed in this book are obvious here.

24. The importance of physical and social distancing from the working class, therefore, was readily apparent. See Walkerdine et al. (2001). Note, again, how members of the working class are still seen as lacking in ambition and, by implication, their lack of ambition explains why they occupy lowly positions in British society. Celia Watson, in fact, was remarkably candid about how she and her husband were pushy parents at first. Neither of their children was educationally or occupationally successful in having high-flying professional or managerial careers. Because of their lack of success, Celia sounded as if she had developed a more critical evaluation of middle-class parents urging their children to get ahead. She had not been successful as a parent in this respect and distanced herself as an outsider from the whole competition. She was not unaware that she would have thought differently if things had worked out for her children.

25. As with the American interviewees, therefore, geographical mobility influenced the networks that parents could mobilise in pursuit of academic success. Like their American counterparts, the British doctors were far more likely to have moved in pursuit of their careers in comparison to the British teachers of this research. The geographically mobile, it seemed, were comfortable in moving across different social spaces, establishing new networks and so forth. On geographical and social mobility, see Savage et al. (1992). Of course, social networks can be crucial in facilitating geographical mobility, as studies of workers on the move have shown. See Grieco (1987) and Devine (1992). Grieco's much overlooked study of steelworkers who relocated from Scotland to Corby in the second half of the twentieth century drew on the classic study of networks by Bott (1957). Bott's work was a huge influence on Granovetter too. For his review of British research on social networks, see Granovetter (1995). It is in the afterword to the second edition of his book that he also discusses the great research undertaken by Chris Harris, Phil Brown, Ralph Fevre and Lydia Morris among others, on the steel industry in South Wales in the 1980s. See Harris et al. (1987). Morris (1994, 1995) went on to explore the social networks of the unemployed in the North East. It is surprising how little recent research has been conducted on social networks and the middle class in Britain. The issue was neglected in the otherwise interesting study by Wynne (1998).

26. The interviewees, in other words, were very conscious of the influence of other children on their children. It is surprising how often the word 'nice' appears in such conversations. The word seems to be a euphemism for many things including issues around class!

27. Note here how Ian Lamb drew on information and advice from his colleagues and friends as a short cut so that he did not have to undertake research on

local schools for himself that would have been very time-consuming. To be sure, I can see Ian's actions might be construed as a rational response to the time constraints he faced.

28. On the strength of weak ties, see Granovetter (1985, 1995).

29. It was apparent that the teachers who had not been geographically mobile drew on their family, long-standing friends and other local people that they just knew from living somewhere for most of their lives. On a local middle class, see Devine *et al.* (2002).

30. Pauline and Martin's strongly held socio-political values clearly shaped their everyday lifestyle practices. In many respects, they were defiant in their belief that their daughter's self-motivation would see her do well. This was coupled with nervousness about the challenges she would meet which made them very vigilant. It was a tough juggling act that they struggled with all the time.

31. The academic reputation of the schools was all-important to the interviewees, without doubt. Issues of social standing, however, had not disappeared altogether in the pursuit of educational success. See Heath (2000).

32. Here, then, was a clear example of social resources being mobilised when all avenues leading to educational success had been pursued unsuccessfully. I would not want to argue against the idea that social resources play a crucial role in such contexts. All I have emphasised in this chapter is that they play a role in the pursuit of educational success too. What is evident, therefore, is that the significance of different types of social resources can vary according to the context and are contingent upon that context. Again, this idea undermines the thesis that economic resources are the all-important resources in whatever circumstances.

33. I was very interested to find that the mobilisation of economic resources was not always successfully converted into cultural capital in the form of educational credentials. Incredible amounts of investment, it seemed, were required to get the necessary returns!

34. The family culture, therefore, emphasised independence and risk-taking. Both of James Brown's grandparents had been self-employed small businessmen and the ethic of self-employment clearly still ran through the family. On a French example, see Bertaux and Bertaux-Waime (1997).

35. Ken and Hilary Butler have two children who have been very successful in school and beyond. They were, however, very sanguine about the issue of success as neither their son nor their daughter was fulfilled in their jobs in accountancy and medicine. As parents, they remained anxious about their children and their lives 'in the round'. On a sociological account of the personal troubles and public issues surrounding personal success, see the novel study by Pahl (1995).

36. Interestingly, Peter and Diane Smith valued medicine and teaching so highly because they were vocational careers. Peter Smith was clearly influenced by his father's background as an engineer who enjoyed work–life mobility in a major chemical company. The emphasis on the vocational and practical nature of medicine could be linked back to this family history. For a critical take on doctors' knowledge, expertise and power, see the fine work by Sinclair (1997).

37. Like their American counterparts, the British doctors and teachers effectively spoke of belonging to occupational communities. Some belonged to very tight communities or networks where their colleagues from work were also their friends with whom they socialised. Others belonged to loose communities or networks where there was virtually no overlap between their work lives and their non-work lives. I suspect the denseness of such communities or networks influenced levels of occupational inheritance, namely, the extent to which daughters and sons followed their children into the same professional careers.

38. Here was an example of the interviewees' children's own networks affecting their job choices. In this instance, Claire's friend reinforced her parents' preferences, which pleased and amused them greatly.

39. It is not difficult to imagine circumstances where parents do not know how to help their children get on in a job or career of which they have little direct experience. Given that some occupations are declining and some are increasing all the time, it would not be unusual for parents to find themselves in such a position. On employment in the British economy, see Gallie *et al.* (1998). At the same time, it was very interesting to hear Janet Jones offer general advice about career advancement, and her assumption that her daughters would find themselves in management positions in the long term.

40. The interviewees, therefore, were very conscious of the fact that their influence on their children declined as they became more independent and moved away from home to go to university. They spoke of how they hoped they had given their children all the opportunities they possibly could and the skills and capacity to make the best of those opportunities. In the end, however, it was their children who decided their own fate in life.

41. It was trustworthy advice that enabled them to understand the choices ahead of them and make decisions about their children's education.

42. Once again, I conclude that the parents mobilised social resources on their children's half but they could not guarantee success in the reproduction of advantage. Parental power, it seemed, was not unfettered, by any means.

8. CONCLUSION

1. Changes in the occupational structure and specifically the growth of high-level professional and managerial jobs have led to fundamental changes, therefore, in the character of America and Britain. These changes and their implications for the structure of class positions and movement between those positions are greatly overlooked. While I agree that continuities in class inequalities are a major research topic – after all, it guided the research discussed in this book – these changes should not be neglected in any study of class inequalities and their reproduction. It is for this reason that although I strongly disagreed with Saunders's (1995) interest in the role of intelligence in the mobility process I was impressed with his interest in change. Not surprisingly, Marshall *et al.*'s (1997) findings on the declining influence of class in securing salariat employment over the last twenty years and Heath's (2000) careful account of the declining effects of class origins on destinations have caught my attention over the years. See n. 15 in the Introduction.

2. In Goldthorpe's (1987) discussion of the experience of social mobility, he readily acknowledged that it is absolute rather than relative changes that people experience personally and these experiences shape people's views' about class. The crucial issue, of course, is the point of comparison. Goldthorpe's consideration of detailed life histories has been overlooked which is a great shame as some very interesting empirical material is discussed. Thinking about the experience of class was not the direct aim of the research discussed in this book. Inevitably, however, in interviewing people in depth, I have discussed their experiences of class mobility and stability across generations. From his analysis of the life histories of some of his respondents, he posits a thesis that the established middle class might be more ambitious in their careers than those mobile from working-class origins into middle-class positions. This hypothesis, along with many other issues in the study of work-life mobility, remain on the research agenda after twenty-five years! It would be interesting to see more research on work-life mobility embracing, without question, the experiences of women and men.

3. In effect, therefore, Goldthorpe argues that the competition regarding education and careers is a form of old-fashioned class struggle or class action! For a long time, I was of the view that some sociologists of class would not notice class action if it hit them in the face. Anything less than the taking up arms at the barricades was not worthy of attention. Fortunately, the increased interest in the sociology of everyday life and how class may be practised in seemingly mundane routines has overcome this problem. On the sociology of everyday life, see Bennett and Watson (2003).

4. It is from the vantage point of today, of course, that it is possible to look back and consider that brief period from the 1940s to the 1970s in terms of its benign economic, social and political climate. Be that as it may, I think Goldthorpe is much too bleak, indeed severe, in his assessment of the Labour government's attempts to reduce inequality. The problems it confronts today reinforce this point. Gordon Brown has made considerable attempts to reduce child poverty by improving the benefits for those on low incomes. In absolute terms, things have improved. However, there will be no register of this in statistics on income inequality as the corporate world continues to reward those at the top with huge salaries. This explains why income inequalities remain the same. See Hills *et al.* (2002). On corporate pay and income inequalities in the USA, see Perrucci and Wysong (2003).

5. Reinforcing the point made in n. 1 above, absolute changes whereby everyone is affected by the bleaker economic and political climate that has existed since the mid 1970s should not go unacknowledged.

6. Whether outcomes cannot be guaranteed because the competition for a good education and a good job is so tough is a moot point.

7. To repeat an earlier distinction, see Devine (1998). First, the focus on economic resources and the neglect of cultural and social resources is problematic. Second, even if attention centres on economic resources, there are limitations to examining income only and not taking patterns of expenditure and consumption tastes into consideration.

8. The comparative research has shown, without doubt, the way in which an education regime and, specifically, different institutional arrangements,

shape the mobilisation of different resources by parents on behalf of their children.

9. Of course, I am well aware that I only interviewed those who were successful in education. I did not interview those who did not do well in school and who then did well in the world of work. Nor did I speak to those of modest origins who did not succeed in school or in employment. The empirical findings apply to a particular group of people – albeit a group who cannot be ignored.

10. My impression, therefore, was that the middle-class physicians in Boston and middle-class doctors in Manchester were exiting the public/state school system.

11. There is an important divide, therefore, between the upper middle class and the lower middle class in both countries although there is a significant overlap between them of course.

12. The differences between Goldthorpe's and Bourdieu's theories are really quite minor and the fact that they both talk about the same three types of resources says it all. Equally, it must be noted that Bourdieu is not consistent about the relative significance of economic and cultural capital in the repro-duction of advantages since he suggests that economic capital is all-important at some juncture and its conversion into cultural capital is all-important at other points. See Bourdieu (1986).

13. Thus, it is not simply the case that economic resources shape cultural cap-ital in an economistic and determinist fashion. Cultural capital influences the mobilisation of economic resources so they exist in a circular relation-ship. They are mutually constitutive of each other. See Devine and Savage (2001).

14. The interrelationship of class, race and gender inequalities has been amply demonstrated in this research.

15. There is a difference, therefore, between expecting success and hoping for success although hopes that are realised can turn into expectations. It is important not to overstate the distinction, as ever. Only slightly differently, Schwartz (1997, p. 11) talks about distinguishing between aspirations and expectations.

16. On a number of occasions, I have drawn on the work of Mare (1995: 160) who has argued that 'each successive generation constructs an educational "floor", below which its offspring are unlikely to fall, that provides a platform for further inter-generational growth'. Importantly, he acknowledges changing family structure and size on opportunities for education too.

17. Thus, I am firmly of the view that middle-class children have to prove them-selves academically also and their success does not depend, as Bourdieu's argument implies, simply on linguistic talents.

18. It is not simply the case, therefore, that the middle class has all the cultural capital and the working class has none. Further consideration needs to be given to the inclusive nature of cultural and social resources and, for that matter, economic resources too.

19. It could be argued that the neglect of social resources is a mundane example of the way in which an increasing preoccupation with issues of 'culture' in

sociology has left a void in the study of the 'social'. See Abbott (2001) for an account of the development of social science knowledge. See also Devine and Savage (2004).

20. I suspect that, like gender segregation and racial segregation, class inequalities are being constantly remade within occupations in complex and subtle ways over time and space.

21. Thus, the class character, like the gendered and racialised nature of social networks, is crucial for any understanding of the reproduction of inequality.

22. In a different fashion, on the interconnections between cultural capital and social networks, see also the work of Erikson (1986) and Petersen and Kern (1996).

23. Issues of social exclusivity and inclusivity, therefore, are an important consideration in an analysis of social networks.

24. Again the inclusive nature of social resources implies that a sophisticated analysis of the ownership of different amounts and types of contacts and ties is required. Arguably, Coleman (1986) addresses these issues in his theory of social capital in the creation of human capital.

25. It is, indeed, somewhat overwhelming to think about the many and different combinations of economic, cultural and social resources that could be found amongst different groups of people. Maybe Pawson (1993) was right in his assessment of the daunting nature of social mobility research! There are plenty of other resources that could be explored too. In a moving study of the young unemployed and their families, for example, Allatt and Yeandle (1990) drew on the concept of emotional resources to consider how parents supported their children emotionally through the different experience of unemployment. (Yeandle was also involved in the research on social networks in South Wales. See Harris *et al.* (1987).)

26. There is, I suspect, much downward social mobility within the middle class that goes unrecognised and downwardly mobile children do not enjoy the same quality of life as their parents – material or otherwise. In other words, there is much flux behind the picture of stability.

27. It is not uncommon for assessments of L. B. Johnson's New Society initiative to be largely pessimistic in tone although this view derives, in part, from Johnson's subsequent involvement in Vietnam that tarnished his political record across the board. See Karnow (1991).

28. I think the issue of middle-class exit, especially from the welfare state project in Britain, is a serious issue and a bad thing in the long run. On the argument of alliances, I have been greatly influenced by the work of W. J. Wilson's (1996) evaluation of the implications for public policy arising from his research on race and class in the USA.

29. Although Third Way politics have been a source of derision, I would contend that Giddens (1995) has developed some radical arguments about inequalities in Britain too.

30. Like Giddens, Fischer and his colleagues (1996), in my view, also provide a critical challenge to the supposed ideal of living in a meritocracy. They also make a strong moral case for thinking about how we treat the so-called 'losers' in the competition for good jobs in contemporary society.

31. As Schwatz (1997, p. 188) rightly says, 'While the individual race for academic credentials has certainly broadened its scope in the postwar period, it is not clear that individual mobility is the only game in town.' That is to say, Schwatz was critical of Bourdieu's focus on education as a form of individual competition and if he had extended his gaze to the workplace, for example, he might have considered other (namely, collective) forms over struggles for privilege and power. The expansion of educational credentials as the entry requirements for professional and managerial jobs has been well documented in Collins's (1979) classic study of credential society.

APPENDIX B

1. The writing of this appendix has been very much influenced by other appendixes written by American sociologists. Here, I am thinking particularly of the work of Lareau (1989, 2000) – which I recommend to all Ph.D. students – and the appendix in Waters (1999), among others. British sociologists are often dismissive of American sociology because it is very quantitative. I would contend, however, that American sociology is also characterised by some great qualitative research. Indeed, it is more ethnographic, drawing on mixed methods including observation, participant observation and in-depth interviewing while a lot of qualitative research in Britain relies on interviews only.
2. Savage et al.'s book (1992) was also hugely influential for its critique of the Nuffield approach to class analysis which was dominant in the 1980s but which is less influential today.
3. I was also influenced by the analysis of social mobility patterns within the middle class by Heath (1981). While it is almost customary for sociologists to predict the decline of social mobility into the middle class in the harsher economic and political climate prevailing since the 1970s (see Roberts 2001), Heath (2000) and Marshall et al. (1997) suggest such a seemingly obvious prediction is not necessarily well founded.
4. For an excellent book on qualitative research, see Mason (2002).
5. It was not hard to see why there is a severe shortage of GPs willing to work in inner-city areas. See Young et al. (2001). It was common to come across GP practices surrounded with lots of barbed wire to prevent burglaries for drugs. One of my GP's practices actually had been burnt down in the past and a whole new practice had to be rebuilt.
6. On the privileged position of hospital consultants within the NHS, see Moran (1999).
7. I tried to make sure that I was not just being passed among a sample of friends in one area so I frequently asked my informants to recommend people in other specialisms and/or hospital departments and/or other hospitals if they could.
8. To put it another way, it seemed as if husbands found it easier to say no. They were not so willing to oblige. They might not have wanted to talk at length either. I confronted this problem in previous research. See Devine (1992).
9. Being flexible does not mean I was unsystematic. On the need for pragmatism, see Devine and Heath (1999).

10. The book from this project will appear in 2004.

11. The Center for Urban Inequality at Chicago was a hive of activity with lots of graduate students doing some great research in the city. See, for example, Patillo-McCoy (1999) and Venkatesh (2000).

12. Often, therefore, informal contacts are very important. See Waters (1999) for a very good discussion of this issue.

13. On the organisation of health care in the USA, see Moran (1999).

14. See Wilson (1996).

15. Indeed, I was very struck by how some informants' strongly held values shaped their lifestyles in terms of the choice of fields in medicine or teaching in which they practised. It reminded me of the classic study by Parkin (1971).

16. On the interconnections between social and spatial mobility, see Savage (1996).

17. I was troubled with ethical issues here, in other words. At the same time, I did not want to spend ages negotiating access for only a small number of people.

18. Sampling was ongoing throughout the project. See Devine and Heath (1999).

19. I was conscious here of debates on how people often want to distance or dissociate themselves from class. On this debate in Britain, see Skeggs (1997), Bradley (1999), Savage et al. (2001) and Devine (2004a, 2004b).

20. See Devine (2004a, 2004b). See also Walkowitz (1999).

21. Thus, although macro-sociological research was the context in which I conducted my micro-sociological work, the intervening meso level in the form of institutional arrangements made a regular appearance in my work.

22. Thus, black history and white history are heavily intertwined. See Roediger (1991, 1998).

23. There is lots of research on work-life mobility in the field of economic life in the USA and the UK but little that considers the issue of class reproduction or otherwise.

24. On the challenge to Affirmative Action policies in the USA, see Reskin (1998). On its crucial role in facilitating the increase in the number of women physicians in the USA in the 1960s and beyond, see Riska (2001).

25. It would have been great, of course, to have talked to the children of my interviewees. No doubt, other researchers will do this in the future. After all, social scientists are more aware of children's agency. See Prout (2003).

26. On sensitive topics, see Lee (1994).

27. I realise I cannot go overboard about the differences between two countries that are very similar in many respects. While I was there I resolved never to read an English newspaper and I read only American novels. Oprah Wimphrey's book club was very helpful!

28. See the debate on class subjectivities made in n. 19. The debate has made me much more sensitive to the issue of 'noise' within qualitative interviews. That said, it is important to guard against seeing class everywhere. This is an accusation frequently levelled at sociologists and I suspect there is quite a lot of truth in the critique.

29. To my shame, I did not use a qualitative package to analyse this interview material even though I have used such packages on other research. I did not,

in part, because the research project grew from something quite small to a bigger comparative project only gradually.

30. Bourdieu is very much in fashion at the moment in sociology (Devine 1992). It amazes me how his work has been extended so far across the discipline in a very uncritical fashion. Years ago, Foucault had the answer to all our questions. Who knows who that theorist will be in ten years' time!

31. Sociologists invariably stress the significance of context. It is rarely stated explicitly, however, that it is people in that context who are all important. It is for this reason that the growing interest in social networks in Britain is very welcome.

32. Thinking does not stop once writing starts. It is while writing that I do my hardest thinking.

33. The issue is regularly discussed in *The Times Higher Education Supplement* (2003).

34. After much delay, the government White Paper was published in early 2003.

35. See Wilson (1996).

References

Abbott, A. (2001) *Chaos of Disciplines*, Chicago: University of Chicago Press.

Allatt, P. and Yeandle, S. (1990) *Youth Unemployment and the Family*, London: Routledge.

Banks, M., Bates, I., Breakwell, G. and Bynner, J. (1992) *Careers and Identities*, Buckingham: Open University Press.

Beck, U. (1992) *Risk Society*, London: Sage.

Bennett, T. and Watson, D. (2003) *Understanding Everyday Life*, Oxford: Blackwell.

Bertaux, D. and Bertaux-Wiame, I. (1997) 'Heritage and its lineage: a case history of transmission and social mobility over five generations' in D. Bertaux and P. Thompson (eds.), *Pathways to Social Class*, Oxford: Clarendon Press.

Bianchi, S. M. (1995) 'Changing economic roles of women and men' in R. Farley (ed.) (1995) *State of the Union, Volume 1: Economic Trends*, New York: Russell Sage Foundation.

Blau, P. and Duncan, O. P. (1967) *The American Occupational Structure*, New York: John Wiley.

Bott, E. (1957) *Family and Social Networks*, London: Tavistock Publications.

Boudon, R. (1974) *Education, Opportunity and Social Inequality*, New York: Wiley.

(1980) *The Crisis in Sociology*, New York: Columbia University Press.

Bourdieu, P. (1973) 'Cultural reproduction and social reproduction' in R. Brown (ed.), *Knowledge, Education and Cultural Change*, London: Tavistock.

(1984) *Distinction*, London: Routledge.

(1986) 'The forms of capital' in J. E. Richardson (ed.), *Handbook of Theory of Research for the Sociology of Education*, New York: Greenwood Press.

(1987) 'What makes a social class? On the theoretical and practical existence of groups', *Berkeley Journal of Sociology*, 32: 1–8.

(2000) *Masculine Domination*, Cambridge: Polity Press.

Bourdieu, P. and Coleman, J. S. (eds.) (1991) *Social Theory for a Changing Society*, Boulder, CO: Westview Press.

Bourdieu, P. and Passeron, J.-C. (1977) *Reproduction in Education, Society and Culture*, London: Sage.

Bourdieu, P. and Wacquant, L. J. D. (1992) *An Invitation to Reflexive Sociology*, Chicago: University of Chicago Press.

Bourdieu, P. *et al.* (1999) *The Weight of the World*, Oxford: Blackwell.

Bradley, H. (1999) *Gender and Power in the Workplace*, Basingstoke: Macmillan.

Breen, R. and Goldthorpe, J. H. (1999) 'Class inequality and meritocracy: a critique of Saunders and an alternative analysis', *British Journal of Sociology*, 50: 1–27.

Brown, P. (1987) *Schooling Ordinary Kids*, London: Tavistock.

—— (1995) 'Cultural capital and social exclusion: some observations on recent trends in education, employment and the labour market', *Work, Employment and Society*, 9: 29–51.

Brown, P. and Scase, R. (1994) *Higher Education and Corporate Realities*, London: UCL Press.

Brown, P., Halsey, A. H. and Wells, A. S. (1997) 'The transformation of education and society' in A. H. Halsey, H. Lauder, P. Brown and A. S. Wells (eds.), *Education: Culture, Economy, Society*, Oxford: Oxford University Press.

Bruce, S. (1995) *Religion in Modern Britain*, Oxford: Oxford University Press.

Bullough, R. V. J. (1997) 'Becoming a teacher: self and the social location of teacher education', in B. J. Biddle, T. L. Good and I. F. Goodson (eds.), *International Handbook of Teachers and Teaching*, Dordrecht: Kluwer.

Burchell, B. J. *et al.* (1999) *Job Insecurity and Work Intensification*, York: Joseph Rowntree Foundation.

Burt, R. (1982) *Towards a Structural Theory of Action*, New York: Academic Press.

Butler, T. (1997) *Gentrification and the Middle Classes*, Aldershot: Ashgate.

Butler, T. and Robson, G. (2003) *London Calling*, London: Berg.

Bynner, J. (ed.) (2000) *Twenty Something in the 1990s*, Aldershot: Ashgate.

Bynner, J. and Roberts, K. (eds.) (1991) *Youth and Work*, London: Anglo-German Foundation.

Chiswick, B. R. and Sullivan, T. A. (1995) 'The New Immigrants' in R. Farley (ed.), *State of the Union, Volume Two: Social Trends*, New York: Russell Sage Foundation.

Chitty, C. (1993) 'The education system transformed', *Sociology Review*, 2: 3.

Clark, T. N. and Lispet, S. M. (1991) 'Are social classes dying?', *International Sociology*, 6: 293–316.

Coffey, A. (2001) *Education and Social Change*, Buckingham: Open University Press.

Coleman, J. S. (1988) 'Social capital in the creation of human capital', *American Journal of Sociology*, 94: 95–120.

—— (1990) *Foundations of Social Theory*, Cambridge, MA: Harvard University Press.

Coleman, J. S. and Hoffer, T. B. (1987) *Public and Private Schools*, New York: Basic Books.

Coleman, D. and Salt, J. (eds.) (1996) *Ethnicity in the 1991 Census*, vol. I, London: OPCS.

Collins, R. (1979) *The Credential Society*, New York: Academic Press.

—— (1994) *Four Sociological Traditions*, Oxford: Oxford University Press.

Conley, D. (1999) *Being Black, Living in the Red*, Berkeley, CA: University of California Press.

Connell, R. W. (1987) *Gender and Power*, Cambridge: Polity.

—— (1995) *Masculinities*, Cambridge: Polity.

Cookson, P. W. and Persell, C. H. (1985) *Preparing for Power*, New York: Basic Books.

Coxon, A. P. and Jones, C. L. (1978) *The Images of Occupational Prestige*, London: Macmillan.

(1979) *Class and Hierarchy*, London: Macmillan.

Crompton, R. (1980) 'Class mobility in modern Britain', *Sociology*, 14: 117–19.

(1992) 'Where did all the bright girls go? Women's higher education and employment since 1964' in N. Abercrombie and A. Warde (eds.), *Social Change in Contemporary Society*, Cambridge: Polity.

Crompton, R. (ed.) (1999) *Restructuring Gender Relations and Employment*, Oxford: Oxford University Press.

Crompton, R. and Harris, F. (1999) 'Employment, careers and families: the significance of choice and constraint in women's lives' in R. Crompton (ed.), *Restructuring Gender Relations and Employment*, Oxford: Oxford University Press.

Crompton, R. and Sanderson, K. (1990) *Gendered Jobs and Social Change*, London: Unwin Hyman.

Crompton, R. *et al.* (1999) 'The restructuring of gender relations within the medical profession' in R. Crompton (ed.), *Restructuring Gender Relations and Employment*, Oxford: Oxford University Press.

Crompton, R., Devine, F., Savage, M. and Scott, J. (2000) *Renewing Class Analysis*, Cambridge: Blackwell/Sociological Review Monograph.

Crossick, G. J. (1978) *An Artisan's Elite in Victorian Society*, London: Croom Helm.

Crouch, C. and Heath, A. F. (1992) *Social Research and Social Reform*, Oxford: Clarendon Press.

Crow, G. (1979) 'The use of the concept of "strategy" in recent sociological literature', *Sociology*, 231: 1–24.

(2002) *Social Solidarities*, Buckingham: Open University Press.

Crow, G. and Mcclean, C. (2000) 'Community' in G. Payne (ed.), *Social Divisions*, Basingstoke: Macmillan.

Davie, G. (1994) *Religion in Britain Since 1945*, Oxford: Basil Blackwell.

Dawkins, R. A. (2003) *A Devil's Chaplain*, New York: Houghton Mifflin Co.

Deem, R. (1978) *Women and Schooling*, London: Routledge and Kegan Paul.

Deem, R. (ed.) (1980) *Schooling for Women's Work*, London: Routledge and Kegan Paul.

Demaine, J. (ed.) (2001) *Sociology of Education Today*, New York: Palgrave.

Dennis, N., Henriques, F. and Slaughter, C. (1956) *Coal is our Life*, London: Eyre and Spottiswoode.

Devine, F. (1992a) *Affluent Workers Revisited*, Edinburgh: Edinburgh University Press.

(1992b) 'Gender segregation in the engineering and science professions: a case of continuity and change', *Work, Employment and Society*, 6: 557–75.

(1997) *Social Class in America and Britain*, Edinburgh: Edinburgh University Press.

(1998) 'Class analysis and the stability of class relations', *Sociology*, 32: 23–42.

(2004a) 'Talking about class in Britain' in F. Devine and M. Waters (eds.), *Social Inequalities in Comparative Perspective*, Oxford: Blackwell.

(2004b) 'Middle-class identities in the United States' in F. Devine, M. Savage, J. Scott and R. Crampton (eds.), *Investigating Social Stratification*, Basingstoke: Palgrave.

(2004c) 'The cultural turn, sociology and class analysis' in F. Devine *et al.* (eds.), *Investigating Social Stratification*, Basingstoke: Palgrave.

Devine, F. and Heath, S. (1999) *Sociological Research Methods in Context*, Basingstoke: Macmillan.

Devine, F. and Savage, M. (2000) 'Conclusion: renewing class analysis' in R. Crompton *et al.* (eds.), *Renewing Class Analysis*, Oxford: Blackwell/ Sociological Review Monograph.

Devine, F. *et al.* (2000) 'Professional work and professional careers in Manchester's business and financial sector', *Work, Employment and Society*, 14: 521– 40.

Dex, S. and Shaw, L. B. (1986) *British and American Women at Work*, London: Macmillan.

DiMaggio, P. (1982) 'Cultural capital and school success: the impact of status culture participation on the grades of U.S. High School Students', *American Sociological Review*, 47: 189–201.

DiMaggio, P. and Mohr, J. (1984) 'Cultural capital, educational attainment and marital selection', *American Journal of Sociology*, 90: 1231–61.

Domhoff, G. W. (1970) *The Higher Circles*, New York: Random House.

Eaton, S. E. (2001) *The Other Boston Busing Story*, New Haven, CT: Yale University Press.

Ehrenreich, B. (1989) *Fear of Falling*, New York: Pantheon Press.

Erikson, B. (1986) 'Culture, class and connections', *American Journal of Sociology*, 102: 217–51.

Erikson, R. and Goldthorpe, J. H. (1993*) The Constant Flux*, Oxford: Clarendon Paperbacks.

Evans, G. (1993) 'Class conflict and inequality' in R. Jowell *et al.* (eds.), *International Social Attitudes*, Aldershot: Dartmouth.

Farley, R. (1996) *The New American Reality*, New York: Russell Sage Foundation.

(1995a) (ed.) *State of the Union, Volume 1, Economic Trends*, New York: Russell Sage Foundation.

(1995b) (ed.) *State of the Union, Volume 2: Social Trends*, New York: Russell Sage Foundation.

Featherman, S. L. and Hauser, R. M. (1978) *Opportunity and Change*, New York: Academic Press.

Fine, M. (1991) *Framing Dropouts*, New York: State University of New York Press.

(2001) *Social Capital Versus Social Theory*, London: Routledge.

Fischer, C. S. (1982) *To Dwell Among Friends*, Chicago: University of Chicago Press.

Fischer, C. S. *et al.* (1996) *Inequality by Design*, Princeton, NJ: Princeton University Press.

Frey, W. H. (1995) 'The new geography of population shifts' in R. Farley (ed.), *State of the Union, Volume 2: Social Trends*, New York: Russell Sage Foundation.

Gallie, D., White, M., Cheng, Y. and Tomlinson, M. (1998) *Restructuring the Employment Relationship*, Oxford: Oxford University Press.

Gambetta, D. (1987) *Were They Pushed or Did They Jump?*, Cambridge: Cambridge University Press.

(1990) *Trust*, Oxford: Blackwell.

Gershuny, J. (2000) *Changing Times*, Oxford: Oxford University Press.

Gerwirtz, S., Ball, S. J. and Bowe, R. (1995) *Markets, Choice and Equity in Education*, Buckingham: Open University Press.

Giddens, A. (1973) *The Class Structure of the Advanced Societies*, London: Hutchinson.

(1979) *Central Problems in Social Theory*, London: Macmillan.

(1993) *The Transformation of Intimacy*, Cambridge: Polity Press.

(1994) *Beyond Left and Right*, Cambridge: Polity.

(1995) *The Third Way and its Critics*, Cambridge: Polity.

Gittens, D. (1982) *Fair Sex*, London: Hutchinson and Co.

(1985) *The Family in Question*, London: Macmillan.

Glass, D. V. (ed.) (1954) *Social Mobility in Britain*, London: Routledge and Kegan Paul.

Goldin, C. (1990) *Understanding the Gender Gap*, New York: Oxford University Press.

Goldthorpe, J. H. (1996) 'Class analysis and the reorientation of class theory: the case of persisting differentials in educational attainment', *British Journal of Sociology*, 47: 481–505.

(2000) *On Sociology*, Oxford: Oxford University Press.

Goldthorpe, J. H. (in collaboration with Llewellyn, C. and Payne, C.) (1980) *Social Mobility and Class Structure in Modern Britain*, 1st edn, Oxford: Clarendon Press.

Goldthorpe, J. H. (in collaboration with Llewellyn, C. and Payne, C.) (1987) *Social Mobility and Class Structure in Modern Britain*, 2nd edn, Oxford: Clarendon Press.

Goldthorpe, J. H. and Hope, K. (1974) *The Social Grading of Occupations*, Oxford: Clarendon Press.

Goldthorpe, J. H. and Marshall, G. (1992) 'The promising future of class analysis: a response to recent critiques', *Sociology*, 26: 381–400.

Goldthorpe, J. H., Lockwood, D., Bechhofer, F. and Platt, J. (1969) *The Affluent Worker in the Class Structure*, Cambridge: Cambridge University Press.

Goldthorpe, J. H., Lockwood, D., Bechhofer, F. and Platt, J. (1968a) *The Affluent Worker: Industrial Attitudes and Behaviour*, Cambridge: Cambridge University Press.

(1968b) *The Affluent Worker: Political Attitudes and Behaviour*, Cambridge: Cambridge University Press.

Goodin, R. E. and Le Grand, J. (1987) *Not Only the Poor*, London: Unwin Hyman.

Gottschalk, P. and Smeeding, T. M. (1997) 'Cross-national comparisons of earnings and income inequality', *Journal of Economic Literature*, 35: 633–87.

Granovetter, M. (1973) *Getting a Job*, Chicago: Chicago University Press.

(1985) 'Economic action and social structure: the problem of embeddedness', *American Journal of Sociology*, 91: 481–510.

(1995) *Getting a Job*, 2nd edn, Chicago: Chicago University Press.

Gray, R. Q. (1976) *The Labour Aristocracy in Victorian Edinburgh*, Oxford: Oxford University Press.

Grieco, M. (1987) *Keeping it in the Family*, London: Tavistock.

Grusky, D. and Sorensen, J. (1998) 'Can class analysis be salvaged?', *American Journal of Sociology*, 103: 1187–234.

Hakim, C. (1996) *Key Issues in Women's Work*, London: Athlone Press.

Hall, P. (1999) 'Social capital in Britain', *British Journal of Political Science*, 29: 417–61.

Halsey, A. H., Heath, A. and Ridge, J. (1980) *Origins and Destinations*, Oxford: Clarendon Press.

Harris, C. C. *et al.* (1987) *Redundancy and Recession in South Wales*, Oxford: Basil Blackwell.

Harrison, R. J. and Bennett, C. E. (1995) 'Racial and ethnic diversity' in R. Farley (ed.), *State of the Union, Volume 2: Social Trends*. New York: Russell Sage Foundation.

Hauser, R. M. (1978) 'A structural model of the mobility table', *Social Forces*, 56.

Heath, A. F. (1981) *Social Mobility*, London: Fontana.

—— (2000) 'Social mobility' in A. H. Halsey (ed), *Social Trends in British Society*, Oxford: Oxford University Press.

Heath, A. F., Mills, C. and Roberts, J. (1992) 'Towards meritocracy? Recent evidence on an old problem' in C. Crouch and A. F. Heath (eds.), *Social Research and Social Reform*, Oxford: Clarendon Press.

Herrnstein, R. J. and Murray, C. (1994) *The Bell Curve*, New York: The Free Press.

Hills, J. (ed.) (1996) *New Inequalities*, Cambridge: Cambridge University Press.

Hills, J., Le Grand, J. and Piachand, D. (2002) *Understanding Social Exclusion*, Oxford: Oxford University Press.

Hirschman, E. O. (1962) *Exit, Voice and Loyalty*, Cambridge, MA: Harvard University Press.

Hochschild, A. R. (1989) *The Second Shift*, New York: Avon.

—— (1997) *The Time Bind*, New York: Metropolitan Books.

Hochschild, J. L. (1995) *Facing Up to the American Dream*, Princeton, NJ: Princeton University Press.

Holmwood, J. (1996) *Founding Sociology?*, London: Addison-Wesley.

Hout, M. (1988) 'More universalism, less structural mobility: the American occupational structure in the 1980s', *American Sociological Review*, 89: 1358–400.

Hout, M., Brooks, C. and Manza, J. (1993) 'Classes in post-industrial society', *International Sociology*, 8: 259–77.

Hout, M., Raftery, A. E. and Bell, E. O. (1993) 'Making the grade: educational stratification in the United States, 1925–1989' in Y. Shavit and H. P. Blossfeld (eds.), *Persistent Inequality*, Boulder, CO: Westview Press.

Hunter, J. D. and Rice, J. S. (1991) 'Unlikely alliances: The changing contours of American religious faith' in A. Wolfe (ed.), *America at Century's End*, Berkeley, CA: University of California Press.

Jackson, B. and Marsden, D. (1962) *Education and the Working Class*, London: Penguin.

Jamieson, L. (1998) *Intimacy*, Cambridge: Polity.

Jencks, C. and Phillips, M. (1998) *The Black–White Test Score Gap*, Washington, DC: Brookings Institution.

Jencks, C. *et al.* (1972) *Inequality*, New York: Basic Books.
(1979) *Who Gets Ahead?*, New York: Basic Books.
Jenkins, R. (1991) *Pierre Bourdieu*, London: Routledge.
Karnow, S. (1991) *Vietnam*, London: Viking Penguin.
Kelly, A. (1982) *The Missing Half: Girls and Science Education*, London: St. Martin's Press.
Kerckhoff, A. C. *et al.* (1996) *Going Comprehensive in England and Wales*, London: Woburn Press.
Kingston, P. W. (2000) *The Classless Society*, Stanford, CA: Stanford University Press.
Kluegal, J. R. *et al.* (eds.) (1995) *Social Justice and Political Change*, New York: Aldine De Gruyter.
Kluegal, J. R. and Smith, E. R. (1986) *Beliefs About Inequality*, New York: Aldine De Gruyter.
Kozol, J. (1991) *Savage Inequalities*, New York: Crown Publications.
Lamont, M. (1992) *Money, Morals and Manners*, Chicago: University of Chicago Press.
(2000) *The Dignity of Working Men*, Cambridge, MA: Harvard University Press/New York: Russell Sage Foundation.
Lamont, M. and Lareau, A. (1988) 'Cultural capital: allusions, gaps and glissandos in recent theoretical developments', *Sociological Theory*, 6: 153–68.
Landry, B. (1988) *The New Black Middle Class*, Berkeley, CA: University of California Press.
(1991) 'The enduring dilemma of race in America' in A. Wolfe (ed.), *America at Century's End*, Berkeley, CA: University of California Press.
Lareau, A. (1989) *Home Advantage*, New York: The Falmer Press.
(2000) *Home Advantage*, rev. edn, New York: Rowman and Littlefield Publishers, Inc.
(2002) 'Invisible inequality: social class and childrearing in black families and white families', *American Sociological Review*, 67: 747–76.
Lee, R. M. (1994) *Doing Research on Sensitive Topics*, London: Sage.
Lemann, N. (1991) *The Promised Land*, New York: A. A. Knopf.
(1999) *The Big Test*, New York: Farrar, Straus and Giroux.
Levy, F. (1995) 'Incomes and income inequality' in R. Farley (ed.), *State of the Union, Volume 1: Economic Trends*, New York: Russell Sage Foundation.
Lieberson, S. (1987) *Making it Count*, 2nd edn, Berkeley, CA: University of California Press.
Lipset, S. M. (1996) *American Exceptionalism*, New York: W. W. Norton and Company.
Lockwood, D. (1992) *Solidarity and Schism*, Oxford: Clarendon Press.
Lukas, J. A. (1985) *Common Ground*, New York: Alfred A. Knopf.
Lukas, S. R. (1999) *Tracking Inequality*, New York: Teachers College, Columbia University.
Luker, K. (1996) *Dubious Conceptions*, Cambridge, MA: Harvard University Press.
Mac an Ghaill, M. (1988) *Young, Gifted and Black*, Milton Keynes: Open University Press.
(1994) *The Making of Men*, Buckingham: Open University Press.

Mare, R. D. (1995) 'Changes in educational attainment and school enrollment' in R. Farley (ed.), *State of the Union, Volume 1: Economic Trends*, New York: Russell Sage Foundation.

Marsh, C. and Blackburn, R. M. (1992) 'Class differences in access to higher education' in R. Burrows and C. Marsh (eds.), *Consumption and Class, Divisions and Change*, Basingstoke: Macmillan.

Marshall, G., Swift, A. and Roberts, S. (1997) *Against the Odds*, Oxford: Clarendon Press.

Marshall, G., Rose, D., Newby, H. and Vogler, C. (1988) *Social Class in Modern Britain*, London: Hutchinson.

Martin, J. and Roberts, C. (1980) *Women and Employment*, London: HMSO.

Mason, J. (2002) *Qualitative Researching*, 2nd edn, London: Sage.

Massey, D. S. and Denton, N. A. (1993) *American Apartheid*, Cambridge, MA: Harvard University Press.

McCrone, D. (1994) 'Getting by and making out in Kilkaldy' in M. Anderson, F. Bechhofer and J. Gershuny (eds.), *The Social and Political Economy of the Household*, Oxford: Oxford University Press.

McRae, S. (1991) *Maternity Rights in Britain*, London: PSI.

Miller, R. L. (2000) *Researching Life Stories and Family Histories*, London: Miller.

Mills, C. W. (1959) *The Sociological Imagination*, New York: Oxford University Press.

Moran, M. (1999) *Governing the Health Care State*, Manchester: Manchester University Press.

Morris, L. (1994) *Dangerous Classes*, London: Routledge.

(1995) *Social Divisions*, London: UCL Press.

Newman, K. (1988) *Falling from Grace*, New York: Free Press.

(1991) 'Uncertain seas: cultural turmoil and the domestic economy' in A. Wolfe (ed.), *America at Century's End*, Berkeley, CA: University of California Press.

(1993) *Declining Fortunes*, New York: Basic Books.

(1999) *No Shame in my Game*, New Jersey: Knopf/Russell Sage.

Ogbu, J. U. (1988) 'Class stratification, racial stratification and schooling' in L. Weis (ed.), *Class, Race and Gender in US Education*, Buffalo: State University of New York Press.

Oliver, M. L. and Shapiro, T. M. (1997) *Black Wealth/White Wealth*, New York: Routledge.

O'Neil, O. (2002) *A Question of Trust*, Cambridge: Cambridge University Press.

Pahl, R. E. (1993) 'Does class analysis without class theory have a future: a reply to Goldthorpe and Marshall', *Sociology*, 27: 253–8.

(1995) *After Success*, Cambridge: Polity.

Parkin, F. (1971) *Class Inequality and Political Order*, London: MacGibbon and Kee.

(1979) *Marxism and Class Theory*, London: Tavistock.

Patterson, J. T. (1981) *America's Struggle Against Poverty*, Cambridge, MA: Harvard University Press.

Pattillo-McCoy, M. (1999) *Black Picket Fences*, Chicago: University of Chicago Press.

Pawson, R. (1993) 'Social mobility' in D. Morgan and L. Stanley (eds.), *Debates in Sociology*, Manchester: Manchester University Press.

Payne, G. (1986) *Mobility and Change in Modern Society*, London: Macmillan.

Peach, C. (ed.) (1996) *Ethnicity in the 1991 Census, Volume 2*, London: OPCS.

Penn, R. (1980) 'The Nuffield class categorization', *Sociology*, 15: 265–71.

Perrucci, R. and Wysong, E. (2003) *The New Class Society*, 2nd edn, New York: Rowman and Littlefield Publishers.

Petersen, R. and Kern, R. (1996) 'Changing highbrow taste: from snob to omnivore', *American Sociological Review*, 61: 900–7.

Prandy, K. (1997) 'Class and continuity in social reproduction: an empirical investigation', *British Journal of Sociology*, 46: 340–64.

Prandy, K., Stewart, A. and Blackburn, R. M. (1980) *Social Stratification and Occupations*, London: Macmillan.

Pringle, R. (1998) *Sex and Medicine*, Cambridge: Cambridge University Press.

Prout, A. (ed.) (2003) *The Future of Childhood*, London: Routledge-Falmer.

Przeworski, A. (1990) 'Marxism and rational choice' in P. Birnbaum and J. Leca (eds.), *Individualism*, Oxford: Clarendon Press.

Purvis, J. (1983) *Hard Lessons*, Cambridge: Polity.

(1991) *A History of Women's Education in England*, Milton Keynes: Open University Press.

Putnam, R. D. (2000) *Bowling Alone*, New York: Simon & Schuster.

Reay, D. (1998) *Class Work*, London: UCL Press.

Reay, D. and Lucey, H. (2003) 'The limits of "choice": children and inner city schooling', *Sociology*, 37: 121–42.

Reskin, B. (1998) *The Realities of Affirmative Action*, Washington, DC: American Sociological Association.

(2003) 'Including mechanisms in our models of ascriptive inequality', *American Sociological Review*, 68: 1–21.

Reskin, B. and Roos, P. (1990) *Job Queues, Gender Queues*, Philadelphia: Temple University Press.

Riska, E. (2001) *Medical Careers and Feminist Agendas*, New York: Walter de Gruyter.

Roberts, K. (2001) *Class in Modern Britain*, Basingstoke: Palgrave.

Robinson, V. (1988) 'The new Indian middle class in Britain', *Ethnic and Racial Studies*, 11: 456–73.

(1990) 'Roots to mobility: the social mobility of Britain's black population', *Ethnic and Racial Studies*, 13: 197–8.

Roediger, D. (1991) *The Wages of Whiteness*, London: Verso.

(1998) *Black on White*, New York: Schocken Books.

Roker, D. (1993) 'Gaining the edge' in I. Bates and G. Riseborough, *Youth and Inequality*, Buckingham: Open University Press.

Rose, J. (2001) *The Intellectual Life of the British Working Classes*, New Haven, CT: Yale University Press.

Royle, E. (1987) *Modern Britain*, London: Edward Arnold.

Saunders, P. (1995) 'Might Britain be a meritocracy?', *Sociology*, 29: 23–41.

Savage, M. (1996) 'Space, networks and class formation' in N. Kirk (ed.), *Social Class and Marxism*, Aldershot: Scolar Press.

(1997) 'Social mobility and the survey method' in D. Bertaux and P. Thompson (eds.), *Pathways to Social Class*, Oxford: Oxford University Press.

(2000) *Class Analysis and Social Transformation*, Buckingham: Open University Press.

Savage, M. and Egerton, M. (1998) 'Social mobility, individual ability and the inheritance of class inequality', *Sociology*, 31: 645–72.

Savage, M., Bagnall, G. and Longhurst, B. (2001) 'Ordinary, ambivalent and defensive: class identities in the Northwest of England', *Sociology*, 35: 875–92.

Savage, M., Barlow, J., Dickens, P. and Fielding, T. (1992) *Property, Bureaucracy and Culture*, London: Routledge.

Scase, R. and Goffee, R. (1989) *Reluctant Managers*, London: Unwin Hyman.

Schor, J. B. (1992) *The Overworked American*, Cambridge, MA: Harvard University Press.

(1998) *The Overspent American*, New York: Harper Perennial.

Scott, J. (1982) *The Upper Classes*, London: Macmillan.

(1995) *Sociological Theory*, Cheltenham: Edward Elgar.

(1996a) *Stratification and Power*, Cambridge: Polity Press.

Scott, J. (1996b) 'Comment on Goldthorpe', *British Journal of Sociology*, 47: 507–12.

(2000) *Network Analysis*, 2nd edn, London: Sage.

Sennett, R. (1998) *The Corrosion of Character*, New York: W. W. Norton and Company.

Shapiro, T. M. and Wolff, E. N. (eds.) (2001) *Assets for the Poor*, New York: Russell Sage.

Simon, B. (1991) *Education and the Social Order 1940–1990*, London: Lawrence and Wishart.

Simon, H. (1982) *Models of Bounded Rationality*, Cambridge, MA: Harvard University Press.

Sinclair, S. (1997) *Making Doctors*, New York: Berg.

Skeggs, B. (1997) *Formations of Class and Gender*, London: Sage.

Skorupski, J. (1998) *The Cambridge Companion to Mill*, Cambridge: Cambridge University Press.

Smart, C. and Neale, B. (1999) *Family Fragments*, Cambridge: Polity Press.

Smith, D. and Tomlinson, S. (1989) *The School Effect*, London: PSI.

Smith, J. (1987) 'Men and women at play: gender, life-cycle and leisure' in J. Horne, D. Jary and A. Tomlinson (eds.), *Sport, Leisure and Social Relations*, Sociological Review Monograph 33, London: Routledge and Kegan Paul.

Smith, V. (2001), *Crossing the Great Divide*, Ithaca: IRL Press.

Sorensen, A. B. (1986) 'Theory and methodology in social stratification' in U. Himmelstrand (ed.), *Sociology from Crisis to Science*, London: Sage.

Stacey, J. (1991) *Brave New Families*, New York: Basic Books.

(1996) *In the Name of the Family*, Boston, MA: Beacon Press.

Strathern, M. (1992) *After Nature*, Cambridge: Cambridge University Press.

Swartz, D. (1997) *Culture and Power*, Chicago: University of Chicago Press.

Swift, A. (2003) *How Not to Be a Hypocrite*, London: Routledge.

Taylor, S. J. L. (1998) *Desegregation in Boston and Buffalo*, Albany, NY: Suny.

Tilly, C. (1998) *Durable Inequality*, Berkeley, CA: University of California Press.

Turner, S. J. (2000) *The Cambridge Companion to Weber*, Cambridge: Cambridge University Press.

Venkatesh, S. A. (2000) *American Project*, Cambridge, MA: Cambridge University Press.

Waite, L. and Gallagher, M. (2001) *The Case for Marriage*, New York: Broadway Books.

Walkerdine, V., Lucey, H. and Melody, J. (2001) *Growing Up Girl*, Basingstoke: Palgrave.

Walkowitz, D. J. (1999) *Working with Class*, Chapel Hill, NC: The University of North Carolina Press.

Wallace, C. (1993) 'Reflections on the concept of "strategy" in D. Morgan and L. Stanley (eds.), *Debates in Sociology*, Manchester: Manchester University Press.

Warde, A. (2002) 'Constructions of Pierre Bourdieu', *Sociology*, 36: 1003–9.

Waters, M. C. (1990) *Ethnic Options*, Berkeley, CA: University of California Press.

 (1999) *Black Identities*, Cambridge, MA: Harvard University Press/New York: Russell Sage Foundation.

Weiner, G., Arnot, M. and David, M. (1997) 'Is the future female? Female success, male disadvantage and changing gender patterns in education' in A. H. Halsey *et al.* (eds.), *Education: Culture, Economy and Society*, Oxford: Oxford University Press.

Westergaard, J. and Resler, H. (1975) *Class in a Capitalist Society*, London: Heinemann.

Whitty, G. (1997) 'Marketization, the state and the re-formation of the teaching profession' in A. H. Halsey *et al.* (eds.), *Education: Culture, Economy and Society*, Oxford: Oxford University Press.

Williamson, B. (1990) *The Temper of the Times*, Oxford: Basil Blackwell.

Willis, P. (1977) *Learning to Labour*, Farnborough: Saxon House.

Wilson, W. J. (1978) *The Declining Significance of Race*, Chicago: Chicago University Press.

 (1987) *The Truly Disadvantaged*, Chicago: University of Chicago Press.

 (1996) *When Work Disappears*, New York: A. A. Knopf.

Witz, A. (1991) *Professions and Patriarchy*, London: Routledge.

Wolfe, A. (1991) *Marginalised in the Middle*, Chicago: University of Chicago Press.

 (1999) *One Nation, After All*, New York: Viking Penguin.

Wolff, E. N. (1995) *Top Heavy*, New York: The Twentieth Century Fund Press.

Wright, E. O. (1996) *Class Counts*, Cambridge: Cambridge University Press.

Wuthrow, R. (1988) *The Restructuring of American Religion*, Princeton, NJ: Princeton University Press.

 (1998) *Loose Connections*, Cambridge, MA: Harvard University Press.

Wynne, D. (1998) *Leisure, Lifestyles and the New Middle Class*, London: Routledge.

Young, R., Leese, B. and Sibbald, B. (2001) 'Imbalances in the GP labour market in the UK: evidence from a postal survey and interviews with GP leavers', *Work, Employment and Society*, 15: 699–719.

Zwieg, M. (2000) *The Working Class Majority*, Ithaca, NY: ILR Press.

Author index

Subject index

academic success 44, 62, 63, 83, 153
  and alternative talents 189
  investment conditional on 63
  lack of 104
  social capital and 120, 146, 153
  social pressures towards 122, 134
adolescents 96, 101, 111
Advanced Placement (AP) courses, as
  credits 27
African Americans 13, 25, 29, 47, 49, 187
  women 74
ascriptive processes 8
Asians 151
Attention Deficient Disorder (ADD) 98,
  102
Attention Deficient and Hyperactivity
  Disorder (ADHD) 102
Australia, social mobility trends 3
autobiographical example 1, 171

'bell curve myth' 188
blue-collar occupations 25, 31, 119
Boston 11, 46, 48, 123, 149
Brown University 103

Cambridge, University of 65
careers 14, 40
  choice 106, 117, 164, 167
  combining with children, for women
   141
  contacts and 120–45, 147, 183
  progression and family connections 129,
   140
  social networks and success in 120–45
  weak ties and 132, 143
Catholic schools 22, 50, 114
Catholics 13
childcare 107, 130
China 151
choice
  branching points in educational
   system 7

of career 106, 117, 164, 167
  and cost–benefit analysis 7
  income spending 7, 44–68, 175
  of residence 47, 58, 60, 147
  of schools 60, 137, 148, 150, 163
  of university or college 155, 157, 164,
   176
class advantage
  Goldthorpe's types 5
  mobilisation of cultural resources
   178–82
  mobilisation of economic resources
   174–78
  mobilisation of social resources 182–5
class backgrounds 13, 18–43, 70,
  174
  advantaged 15
  and occupational dispositions 81
class inequalities 3, 4, 6
  individual resistance to policies to
   reduce 6
class relations, stability in context of
  change 3, 4, 6, 172–89
class reproduction 18
  see also middle-class reproduction;
   working-class reproduction
class sizes in schools 46, 57
class structure
  effect of changes in occupational
   structure on 3
  resistance to change 5, 8
class subordination 181
college, preparation programme, Upward
  Bound 126
colleges of further education 14, 62,
  114
community, as social capital 121,
  185
comparative research 11, Appendix B
competition 8, 10, 11, 174, 186,
  188
comprehensive schools 36, 59

279